BEHIND THE LINES

Behind the Lines
Pieces on Writing and Pictures
MICHAEL HOFMANN

faber and faber

First published in 2001
by Faber and Faber Limited
3 Queen Square London WC1N 3AU
Published in the United States by Faber and Faber, Inc.,
an affiliate of Farrar, Straus and Giroux, New York

Phototypeset by Intype London Ltd
Printed in England by Clays Ltd, St Ives plc

A CIP record for this book
is available from the British Library

ISBN 0-571-19523-7

2 4 6 8 10 9 7 5 3 1

to the memory
and grandchildren
of Gert Hofmann
(1931–1993)

CONTENTS

Introduction ix

Wallace Stevens 1
Frederick Seidel 5
Randall Jarrell: Poetry 10
Randall Jarrell: Letters 17
John Berryman 21
Robert Lowell's Prose 35
Weldon Kees 40
Elizabeth Bishop: Prose 41
Elizabeth Bishop: Letters 44
Frank O'Hara 47
C. K. Williams 55

Rilke: Poetry and Letters 60
Rilke: Life and Uncollected Poems 68
Gottfried Benn 74
Georg Trakl 84
Bertolt Brecht: Life 90
Bertolt Brecht: Letters, Poems and Songs 98
Paul Celan 105
Anna Akhmatova 116
Joseph Brodsky 119
Max Beckmann and Joseph Brodsky 132
Eugenio Montale 133
Ian Hamilton 142
Tom Paulin 149
Paul Muldoon 156
Seamus Heaney 164

Otto Dix 172
Anselm Kiefer 183
Egon Schiele 189
George Grosz 193

Edvard Munch 197
Arturo Di Stefano 203

Pericles 209
Eugene O'Neill 212
Ödön von Horváth 214
Thomas Bernhard 216
Friedrich Dürrenmatt 218
Voyager 221
Wings of Desire 223
Until the End of the World 225
The Sacrifice 228

James Buchan 230
Malcolm Lowry: Letters and Studies 237
Malcolm Lowry: Life and Poetry 244
Paul Bowles 252
Christa Wolf 260
Gert Hofmann 267
Wolfgang Koeppen 272
Bohumil Hrabal 279
Adam Czerniawski, Jakov Lind,
    Manes Sperber 285
George Konrad 292
Péter Nádas 297
Tadeusz Konwicki 303
Robert Musil 313
Joseph Roth 317
Ryszard Kapuściński 322

INTRODUCTION
From A to B, Freestyle

I started to write book reviews in 1980, a few months after my first poems started to appear. It suggested itself to me, and was suggested to me, as a further field of literary endeavour, as a way of keeping my hand in and my name before the public. The performance of random tasks, which is pretty much what they were to begin with, was pleasant, useful and distracting. It was a way of living by the initiative of others, I was like a kind of executive arm. I was at the time a postgraduate student, but before long I came to depend on and live for these literary assignations that were contrived for me. I was always prepared to drop everything if a book came through the post with a little review slip – whereas I never gave much for libraries, and the larger the less. I relished what seemed to me the freedom of reviewing, and the multiple address (of which more later) – even if it did mean the end of any academic hopes I might have entertained. Seeking to direct opinion, making my contribution to debate, was much more to my liking than the 'contribution to knowledge' that was required for a Ph.D. It was first thoughts and second thoughts, *'flashes' e dediche* in Montale's phrase, flashes and inscriptions, swift, provisional, personal responses, as universal or local, as beautiful or utilitarian as I cared to make them – rather than having the last word in a way that struck me as being halfway between posthumous and picayune.

I thought of reviewing then – and I don't think of it much differently now – as getting from one pair of co-ordinates to another, from A to B freestyle. In one way or another, I cover the ground, I have my say, I use up my word-limit – in those days, 800 words seemed vastly longer than 600; although I'm pleased to say I still haven't entirely got over my stagefright at writing. (Klöterjahn, the writer in Thomas Mann's *Tristan*, is my type: someone who writes unimpressively, illegibly, and with great difficulty.) Reviewing seems to me to be (perhaps wrongly) as unrepeatable, as 'hot' and as improvisational an activity as writing poems. Judgment isn't reliably 'there', like a geological stratum. A lot of the articulacy and the connections and the nerves that might have gone on poems, have gone on these pieces. Sometimes I even fancy it shows: the hindered poem. I regularly felt – probably all reviewers or critics do – that I was going far beyond the needful. Hence my inordinate pleasure at seeing them here collected and in book form. It's the salvaging of – Malcolm Lowry's phrase – 'all the lost prose'. Besides, I think it's probably the only way of getting a book out of myself, and it's probably the only other sort of book I can write, a collage, a mosaic, not a bronze or a lump of marble. To put it another way, as a poet or sometime poet, I'm not a distance merchant, but a sprinter, a bend runner.

The other thing I thought about was who it was for – for whom, in addition to my trusting editors, was I writing? My possible readership struck me as interestingly, if not dauntingly, broken up. I had to cater for people who had read or seen whatever I was writing about, who might yet read or see it, and who were rather unlikely ever to. All these three groups, and the author as well. (Hence my irritation with Rilke for claiming not to read reviews, on the grounds that they were personal missives intended for others. Rilke is, as it were, my addressee as much as any live reader. Certainly, when I've been at the receiving end of the process, I had – often disappointed – expectations of being interestingly addressed.) So, one had a duty both to inform and entertain people who were resolutely uninterested in one's subject and to hold the interest of those who might reasonably feel they knew all there was to be known about it. Hence, perhaps – though there are other reasons for them too – the mobility, the flightiness and skippiness, the variety of address, the pleasure in quoting, the sketches, facts, dates. I like detail, and I like bold outlines. I like to know something about the people I read. Among other things, I was interested in getting an education. Reviewing stretched me and consumed me as much as poetry did. It was as a reviewer that I first read Roth and Celan and Trakl; that I saw Wenders making ever dodgier films while (in the books of his I was translating at the same time) talking better and better ones; that I got my first proper sight of Kiefer; that gave me a chance to pay my respects to O'Hara, to Musil, to Brodsky, to Konwicki.

After several – I now see – hopelessly aberrant shots at titles, I settled on *Behind the Lines*. That combines the usual promise of scrutiny and study and possible revelation with perhaps an uncommon wariness and transgressiveness. You see, of the various fields I peruse here, American poetry, European poetry, painting, stage and screen, prose fiction, I am not really entitled to any of them. None of them are 'mine'. Wherever I go, I find myself treading on other people's turf, if not toes. Much more, I tend to think, disqualifies me than qualifies me: I am not British, I am not American, I am not a novelist, never raised a brush, never studied German. Nor do I make any appeal to my authority – if any – as a poet. I am not interested in producing a sort of Arcimboldo self-portrait made of book reviews, I write as a reader and observer, and if I have any authority it is the nervous authority of the reader. (Although, as witness Randall Jarrell, whose opinions one might well choose to adopt *en bloc*, there is no substitute for being right about things.)

My subjects may have been offered or suggested to me, but in every case, I devoted myself to them – those I vilified as much as those I extolled. They became my detail, my piece of paper that I chewed up and gulped down, my theatre of operations as a reviewer, off to one side, or perhaps off to several sides of the current major preoccupations of Britain and the United States. And my methods? It seems to me I am probably alarmingly ready to go back to first principles, or, as civil servants say, to 'think the unthinkable'. I have always written out of curiosity to find out what I thought of something. (Writing uninformed, as it were, by such curiosity strikes me as either unscrupulous or unnecessary. Perhaps what I learned about Dix as a portraitist – first impressions, followed by bags of technique – holds true in a general way.) This position, of heightened alertness, of being on occupied territory, of vulnerable blundering at worst, of making unexpected discoveries at best, is all in my title. Whatever I do here, I would like to think it's not the usual troop inspection.

The pieces included here come to roughly half of what I wrote in those twenty years (ideally, this book should be too short as well as too long). I was in no particular rush to begin – the earliest subjects here, I think, are Elizabeth Bishop from 1984

(and '94) and Georg Trakl from 1985; and the latest is Paul
Bowles from 1999. They are minimally edited: essentially they
are left in whichever form I happened to find them in, carbons,
photocopies, newsprint. Where a different subject heaves into
view – with Rilke, with Jarrell, with Lowell's prose – I have cut;
and on two or three occasions, I've substituted quotations to
avoid the most egregious repetition. (After thinking about it for
a long time, I also included three or four of the introductions I
have written more recently; they are, I concede, a slightly dif-
ferent kind of animal, but, I hope, just as objective and
exploratory as the reviews.) Forays into art and showbiz are
also included; the broader vocabulary, the licence to describe
physical objects, sights and sounds – asparagus, Sam Shepard,
Berlin! – felt wonderfully liberating, though in fact the difference
probably comes down to having to identify and re-make in my
own words what, if I had still been writing about books, I would
have been able to quote. Quoting is very much to the point.
I have gravitated to the longer pieces, not so that I can the more
effectively overwhelm you, as the wolf might have said to Little
Red Riding Hood, but if anything for the opposite reason:
to allow me to supply more context, more information, more
quotation, so that what I write becomes something more than
the transmission of an opinion. I am not chary of opinions, and
have at least as much faith in my own as the next person, but
if this is to amount to anything as a book, I will have to do a
little more than give points out of ten.

Given such an emphasis, I have also moved away from making
this a book on contemporaries; the line of the present is, if you
like, one of those lines I am going behind. I can quite see that
writing an early response to something brand new is one of the
more exhilarating things one can do in print, and while there
are some pieces like that here – Seidel, Buchan, Konrad, Heaney
– the bulk of it is what I might call Late Modern: the American
generation of the mid-century, German and European poets a
little before that, broadly fauve or expressionist painters. It was
also part of my purpose to present a small minority of English
writers: I have Malcolm Lowry as a classic, and one novelist
and one poet, James Buchan and Ian Hamilton. England is at
the edge of my circle rather than at the centre of its own, where

it unalterably weens itself. Both history and geography are to do with my – transient's or magpie's – location of value, which, in literary terms, is interest.

This book owes its existence to not one, but three poetry editors at Faber: to Craig Raine, for whom it was first a twinkle (though it was his anxious stipulation that I should wait until I was forty – safely long past), to Christopher Reid, who talked it on and up, and to Paul Keegan, whose interest in the project actually preceded his arrival at Faber, and to whom it happily fell to see it through. The trustingness of editors – to which I have already paid tribute – is one of the amenities of the British scene. I am grateful, in addition to those mentioned, to the editors of the *London Review of Books*, *Modern Painters*, the *New Statesman*, the *New York Times, PN Review*, the *Times*, and the *Times Literary Supplement*, for having commissioned these pieces or having been prepared to entertain them. It is these same people – single individuals in some cases, members of a dynasty or collective in others – who have also largely shaped this book, by generously and imaginatively thinking what might interest me, offering me bigger subjects, longer pieces, remoter deadlines. It has given me a sense, rare in life – because what else is there that would provide it – of things steadily gaining in interest, in value, in resonance. The experience of meliorism in action. The freelance's equivalent of promotion. 'A tiny area of *joie de vivre*', in a phrase I remember reading once, in an utterly different context, in the German writer Anna Duden.

Michael Hofmann
March 2001

WALLACE STEVENS

Poets and others are always talking about the essential thisness or thatness of poetry, but surely no one but Wallace Stevens would have come up with 'gaudiness' as the thing. He did, though: 'the essential gaudiness of poetry', and it's what one loves him for, and what sets his work apart from that of his peers, the great modernists. It makes him something like the Matisse among poets.

For sheer delight, there is no one like Stevens. No poet has better titles ('Nomad Exquisite', 'The Revolutionists Stop for Orangeade', 'Loneliness in Jersey City', 'Late Hymn from the Myrrh-Mountain', 'Lytton Strachey, Also, Enters Heaven', 'Metaphor as Degeneration'). No verse contains as many colours, musical instruments, birds and fruits, seas and skies and suns. ('There has never been a travel poster like *Harmonium*,' wrote Randall Jarrell, harking back to Stevens's first book.) None is so regularly couched in the forms of exclamation or address – which come to seem pleasing in themselves. None uses exotic place-names more alluringly or domestic place-names more unconsolably ('Home from Guatemala, back at the Waldorf)'. None endows its speakers and its addressees with such fragrantly invented names as 'Mrs Alfred Uruguay', 'The Canon Aspirin', 'Professor Eucalyptus' or 'Chieftan Iffucan' (like a children's book one would love to get one's hands on to). No other poet has made the startling claim that 'French and English constitute a single language' as Stevens has, and then proceeded to write as though he believed it, or, at any rate, accordingly. No modern poet has a more delicious vocabulary or a wittier diction, or combines words in a more surprising manner. No one (not since Edward Lear anyway) has dived more enthusiastically into non-verbal sounds, nonsense, baby-talk. Stevens writes, to put it at its briefest, a ravishing idiolect. He sounds like a man imitating a whole orchestra, not despising the triangle.

Stevens's appointed theme or mission is to write a lay hymn to the joys of living in this world. In a very early journal entry,

Review of Wallace Stevens, *Collected Poetry and Prose*
(Library of America, 1997)

written in 1902 when he was just 22, he notes: 'An old argument
with me is that the true religious force in the world is not the
church but the world itself', and this remains true throughout
his long life and longer work. He is after 'an aesthetic tough,
diverse, untamed,/ Incredible to prudes, the mint of dirt,/ Green
barbarism turning paradigm'. But before he can get there, he
needs to scrape away all the sheets of varnish that man, over
the ages, has applied to the world, the prophylactic layerings of
religion and myth and meaning, the blackening deposits of cliché
and ingratitude, and so 'Exit the mental moonlight, exit lex,/
Rex and principium, exit the whole/ Shebang. Exeunt omnes.'
How many of the poems have fighting or debunking titles:
'Invective Against Swans', 'The Plot Against the Giant', 'Of
Heaven Considered as a Tomb', 'Poetry Is a Destructive Force',
'Evening Without Angels'. Once they have done their work,
Stevens is left to face the world as whole-hearted and gleeful
and unconditional as an infant, unable to distinguish inside
from outside, awash with sensation, not merely responding to
a stimulus but participating in it and helping to create it: 'As
the immense dew of Florida/ Brings forth/ The big-finned palm/
And green vine angering for life,/ (. . .) So, in me, come flinging/
Forms, flakes, and the flakes of flames.' An alternative mode to
this pure and orgiastic – Dionysian – celebration of life is when
Stevens, now in the role of malign and ironic observer, watches
the exquisite discomfiture of the adult, the puritan and the bigot
in the face of a world that their categories are unable to cope
with: it is the giant, undone by 'Heavenly labials in a world of
gutturals', the doctor of Geneva quailing at the sight of Pacific
rollers ('an unburgherly apocalypse'), using his handkerchief
and sighing, and even God Himself feeling 'a subtle quiver,/
That was not heavenly love,/ Or pity. This is not writ/ In any
book' as he receives the sacrifice of Saint Ursula.

Among Stevens's 'Adagia' – his addictively wonderful aphor-
isms about poetry and life – you will find such things as 'La vie
est plus belle que les idées' and 'Perhaps it is of more value to
infuriate philosophers than to go along with them', but in his
poetry of the thirties and forties he seemed to lose sight of
them. The middle-period Stevens is largely a bore. He loses his
freshness and gaiety and unpredictability as his philosopher's

bow tie gets him in a stranglehold. The author of the essay 'The Irrational Element in Poetry' comes on like a logician. The man who describes poetry as 'an unofficial view of being' seems to be writing under sanction. The man who amiably says, 'I dislike niggling, and like letting myself go' is hard to square with the man who writes 'The Man with the Blue Guitar', which reads like a precursor of Dr Seuss, a protracted twenty-page niggle:

> So that's life, then: things as they are?
> It picks its way on the blue guitar.
>
> A million people on one string?
> And all their manner in the thing,
>
> And all their manner, right and wrong,
> And all their manner, weak and strong?

Even the revels in reality are now conducted with careful sobriety: 'It was the importance of the trees outdoors,/ The freshness of the oak-leaves, not so much/ That they were oak-leaves, as the way they looked.' Where once 'the only moving thing' had been 'the eye of the blackbird', it is now in the regular sounding of a note of remorse or warning: 'a beau language without a drop of blood', 'This structure of ideas, these ghostly sequences/ Of the mind, result only in disaster', 'The greatest poverty is not to live/ In a physical world'.

Out of this, Stevens manages to raise and collect himself once more in the poems he wrote in his seventies, those in *The Rock* and *Late Poems*, which take their place among the greatest achievements of our century. They have a plainness and a grandeur that are perhaps only ever to be found in the work of the very old: of Yeats and Pound, of Robert Penn Warren and the German poet Gottfried Benn. All his life, Stevens had been a poet of the verities of the seasons and the cardinal points, and the great antinomies of day and night, heat and cold, reality and the imagination; his oeuvre had been a kind of tree – fruit, flowers, colours, burgeoning, expanse, leafage, shade – and now all that is left in the long lines of his late manner are the bare and richly desolate branches:

> It makes so little difference, at so much more
> Than seventy, where one looks, one has been there before.

Wood-smoke rises through trees, is caught in an upper flow
Of air and whirled away. But it has been often so.

The trees have a look as if they bore sad names
And kept saying over and over one same, same thing,

In a kind of uproar, because an opposite, a contradiction,
Has enraged them and made them want to talk it down.

('Long and Sluggish Lines')

Over the years, I have become used to reading Stevens in his much-loved *Collected Poems* (first published by Knopf for his seventy-fifth birthday in 1954, and reprinted many times since): I loved the purity of it, the fact that – just like Whitman's *Leaves of Grass* a century before – it contained only the poems and a picture of the man who wrote them. The editors of this new Library of America edition, Frank Kermode and Joan Richardson, have produced a book that's half prose and twice as long and, for both reasons, will take me some time to get used to. Stevens's philosophical essays, in particular, are heavy going. But then, having all his poems – especially all his late poems – in one volume is a great thing (previously, one had to seek them out in three different books); his 'Adagia' and his replies to questionnaires are marvellous; and even in the somewhat turgid and dated prose he wrote for publication, he sometimes expresses himself with exemplary force and concision. 'There is not a poet whom we prize living today,' he writes, 'that does not address himself to an élite'. Or: 'We say that we perfect diction. We simply grow tired.' Or: 'A man has no choice about his style.' Or: 'The last thing in the world that I should want to do would be to formulate a system.' You see, Stevens is not really a theorist at all. In my favorite adage of his, he writes: 'One reads poetry with one's nerves.' Amen.

FREDERICK SEIDEL

Unless it were Grey Gowrie ten or fifteen years ago, there is no one in Britain who writes or could write like Frederick Seidel: from an easy first-hand acquaintance with the great people and places and spectacles of his time. He is like Lowell with a mean streak; St Louis Jewish for Boston Brahmin; matching him Harvard for Harvard and New York for New York; and with money and power for Lowell's frog-like identifications with the princes of history – with a cast of movie stars, grand-prix riders, politicians and millionaires for the other's grand traditions of family and culture. 'Voilà donc quelqu'un de bien quelconque!' he says mockingly to the failed writer who is his subject in the vicious poem 'What One Must Contend With'. And all the men at least in *Men and Woman* are assuredly 'bien quelconque'. Or Seidel is like Patrick White, effortlessly conveying the impression of a man of the world, the half-disaffected half-insider, omniscient, discriminating and damaging. Is it a character in the ambisexual novel *The Twyborn Affair* or the author of *Men and Woman* who appraises the room in front of him like this: 'Some of the women here would be more use than most of the men'?

Seidel's subject is little less than the present condition of the world, private and public, acknowledged and unacknowledged. Narrowed down a little, it would be something like the oligarchy within American democracy, the 'first four hundred', even these further whittled down in these lines from '1968':

> Fifty or so of the original
> Four hundred
> At the fundraiser,
> Robert Kennedy for President, the remnants, lie
> Exposed as snails around the swimming pool, stretched
> Out on the paths, and in the gardens, and the drive.
> Many dreams their famous bodies have filled.

Though the last line is weakly ambiguous (to avoid being unam-

Review of Frederick Seidel, *Men and Woman* (London: Chatto and Windus, 1984)

biguously weak), the scene is bleakly privileged and powerful. It is interestingly different from other American writing on this and related topics over the last thirty years: Lowell's blankly ferocious Eisenhower and Berryman's sweetly sorrowing 'O Adlai mine'; Bishop's elective deafness to Washington's brass bands; or again Lowell's portraits of Kennedy and Johnson, still heroes, still in control, still personal, still extricable – 'swimming nude, unbuttoned, sick/ of his ghost-written rhetoric!' None of the other poets see their subjects as levelly as Seidel sees the campaign nexus of money, drugs, pop, sex, power and violence. All of them, it seems to me, would have offered a little of their personal sorrow, personal irony, over and above that of history. Seidel doesn't. He stays clear of his poem, of hope and despair, engagement and disengagement. '1968' ends with an entrance:

> A stranger, and wearing a suit,
> Has to be John the Baptist,
> At least, come
> To say someone else is coming.
> He hikes up his shoulder holster
> Self-consciously, meeting their gaze.
> That is as sensitive as the future gets.

Only the last line can truly be construed as commentary, and it is no more sensitive than what it describes: the bodyguard – the assassin? – and the future. It is, if you like, no more the last line of a poem than the man in the suit is John the Baptist.

Seidel's sensitivity serves his subject – a terrible mixture of over-civilization and barbarity – not to set himself apart from it. He is never 'sensitive' in the sense of decent, feeling, moved. Perhaps it is a concomitant of that – the absence of the organic, the squirming, in his work – that his subjects and ambiences so often seem mechanical, cold and clean. Even the kind of nausea his poems often seem to contemplate, and to convey, is strangely pure, unarguable and unmessy. Two more endings, of 'The New Cosmology' and 'Empire' are representative: 'The last nano-second of silence twenty billion years ago/ Before the big bang is endless.' and 'Rank as the odor in urine/ Of asparagus the night before,/ This is empire waking drunk, and remembering in the dark.'

Seidel first attracts the reader's attention by his range of exclusive settings and privileged characters: the fundraising, a film-shoot, travel by 'Astrojet' or 'Metroliner', the Finnish Grand Prix at Immatra, the New York of 'Pressed Duck' and 'Fucking': 'This is New York – / Some mornings five women call within a half hour.' But the authority of these settings and the human types they contain – it tends to be a sensual, experiential authority, not moral authority, not 'sensitivity' as '1968' showed – is also a function of style, and hence is transferrable to quite ordinary subjects, like adolescence, *Time* magazine and the television news. With the style, again, it is its factuality and discrimination that one notices first: a style that names names, that refers to the crucial men and places of the age, a connoisseurial, disabused, sometimes brutal style. Coming from an aesthetic response to life, nevertheless its biggest temptation is phrase-making: 'Rusk's private smile that looks like incest', 'The hideous and ridiculous are obsessed/ By the beautiful which they replace.' This autocratic, outspoken, epigrammatic manner has the effect of leaving the poet quite exposed, with nowhere to hide in his poems. Sometimes it is his mighty lines that fail, sometimes it is that those around them appear astonishingly feeble; on occasion, whole poems, written more 'lyrically', and in shorter lines, are entirely vaporous: 'The Soul Mate', 'The Girl in the Mirror' and 'Robert Kennedy'.

These limitations and shortcomings perhaps leave one unprepared for Seidel's greatest asset as a poet, in my view: his ability, in longer passages, to link four or five ideas and images together, brazenly, even obviously, but quite irresistibly. He does it in the title-poem, in 'Wanting to Live in Harlem', and six or seven others, but I want to quote from 'Death Valley':

> Antonioni walks in the desert shooting
> *Zabriskie Point*. He does not perspire
> Because it is dry. His twill trousers stay pressed,
> He wears desert boots and a viewfinder,
> He has a profile he could shave with, sharp
> And meek, like the eyesight of the deaf,
> With which he is trying to find America,
> A pick for prospecting passive as a dowser.
> He has followed his nose into the desert.

I find this brilliantly audacious, modest and economical. The second, short sentence is a miraculous creation: one would have expected it to be trite, but it is fascinating, at once slow and witty! The scene shows a man struggling to master an alien element. His equipment is partly out of place (*twill* trousers?), partly ironically apposite (*desert* boots). The dominant idea of the stanza is that of Antonioni's sight, which, because of his being a film-director, and by association with his profile, Seidel conceives of as pronounced, even protuberant: that idea runs through 'shooting', 'Point', 'viewfinder', 'sharp', 'eyesight', 'pick' and 'dowser'. It culminates in the last short sentence, a kind of outrageously simple summing-up. Throughout the stanza, there are little subliminal plays: 'dry' and 'stay pressed', 'pick' and 'nose', 'desert boots', 'viewfinder'. The simile, 'like the eyesight of the deaf' is startlingly effective, combining the ideas of a gift and a disability to evoke both the inadequacy (in other respects) of genius, and Antonioni's simultaneous alienation and discovery of America. And it is decorously simple – in a later poem, Seidel writes 'The ears for eyes of a bat on the wings of a dove', a type of overloading he tends to go in for.

Men and Woman is an odd mixture of passages like these, and lines of variable, fallible power. Seidel's starting-point is clearly Robert Lowell, whom his poems recall at every point; sometimes they even look like counterweights to Lowell poems, 'Sunrise' to 'Waking Early Sunday Morning', 'Wanting to Live in Harlem' to a lot of *Life Studies*. The sounds and rhythms, turns of phrase, flourishes, the jokes and puns all seem like Lowell's: 'my rival Lief,/ Boyfriend of girls and men, who cruised/ In a Rolls convertible'. No wonder, the cynic might say, that Lowell felt 'jolted' on seeing Seidel's first book. But familiar though these features are, I would argue that they only represent the way for Seidel to write his own poems. He is more acidic than Lowell, and more blatant, and he lacks the personal centre or mythology that Lowell developed. What he cultivates instead is a kind of encyclopaedia of modern atmospheres, occurrences, appearances. Of the thirty poems here, there are at least a dozen that one would be glad to see in anthologies, or on desert islands. *Men and Woman*, his 'new and selected', is drawn from the two American volumes that are all he has published. It may be a while till his next one, and who knows if that will be published here? So why wait? We have no one like him here.

RANDALL JARRELL
Poetry

Like Delmore Schwartz, Jarrell was not in the first rank of American poets, but he was a talismanic figure for his generation, as Schwartz was. Only Schwartz, I feel, could have inspired a collection of tributes – think of Saul Bellow's *Humboldt's Gift*, of the poem by Lowell in *Life Studies*, of Berryman's ten Dream Songs, 'one solid block of agony' – to compare with *Randall Jarrell, 1914–1965*, a collection of reviews, articles and tributes of rare fervour and incredible diversity, published in 1967. It means, I think, that he will always be defined, like Schwartz, by his generation, by his relationships with it – which makes that book of tributes uniquely appropriate and also uniquely expressive of him. What is special about Jarrell, the personal style, involvement, charm, delicate spidery threads survive in that collective form, and not necessarily in any individual work of his nor yet in his biography. Some of this, again as with Schwartz, is to do with his youth, intensity, early brilliance, unfulfilled promise, even though his career didn't go so terribly awry as Schwartz's. Mature, orderly, well-regulated figures, even mature, orderly, well-regulated geniuses, somehow don't leave such holes. Not just contemporaries, practically all who knew him were in thrall to him. An *enfant terrible* was what his teacher John Crowe Ransom ('*Mr* Ransom') called him; he was 'Child Randall' in the mediocre poems Lowell wrote about him later.

Just as a child has the ability to be more than a child – it may become the Spirit of Childhood, or Youth, or Hope – so Jarrell, Child Randall, always had it in him to be more than Jarrell, a figure of more general significance, something allegorical, an enduring function. In one title of his, 'Thinking of the Lost World', he is the lost world; in another, *Poetry and the Age*, he is the age. He has, I think, a kind of immortality, not that of personal achievement and warts-and-all greatness, but the apotheosis of his qualities: his passion, wit, grace and discrimination. It is pleasant and oddly easy to think of him living on,

Review of Randall Jarrell, *Selected Poems*, ed. William H. Pritchard
(New York: Farrar, Straus and Giroux, 1990)

doing not only the things he had planned, a new book of poems called *Women*, a psychoanalytical book on Eliot, a book on Auden (William H. Pritchard aptly calls him a 'Coleridgean projector of schemes'), but also continuing his critical work (even though in the last three years of his life he published nothing at all on modern poetry), with a pitchfork in one hand and a tuning-fork in the other. What might he have made of late Lowell, of Plath, or Ashbery or C. K. Williams? Surely he would have had years as a superb anthologist (he only ever got a chance with prose, with Kipling and the Russians), a popular-izer and all-round pundit – fashion critic, motor-racing correspondent, tennis writer – a lecturer, even perhaps a tele-vision evangelist on book programmes.

There was something immoderate, intransigent, exorbitant about Jarrell, as his memorialists say, one after another:

> He always seemed more alive than other people, as if constantly tuned up to the concert pitch that most people, including poets, can only maintain for short and fortunate stretches. (Elizabeth Bishop)

> What had fascinated me, provoked me, even made me envious, was the overwhelming, inexpressible importance that Randall attached to taste, to his own taste, to right reading and to right thinking about what one had read. (Alfred Kazin)

> Gordon Chalmers, the president of Kenyon College and a disciple of the somber anti-Romantic humanists, once went skiing with Randall, and was shocked to hear him exclaiming, 'I feel just like an angel.' Randall *did* somehow give off an angelic impression ... His mind, unearthly in its quickness, was a little boyish, disembodied and brittle. His body was a little ghostly in its immunity to soil, entangle-ments and rebellion. (Robert Lowell)

> The manuscripts of Randall Jarrell, whether poems or prose, were the only perfect manuscripts I ever saw. I mean that they were letter-perfect. There was no question of a typo or any other kind of graphical error. He was my only scrupulous poet ... (Karl Shapiro)

In this last, as in one or two other ways – Hannah Arendt's husband thought there was a physical resemblance, which delighted Jarrell, and there are certain repetitive rhetorical struc-tures – Jarrell recalls Rilke, whom he adored and, adoring and without much German, translated. All these qualities, immoderation, intransigence, exorbitance, a feeling of being out-of-this-world, or better-than-this-world, are the reasons for which one reads Jarrell: the Olympian laughter and Olympian excitement of the reviews, conferring immortality upon some and hurling thunderbolts of derision upon others; the miraculously deft touches in the poems. Even Benton, the campus, the 'Institution' in *Pictures from an Institution*, seems like an Olympus staffed by witty girls.

I embarked upon this review, many months ago, thinking I would like to strike a blow for Randall Jarrell's poetry, whether *in extenso* or as selected by Professor Pritchard. I no longer feel that way, as indeed I think Pritchard himself may have become unsure, saying at the beginning of the *Selected Poems* that Jarrell 'ranks with Robert Lowell and Elizabeth Bishop as one of the leading poets of that generation', but in the course of his biography making many damaging and deprecatory comments on the poetry and on individual poems.

Helen Vendler once wrote, rather too patly, as though they were ingredients for two cakes, that Jarrell 'put his genius into his criticism, and his talent into his poetry'. I incline to think the trouble was more fundamental. Despite tennis and motor cars and elegant clothes and music and all the rest of it, what was important to Jarrell was books; the world came to him between hard or paper covers. Books were the ultimate reality, and the ultimate good. As a critic, he was a moralist of books, and perhaps that is the most striking and the best thing he ever was. There was no question ever about his doubting that part of his vocation – though he could still suggest, in his elegant way, that it might be as futile to write criticism as it was to rain into the sea. His poetry, though, and his career as a poet, seem vulnerable to doubt. Reviewing an early volume, Malcolm Cowley wrote that the poems seemed to lack 'a central core of belief'. Lowell wrote that Jarrell made 'others feel that their realizing themselves was as close to him as his own self-realization', a genuine and rare and admirable condition that, however, makes poetry all but impossible to write.

What speaks against Jarrell's poems is their uneventfulness, or more clumsily and more accurately, their unevent-ishness. Apart from 'The Death of the Ball Turret Gunner', how many of his poems are there one can name or separately allude to? Compared to those by his peers? One has a sense of wartime, of dreams and *Märchen*, of women discontented with their lives. It is excessive to say that Jarrell's poetry is all gimmicks, but its traits do seem over-defined, centrifugal, weird, apparent, perhaps overbred. In an answer to a 1950 questionnaire, he listed the subjects of his poems in nine lines, and in alphabetical order: 'airplanes and their crews, the dead and dying, dreams, forests, graves, letters, libraries, love, *Märchen* . . .'. I don't know if it is the length of the list or its brevity that is alarming, but the knowledge and the degree of detail surely are. Surely a poet shouldn't be his own concordance too? And yet with all this detail, the poems lack conviction and specificity – the number of last lines with words like man, death, change, pain, life and sleep in them. They don't have the power of Lowell's, or the salt and colour of Bishop's.

Jarrell can seem the most contradictory of poets. A prodigy among late developers – he was writing poems at a time when Lowell probably still wanted to be a football player – and yet his early work is unreadable, solemn and botched: only Allen Tate, for whatever reason, claims to prefer it. (Pritchard allows him only one poem before the war poems.) The war poems, then, have this strange impersonality. At times, the narrator's voice seems to be in a different medium from the rest of the poem, he's like the narrator of a film, and the poem seems like a creation of the dubbing studio. Given a choice between the poem and prose, one would surely choose the prose every time:

> And the man awakes, and sees around his life
> The night that is never silent, broken with the sighs
> And patient breathing of the dark companions
> With whom he labors, sleeps and dies.
> ('Absent with Official Leave')

The barracks is queer at night; you're in the middle of a just-moving sea of sleeping people who cough, or make little snoring sounds, or give little moans – at any time you wake there is someone making some sound. At 4.30 you are wakened by a *very* queer sound: somebody running down the street as fast as he can blowing a whistle – the whistle gets louder and louder (accompanied by footsteps) and then vanishes away. (A letter of 1943)

The poems, as above, seem to end with a headlong dash for abstraction and generalization – 'imperilled perhaps by an arid, abstracting precocity', Lowell wrote in his eulogy. Sometimes it even seems to me as though they were written by a committee, like a committee of devils or fairies: one does the rhymes, another the alliteration, a larky one does digressions and asides, a dull, po-faced one tacks on the heavy, depressed, 'Archaic Torso'-type endings, like 'It is terrible to be alive' or 'change me, change me!' Even quite long poems by Jarrell end with otherwise quite inexplicable abruptness.

Two more sets of contradictory qualities or conundrums define a response to Jarrell. The poems written, as I would have it, by syndicates, are obviously laboured, but elsewhere Jarrell is capable of a wonderful, effortless, seemingly irresponsible fluency. In those poems, generally written in the 1950s and later, Jarrell does have his own voice – not just gimmicks – and faith in what he's doing.

> To prefer the nest in the linden
> By Apartment Eleven, the Shoreham
> Arms, to Apartment Eleven
> Would be childish. But we are children.

> If the squirrel's nest has no doorman
> To help us out of the taxi, up the tree,
> Still, even the Shoreham has no squirrel
> To meet us with blazing eyes, the sound of rocks knocked together
> At the glass door under the marquee.

'Hope' carries on with these typical Jarrell arabesques for eight pages: all Pritchard will say about it is that it is 'egregiously overlong', and he leaves it out of his *Selected*. But it seems to me precisely here that one finds Jarrell at his best, still labouring perhaps, but at least labouring with some congenial material like the 'knitting from sweet champagne' that is described in another of these long, fluent poems, 'A Man Meets a Woman In the Street'.

The second, perhaps related, quality or conundrum concerns Jarrell's tidiness or messiness as a poet, and again, as with the labour and fluency, the answer seems to be that he is both. Reading intricate, sheer-tissued passages like those just quoted, one thinks what a sublimely deft and supple poet. And yet, to look at, the poems can be surprisingly full of dots and dashes, proper nouns, italics and quotations, question marks and shriek marks, raggedy lines and frayed paragraphs. Occasionally, a poem will begin with so much data and lingo, it could equip a *veriste* short story:

> Summer. Sunset. Someone is playing
> The ocarina in the latrine:
> You Are My Sunshine. A man shaving
> Sees – past the day-room, past the night K.P.'s
> Bent over a G.I. can of beets
> In the yard of the mess – the red and green
> Lights of a runway full of '24's.
> The first night flight goes over with a roar
> And disappears, a star, among mountains.

Only the last four words, one would have said, come from a poem: the rest, all capitals and initials and figures, could be the small print on a flour-sack.

At its best, I think Jarrell's poetry combines such hardness and leisureliness – something specific and the kaleidoscopic sweep and play of his mind upon it. He is a poet of odd passages rather than whole poems, one reads him for the surprise and grace of certain constructions, rather than for the sum of his alphabetically indexed subjects. He seems to me likely to remain a special taste: sweetness and jumpiness and softness, hesitation, the catch in the throat:

> This spoonful of chocolate tapioca
> Tastes like – like peanut butter, like the vanilla
> Extract Mama told me not to drink.
> Swallowing the spoonful, I have already traveled
> Through time to my childhood. It puzzles me
> That age is like it.

It is only in the poems of *The Lost World*, a handful of posthumously published poems ('Gleaning', 'Say Good-bye to Big Daddy', 'The Player Piano') and one or two earlier things ('Transient Barracks', 'A Girl in a Library'), that he attains the breadth and the freedom and the quality that his essays had from the start. One could say it took him the best part of thirty

years to expunge from his poetry a limitedness and conventional
sagacity that were never in his prose. He read before he wrote,
and perhaps writing never had the importance, the vivid urgency
of reading: 'There were never enough books to fill [my time] –
I lived on the ragged edge of having nothing to read', he once
said of his childhood. In his abbreviated, brilliant and productive
life, what he wrote about best was reading and books: there's
no disgrace in that. Paradoxically, he loved books so much that
he would have preferred it otherwise. I am sure his best poems
were still ahead of him when he died.

RANDALL JARRELL
Letters

Externally anyway, Randall Jarrell's life was less fraught, less eventful, than the lives of some of his contemporaries. In 1935, when these letters begin, he was twenty-one, a brilliant student of psychology at Vanderbilt, and just beginning to publish poems and reviews under the admiring eyes of Allen Tate and Robert Penn Warren. He followed John Crowe Ransom to Kenyon, where he roomed with Robert Lowell and Peter Taylor (both firm friends for life). His first teaching job was at Austin, where he also met his first wife Mackie. He spent the war training and teaching (and receiving photographs of his cat) at various airfields. After a year as literary editor of the *Nation* in 1946, he spent the rest of his life teaching at the Woman's College of North Carolina, at Greensboro – with sabbatical years in Princeton and Washington, DC. He married Mary Von Schrader, his second wife, in 1952. His death in 1965, when he was hit by a car, was thought to have been suicide by those who were so minded (like John Berryman): Mary Jarrell believes it to have been accidental, as the coroner did.

The *Letters* are as attractive as Jarrell's celebrated reviews and as the poems in his last, best book. *The Lost World*. What they share is quickness and agility of mind, an unlikely grace, forthrightness without coarseness, a magnetic attraction towards goodness and love of life. All these go into the characteristic Jarrell tone, and it seems as wicked to call the poems infantile as to find the reviews malicious:

> Garbo,
> A commissar in Paris, is listening attentively
> To the voice telling how McGillicuddy met McGillivray,
> And McGillivray said to McGillicuddy – no, McGillicuddy
> Said to McGillivray – that is, McGillivray . . . Garbo
> Says seriously: 'I vish dey'd never met.'

The much-borrowed note on Oscar Williams begins: 'Oscar Williams's new book is pleasanter and a little quieter than his

Review of *Randall Jarrell's Letters: An Autobiographical and Literary Selection*, ed. Mary Jarrell (London: Faber and Faber, 1986)

old, which gave the impression of having been written on a
typewriter by a typewriter.' They are recognizably by the same
hand: the bold repetitions, the serious, unreasonable tone, the
surprising, imaginative, inescapable conclusions. And yet they
are not 'professionally surprising in the way that, say, Misting-
uette's legs are' (Jarrell on E. E. Cummings). It is the careful,
faithful movement of a rare and particular spirit.

The *Letters* are full of Jarrellisms: expressions of excitement
like 'Gee!' or 'crazy about', and of rejection, like 'dumb' or
'dopey'. There are his imaginative conceits, acute and slightly
florid: a vintage bottle of *Spätlese* 'like a raisin's day-dream', his
loneliness at Princeton, 'If I had a lion I'd be just like St Jerome.'
His prodigious cultural range is a source of more mirth and
peculiarity: 'One sees lots of criticism by William Carlos
Williams these days, but very little by Baby Snooks; it's an unjust
world.' (Mary Jarrell explains who Baby Snooks was.) Or he is
reminded of a sentence of Emerson's:

> 'Today I saw two snakes gliding back and forth in the sunlight – not
> to eat, nor for love, just gliding.' Someone used that for an epigraph
> for a novel about Harvard.

This is varied in another letter, describing a faculty do: 'No
word of interest was said, so I ate quite a bit. So you see: no
love, no gliding, just to eat.' There are innumerable occasions
in these letters of such motiveless joy in expression: as we saw,
even Oscar Williams could serve as one. How could anyone be
accounted malicious who was capable of ending a review: 'And
now I have so little space, and so much enthusiasm, for Adrienne
Cecile Rich's *The Diamond Cutters* that I can only make boiling
and whistling noises like a teakettle'?

At times, Jarrell thought writing reviews was as futile as
raining into the sea: it remained as salty as ever. Perhaps it was
even worse than that, it made the waves reach for the sky: Oscar
Williams retaliated for his review by leaving Jarrell out of his
anthologies, even removing him from reprinted editions. For
Jarrell, though, it was always the expression of enthusiasm that
was most important; and this is carried on just as much in the
letters as in the reviews. There are detailed considerations of
their poems addressed to Lowell, Elizabeth Bishop and Adrienne

Rich, as well as the far more rapid and generalized promulgation
of preferences to other correspondents. He gave a page-long
reading-list to an Austrian friend. He found himself defending
Robert Lowell to a Sister Bernetta Quinn, who preferred Jarrell's
own work. If by now his modern canon – Frost, Stevens,
Williams, Moore, Bishop, Lowell – seems classically obvious
and unarguable, it is worth bearing in mind that it wasn't at
the time, that the sea really *was* salty. Mary Jarrell's short foot-
notes bring this out rather more than her husband's letters; he
was, as he says himself, 'cheerful and determined' in them. She,
though, is free to point out that an anthologist 'chose neither
widely nor too well', or to inform us that 'The year Jarrell
nominated Bishop, the Poetry Society of America prize went to
Joyce Horner.'

As a correspondent or a confederate, Jarrell is wonderfully
bracing: staunch, exuberant, witty and serious. He has the gift
of being genuine, without being dull or lavish or incredible.
Mary Jarrell quotes Robert Lowell:

> Randall was the only man I have ever met who could make other
> writers feel that their work was more important to him than his
> own . . . What he did was to make others feel that their realizing
> themselves was as close to him as his own self-realization, and that
> he cared as much about making the nature and goodness of someone
> else's work understood as he cared about making his own
> understood.

He none the less kept his independence, rejecting, for instance,
Lowell's prose-memoir '91 Revere Street'. (' "What's wrong with
it?" And Jarrell said, "But it's not poetry, Cal." ') He could be
impatient and intolerant but never immodest. His own notes for
his *Selected Poems* explain – to an American audience – what a
'blind date' is, and what it is to be 'stood up'. Perhaps the best
way of appreciating what Jarrell stood for is to understand what
he found regrettable or impermissible. 'I think they ought to say
"What shall it profit a man if he gain his own soul and lose the
whole world?" and give that to people along with the other.'
He objected to some of Allen Tate's poetry on the grounds of
'lack of charm, feeling, tone of forbidding authority'. He wrote
of R. P. Blackmur: 'He's a queer man: if he traded a little

intelligence for a little goodness or sweetness he'd certainly be better off.' In an early letter to Allen Tate – but then, charmingly, he hardly seems to have changed at all as he grew older – he wrote: 'I think all in all I've got a poetic and semifeminine mind, I don't put any real faith in abstractions or systems.' It is a mind of rare responsiveness and tenderness capable of detecting Auden in the work of his contemporaries, even when absorbed indirectly, and at very low concentrations; and of worrying at a sight or sound or taste in a poem even if it means overturning a whole life to find it:

> This spoonful of chocolate tapioca
> Tastes like – like peanut butter, like the vanilla
> Extract Mama told me not to drink.
> Swallowing the spoonful, I have already traveled
> Through time to my childhood. It puzzles me
> That age is like it.

In dedicating this book to her husband and his generation, some alive, mostly dead, Mary Jarrell quotes two lines from one of his poems: 'For all we said, and did, and thought – / The world we were', omitting the line preceding, 'There is no one left to care'. In the event, she is right and he is wrong. It is impossible not to care for that lost 'world we were', so vividly brought to life in these letters, beautifully edited to constitute a mixture of biography, autobiography and group portrait.

JOHN BERRYMAN

The Dream Songs are John Berryman's overriding achievement as a poet. The poems he wrote before and after – they make up the *Collected Poems 1937–1971* – remain just that, they lead up to or down from the Dream Songs. Berryman's prose – the essays and stories collected in *The Freedom of the Poet* (1977) – is as scintillating as that of any of his gifted contemporaries, and more disciplined, but I don't have the feeling he is read as a prose writer, he lacks gaiety, he is too tough. The Dream Songs remain central. I would guess that Robert Lowell had them in mind when he wrote of himself that he 'somehow never wrote something to go back to'.

John Berryman was born in 1914 in Oklahoma as John Smith:

> My father was a banker and my mother was a school-teacher; they were the only people who could read and write for hundreds of miles around and they were living in the same boarding house, so they got married; so I arrived. Son number one. Then we moved to Florida, and my father killed himself.

Thus the poet's description of his formative years, given at an unhealthy speed in a rattling, breezy interview with the *Harvard Advocate*, and reprinted in *Berryman's Understanding*. Son number one was just eleven, and there was a number two also. His mother quickly remarried, their landlord, an older man by the name of Berryman, and the reconstituted family moved north to New York. The poet was sent away to school (from where he wrote the first of the letters to his mother), then to Columbia. After mildly cliffhanging circumstances related in *Love & Fame* ('Crisis'), he eventually took his degree and a Kellett Fellowship to Cambridge, already firmly committed to a life as a writer and intellectual.

On his return from England in 1938, a half-miffed Berryman set about pursuing the 'generic' life of his generation:

> first students, then with our own,
> our galaxy of grands maîtres,

Review of John Berryman, *The Dream Songs* and *Collected Poems 1937–1971*
(London: Faber and Faber, 1990)

our fifties' fellowships
to Paris, Rome and Florence,
veterans of the Cold War not the War –
all the best of life.

The ostentatious ease of these lines from Lowell's 'For John
Berryman' (in *Day by Day*) exemplifies Lowell's 'mysterious
carelessness'. For the fact is that 'all the best of life' never
came to Berryman in quite the same way as it came to Lowell.
Berryman's life was incomparably harder. Outwardly there seem
to be similarities – the books, the honours, the university posts,
the marriages, the breakdowns and hospitalizations – but the
differences are critical. Berryman's 'grands maîtres' had feet of
clay (R. P. Blackmur), or were fragile (Dylan Thomas, Delmore
Schwartz) or turned poisonous on him (Allen Tate). His 'fellow-
ship' didn't get him to Florence or Rome, but to Dublin, and
not until the 1960s. When he went to Italy, he financed the trip
himself, editing a colleague's art-history book in Rome in order
to stay on there. He had to borrow the return fare from his
mother. The pathetic bragging insistence on 'money in the bank'
in some of Berryman's late poems – upsetting to American critics
like Hayden Carruth – was because it was the first time in his
life he had any there. He won awards, but only after they had
been won by others. He knew it and said it: 'Somehow the
prizes/ come at the wrong times to the proper people/ & vice
versa' (Dream Song 361). There is one wretched photograph in
We Dream of Honour of 'JB receiving the Russell Loines Award
for Poetry from Robert Lowell, May 20, 1964'. The two men
are shaking hands, Berryman has piled his left hand on top of
Lowell's right; it's as though one of his hands isn't enough.
Lowell's congratulatory smile looks almost pitying.

The course of Berryman's life was arduous, uneven, provin-
cial. He spent years on projects that either remained unfinished
(his repeated attempts at writing a play, his edition of *King
Lear*) or that couldn't really justify the effort he put into finishing
them (his biography of Stephen Crane). Where Lowell was able
to teach 'whatever I happen to be working on', Berryman's
academic labours were Herculean. His biographer, John Haf-
fenden, lists them: 'courses in St Paul, Luther, Cervantes, Dante,
and New Testament scholarship, and one course . . . called

"Humanities in the Modern World"'. Then, in spite of his gifts and his application as a teacher and lecturer, Berryman was never secure anywhere he worked; to others it may have looked like musical chairs, not to him. In 1943, he was pushed out of Harvard into unemployment. He was in and out of Princeton for a decade. Even at the University of Minnesota, where he was employed from 1955 to his death in 1972, and where in 1969 he was finally honoured with the title of 'Regents' Professor of Humanities' and given a lighter teaching load, he was insecure most of the time, between departments, sometimes without one, a lone sheep among tenured wolves. In 1971, he even sent a personal ad to the *New York Review of Books*:

> POET-BIOGRAPHER-CRITIC-SCHOLAR, Pulitzer, NBA, etc, top tenure major university, paperback reprints selling briskly, readings & lectures country-wide, stonewalling seminar-leader, might be interested contributing radiance & the facts to an occasional change of scene.

The credentials may have been improved, the block capitals multiplied, and achievements taken the place of irony, but the need and anguish were no different from those of 1943, half a lifetime earlier:

> POET, 28, married, 4F, educated here and abroad, critic, editor, an experienced and competent university instructor, would like to continue living and writing if possible.

That appeared in the *New York Times*. At either end of one of the most visible careers in American poetry, here was a man casting his bread upon the waters.

This insecurity was all-pervasive. In the way he wrote, Berryman swung between periods of idleness and bursts of frightening self-destructive energy. There is no reason to disbelieve his first wife, Eileen Simpson, when, in her book *Poets in Their Youth* (1982), she gives her reason for leaving him as 'his need to live in turbulence . . . the way he worked on *Lear, Crane* and *Bradstreet*', not merely the simple rogue male grounds he advanced, 'drinking and bad sex'. Even going by that most humdrum of indicators, the number of times he broke an arm or a leg, Berryman was exceptionally at risk:

Three limbs, three seasons smashed; well, one to go.
Henry fell smiling through the air below
and through the air above,
the middle air as well did he not neglect
but carefully in all these airs was wrecked
which he got truly tired of.

His friends alas went all about their ways intact.

Lest all this wildness seem contrived, over-gunned, histrionic – it wasn't. In Saul Bellow's short memoir of his friend – far and away the best thing ever written on Berryman, it appears as a preface to *Recovery*, his posthumously published novel, and is included by Harry Thomas in his first-class selection of interviews, memoirs, essays and reviews,* – he writes:

> Out of affection and goodwill he made gestures of normalcy. He was a husband, a citizen, a father, a householder, he went on the wagon, he fell off, he joined AA. He knocked himself out to be like everybody else – he liked, he loved, he cared, but he was aware that there was something peculiarly comical in all this.

The effort was all the other way: 'he knocked himself out to be like everybody else'.

The earliest poems in the books under review are four sonnets on his mother's fortieth birthday, written when Berryman was nineteen (they are included in *We Dream of Honour**). They are striking for a kind of dim and unwanted erotic charge, 'Her waist a slender charming line between/ God's twin mysteries in woman'. Berryman's sense of himself was that he was 'very late in developing'. But starting at nineteen is not late. The lateness comes later, as it were, in the string of awful poems he wrote in his twenties and early thirties, full of self-conceit: twenty-one and only just arrived at Cambridge, he was writing with clipped urgency to his mother, 'Would like a book out, here or there, next fall at the latest.' In the event, he was first published in 1940 (again, this is hardly late), in a New Directions volume called *Five Young American Poets*, which Elizabeth Bishop

*Harry Thomas, ed., *Berryman's Understanding* (Boston: Northeastern University Press, 1988)
*Richard J. Kelly, ed., *We Dream of Honour: John Berryman's Letters to his Mother* (Norton, 1988)

slipped out of at a late stage. Then there was a New Directions booklet, *Poems*, in 1942, and in 1948 his first full-length – also his first overlong – book, *The Dispossessed*.

It is curious how, throughout his career, bad Berryman is well-nigh unreadable, and indeed, how much bad stuff he wrote at all stages of it. This suggests that Katha Pollitt, writing in the *New York Times*, is right in seeing him as the epitome of a poet self-made rather than born. His early poetry is a warped fustian. His friend Dylan Thomas, pure inborn instinct, would wickedly offer him lines with which to spice it up, things like 'A bare octagonal ballet for penance'. Reviewing *The Dispossessed*, Randall Jarrell wrote that early Berryman was 'possessed' (ha!) 'by a slavishly Yeatsish grandiloquence'. Eight lines do the work of two. Syntax is abruptly suspended to permit the entrance of padding phrases. Words like 'discomfortable' and 'trivide' appear. Adjectives are polysyllabic holes, 'Extravagant perception of their failure', the 'absolute' butler. The premonitory war poems have to be validated – can only be validated – by the '1938' or '1939' at the foot of them. Amid sheerly neutral poems – 'statues talking like a book', another phrase of Jarrell's – there are passages of almost incomparable bungling:

> The fireflies and the stars our only light,
> We rock, watching between the roses night
> If we could see the roses. We cannot.
>   ('The Spinning Heart')

The later poems are distinctly better: 'New Year's Eve' of 1947, 'Canto Amor' (Eileen Simpson says he worked on it for two years), some of the 'Nervous Songs' (the Professor's especially). But even in the earlier work there is the ability occasionally to generate quite exceptional momentum, particularly at the end of poems. The selfsame 'Spinning Heart' ends:

> No time for shame,
> Whippoorwill calling, excrement falling, time
> Rushes like a madman forward. Nothing can be known.

The turning-point came in 1947 and 1948, though it can have felt little like it to Berryman at the time: once more, he was out of a job at Princeton; once more embarked on a play; and for a smallish advance he took on a biography of Stephen Crane that was to take him the next three years to write. It was in these years too that he began drinking and became sexually promiscuous. At the same time, however, he wrote the first two stanzas of his long poem, *Homage to Mistress Bradstreet* – though that wasn't finished until 1953, and didn't appear between covers until 1956, another instance of the tiresome delays his career was subject to – and he wrote a sequence of sonnets about his first illicit affair, that was published twenty years later as *Berryman's Sonnets* (the title was suggested by Robert Giroux, the publisher and dedicatee of the volume).

I can't imagine anyone familiar with the old *Sonnets* being very keen to read them as *Sonnets to Chris*, which is how they appear in the *Collected Poems*. *Berryman's Sonnets* was a brilliant title, and the name of his paramour, 'Lise', was flowery and fictional; renaming her is like changing Catullus' Lesbia to 'Clodia'. The blurb celebrates Berryman's ear 'so delicate/ he fainted at a trumpet call'. 'Chris! Be our bright surviving actual scene' would knock a dead man cold. The editor of the *Collected*, Charles Thornbury, has as his principle to return to Berryman's last thoughts on his texts. Some of the changes are to be welcomed: 'before he went a-conning across the sea-O' is both a nautical and an erotic refinement on 'a-coming across'. Others are for the worse, or merely indifferent. To have 'conning' at the price of a retitled *Sonnets* – one has to wonder. And that isn't all. Thornbury has included almost sixty pages of editorial matter, and a forty-page introduction. This seems to me unwarrantable. Berryman is difficult, but he's hardly vellum; information on him is plentiful. The *Collected Poems* of a modern poet should not have an academic turnstile in front of them. One paragraph in the introduction invokes comparisons with Eliot, Cervantes, Shakespeare, Joyce, Whitman, Coleridge and Keats. Thornbury has really gone to town (to his home town of Collegeville, Minnesota). If this is to be a trend, I should like to deplore it. The more nearly invisible an editor makes himself in such an such an undertaking, the better: Robert Giroux set a good example with the prose of Bishop and Berryman. Let a Dream Song (119) have the last word: 'There's always the cruelty of scholarship./ I once was a slip.'

There are times when I would rather read the *Sonnets* than anything else of Berryman's. They show what he can do with a plot and a setting. They are the first time he enjoys himself within a form, acquires colour and character, becomes learned and compendious and allusive, dramatizes his themes of anxiety and guilt. His lines are full of music and play, he becomes lexically interesting, revelling – as he does again in *Bradstreet* – in the connection between seventeenth-century English and twentieth-century American, say in the phrase 'writhe in silly ecstasy', where an old sense of 'silly' emerges, related to the German *selig*, 'blissful', from *Seele*, 'soul'. It is in the *Sonnets* that he overcomes perhaps most compellingly what Joseph Warren Beach calls his 'sin against the reader (a scornful disregard for communication)', becoming at once interesting and believable. I wonder what other poet is so dependent on having – and so expert at getting – the unconditional trust of his readers, as Berryman, who noted 'When Shakespeare wrote, "Two loves I have", reader, he was *not kidding*.' In the *Sonnets*, Berryman manages vehemence and a whole voice. He left behind him the language of 'kidding', the single, affected mode of 'poesy', and took up a gloriously mixed diction. He was not, at least to begin with, writing for publication, and so was not inhibited. The more flamboyance he could achieve, the better for the project:

> How shall I sing, western & dry & thin,
> You who for celebration should cause flow
> The sensual fanfare of D'Annunzio,
> Mozart's mischievous joy, the amaranthine
> Mild quirks of Marvell, Villon sharp as tin
> Solid as sword-death when the man blinks slow
> And accordions into the form he'll know
> Forever –

Berryman sets a multiple course, makes his 'form' jagged, cross-questions himself on this ancient tradition – and does it all out loud. He ribs the sonnet ('the octet will be weaker'), he quizzes his material ('Some horse-shit here, eh?'), he marshals his songs ('kids') as he will the Dream Songs later, a man among multitudes. The *Sonnets* roll up material like cracked pepper, Chaplin, Plutarch, Anne Frank, Bach, whatever. They invert ('I

sit/ Or smoking pace'), they space ('and every word that I
have gasped of you is true'), they sing ('Blonde, barefoot,
beautiful/flat on the bare floor rivetted to Bach'). Their
endeavour throughout is to be as expressive and believable as
possible:

> A 'broken heart' . . . but *can* a heart break, now?
> Lovers have stood bareheaded in love's 'storm'
> Three thousand years, changed by their mistress' 'charm',
> Fitted their 'torment' to a passive bow,
> Suffered the 'darts' under a knitted brow,
> And has one heart broken for all this 'harm'?
> An arm is something definite. My arm
> Is acting – I hardly know to tell you how.
>
> It aches . . . well, after fifteen minutes of
> Serving, I can't serve more, it's not my arm,
> A piece of pain joined to me, helpless dumb thing.
> After four months of work-destroying love
> (An hour, I still don't lift it: I feel real alarm:
> Weeks of this, – no doctor finds a thing),
>   not much; and not all. Still, this is something.

The combination of technical ambition and modesty in taking
the rhyme on into the sestet from the octet – it's a simple rhyme
on 'arm', and in his stricken fashion he even repeats the word;
the doubled-up last line mimics the 'helpless dumb thing' men-
tioned above – is typical of Berryman's fight for the belief of the
reader in the *Sonnets*. He razes tradition, and puts up something
true – he asserts – in its place that tops it: Berryman and his
arm taking his place among, not the writers of Odes and their
loved ones, but the symptoms of love and the parts afflicted.

Homage to Mistress Bradstreet is mature Berryman: the
flowering of the ampersand, the crocked – crockt – spellings,
the inversions and archaisms, incorporations of allusions, flit-
tings in and out of character. The ampersand I think especially
is an embodiment of Berryman: it's accelerated, emphatic, indi-
vidual and – both senses, really – unconsidered, a *tic. Berryman's
Understanding* contains two of the best and most celebrated
articles on the poem, by the poets J. F. Nims and Stanley Kunitz,
sane, diligent, technically exhaustive pieces, resolutely less than
impressed by the poem. It remains, though, a startling piece of

writing – even less compromising in a way than the Dream Songs. At times I half-see a rationale in the style – seventeenth-century German word-order, maybe? – but then these chimeras recede. Sensation and faith seem to hold each other in balance. Berryman writes of trouble and pain, endeavour and time passing, lit by tiny moments of domestic joy, as here: 'I pare/ an apple for my pipsqueak Mercy and/ she runs & all need naked apples, fanned/ their tinier envies'. The point here, I suppose, is 'pipsqueak', the way 'naked' seems to modify both 'apples' and 'all', and the realization that a little Fall or a little Judgment of Paris has just been enacted, and no Golden Age is about to begin in the New World, whatever some have hoped. 'Pioneering is not feeling well.' Both Nims and Kunitz have the same objection to the poem, that it is really more about Berryman than Bradstreet ('feelings persist in belonging to the poet instead of becoming the property of the poem'), and both jib at the central stanzas in which the modern poet advances into his poem to make love to his subject. 'Myth too is common sense', says a pained Nims. Still, I suppose it is what Conrad Aiken called it, 'a classic right on the door step' – with all the oddity that that implies.

Only a matter of months after finishing *Homage to Mistress Bradstreet* (which took him five years, all told), Berryman embarked on another long poem: 'It begins in Iowa City, part of it is in Hebrew, and it ends (so far) in the Pleiades – with the best passage I ever wrote.' This venture was mercifully discontinued, but soon another, no less strange, began to take shape, drawing on several different sources. One was the eighteen-line monologue form of the 'Nervous Songs' in *The Dispossessed*. Another was the analysis of dreams Berryman started making in 1955: 'Some of my simplest (in appearance) dreams have proved over the long hours of assoc. and analysis more complete than any poem I have ever read; a great deal to say; I have almost a new idea of the mind's strength, cunning, & beauty.' He kept a journal of these, by the weird and wonderful name 'St Pancras Braser'; it topped 600 pages, and for a time he thought of publishing part of it. A third source was the birth of his son Paul in 1957; the letters to his mother show what a rapt and delighted father and baby-talker Berryman was. Then there is 'Henry' – apparently it was his second wife's nickname for him, as his for her was 'Mabel'. Both star in the first of these new poems, 'The jolly old man is a silly old dumb', but Mabel fell by the wayside quite soon. Then there are other readings of Henry: William Wasserstrom has written an almost divinatory essay on the names and epigraphs of the *Dream Songs*; there are Henrys in Stephen Crane and Hemingway; there was a Jewish dentist Henry in Princeton and even, so it please the court, Henry Helicopter, whose 'happy rotors whirred' in Dream Song 367.

The first Dream Song stanza to survive was written in 1955, and Berryman used the form for almost everything he wrote in the next fifteen years. *77 Dream Songs* appeared in 1964, *His Toy, His Dream, His Rest* in 1968, and there is a choice of posthumous Dream Songs in *Henry's Fate & Other Poems*. The *Dream Songs* contains the first two of these volumes, 385 poems; it was first published in that form in 1969, and why it has taken twenty-one years to reach England I have absolutely no idea.

At first, the selection and order of the songs was provisional: 'These are sections, constituting one version, of a poem in progress', Berryman wrote in a note to *77 Dream Songs*. It was something he entertained thoughts of amending and revising, as Pound did with the Cantos. In the 1940s and 1950s, Berryman was left sitting on his poetry; in the 1960s printers and publishers tore it from his hands. Both Dream Song volumes and *Berryman's Sonnets* (1967) were finished – it seems the wrong word to use – under intense time-pressure. When he dug up the *Sonnets*, after twenty years, he wrote a few more, to round them off. Most made it – they are among the best – but two didn't, and they appear for the first time in the *Collected Poems* as numbers 115 and 116. Hardly surprisingly perhaps, they are both closer to Dream Song concerns of the mid-sixties: one mentions a gun, the other suicide. Similar things happened to the Dream Songs themselves. The idea of publishing a preliminary selection was not Berryman's own, but the suggestion of his peers, Lowell and Wilbur. (Once the genie was out of the bottle – or part of it anyway – Lowell was amazingly equivocal about it. His review of Berryman in the *New York Review of Books* furnished the paperback edition with quotes, but read in its

entirety, it is evasive, critical and uncomfortable. Berryman felt
he had been stabbed in the back.) When plans were reasonably
advanced, there were to be sixty of them. Later this jumped to
seventy-five. When the seventy-seventh poem turned out to be
one he'd already completed, it came as a complete surprise to
Berryman, who fully expected he would have to write it still. A
wild and joky 'Note' of 1961 – not used – shows his ambivalence
towards the whole project:

> The manuscript – of this pseudo-poem or epic – was found in an
> abandoned keyhole and transmitted to me by enemies, anxious to
> thwart my lawful work. It is doubtful whether its author – of whom
> nothing is known, except that he claims (in 67) to be a human being,
> and male – gave it a final form ... The indifferent reader will be
> relieved to learn that I have let loose here only a fraction of the
> manuscript.

Berryman laboured at the serious work of giving the thing a
'final form', studied epic structure and theory – John Haffenden
gives a detailed and sympathetic account of his endeavours in
John Berryman: A critical commentary – but selecting and
ordering the poems was tough and went against the grain: 'I see
why I hate putting the "75" together (I did 51 today – there's
52nd) – the good ones seem to me *so* good I can't bear to hide
them with the inferiors.'

In the end, all but the most imaginative critics and surely
every reader would agree with Louis Martz in saying the Dream
Songs as a whole 'lack plot, either traditional or associative'. If
they are a long poem at all – as Berryman insisted they were –
then it is only in a rather scholastic, unmeaningful way, far
removed from the way people read and think, or simply out of
charity or deference to Berryman's wishes. Harry Thomas writes
in his introduction that 'the impression made by reading several
songs individually ... is greater than that made by reading the
work from end to end'. The two books of them fail for opposite
reasons: *77 Dream Songs* is clearly far shapelier, more manage-
able and memorable, but they are written at such a pitch of
intensity that they cannot be read in a comfortable series. Every
one of them is about – or at any rate reads like – a kind of
ultimate single combat. The only way of organizing them is to

give the reader at least occasional respite; the idea of grouping them by theme, say, the elegies, the poems of lust, of temptation by death, is simply grotesque. By contrast, the 308 Dream Songs of *His Toy, His Dream, His Rest* fail because they are too many and too slack. In a fine and gentle essay, Denis Donoghue makes this point: 'Mr Berryman has proposed to himself the discipline of dramatic character, but he has not, in the later songs, accepted its obligations.' If the 77 are all extreme, all a beginning and ending, all terminal, *His Toy, His Dream* is largely middle, indifferent circumstances lumberingly and unpersuasively put in the third person and hung on Henry:

> The Cabin, Congdon St, & the Old Gristmill
> saw stretches of the long & long work done
> to certain satisfactions,
> including Henry's reluctant still & still
> in spite of the incessant additions.
>   (Dream Song 352)

The later elegies were more coarsely written than those on Roethke and Frost and Hemingway early on; a bluster comes into the phrasing that is more company loyalty than tenderness: 'expression's kings', 'the flaming best', 'that senior genius'. Another indication of the falling-off is the sharply reduced number of appearances by Henry's interlocutor, the man who calls him 'Mr Bones' and who speaks in blackface. He appears eighteen times in the 77, only thirteen more in the remaining 308. And yet his every appearance is a triumph: his harsh ' – Mr Bones, we all brutes & fools' at the end of a charming and innocent song about the behaviour of a rabbit (62); or his cry from the wings, 'Come away, Mr Bones' (77), of which Adrienne Rich has exclaimed: 'Come away! Shakespeare's English and some minstrelly refrain meet, salute and inform each other.'

The Dream Songs are unique in English, and probably any other language:

> this mad amalgam of ballad-idiom (ours via Appalachia), Shakespea-rian rag, Gerard Manley Hopkins in a delirium of syntactical reversals, nigger-talk, blues talk, hip-talk engendered from both, Mil-tonic diction, Calypso, bureaucratiana, pure blurted Anglo-Saxon.

(Adrienne Rich again.) Fumbling for comparisons, one would

reach for late Shakespeare or late Rilke. They are all so broken, and stand in their own spotlight. The dramatic style of their utterance – their poise, both on the page, and the timing when they are said aloud – is exquisite. The endings are utterly hetero-geneous, but of a finality one doesn't find in poetry: 'He fell out of the tree', 'Yes, pal', 'I have said what I had to say'. 'We are all end-men' was another minstrel phrase Berryman thought of using as an epigram. In a way it wasn't necessary. These are all end-poems:

> – I cannot remember. I am going away.
> There was something in my dream about a Cat,
> which fought and sang.
> Something about a lyre, an island. Unstrung.
> Linked to the land at low tide. Cables fray.
> Thank you for everything.

Berryman published two more books of poems, *Love & Fame* and *Delusions, etc* (though he died before the latter appeared). They are near replicas of one another, going through remi-niscence, breakdown and Christian witness. *Love & Fame* is by far the better book, of a transparency and fluency not previously achieved (or striven for) by Berryman, with flashes of his old wit and fire and gorgeousness: '& a short about Oxford was greeted one evening/ with loud cunning highly articulate disdain'; 'Well, hell./ I am not writing an autobiography-in-verse, my friends';

> Bear in mind me, Who have forgotten nothing,
> & Who continues. I may not foreknow
> & fail much to remember. You sustain
> imperial desuetudes, at the kerb a widow.

E. M. Halliday's half-gallant, half-racy memoir* is good to read alongside the poems in this book about his Columbia days.

Berryman's legacy is, I suppose, twofold, the theoretical and the practical. The theory, developed against Eliot's, is that per-sonality and the personal have a role to play in poetry: 'I am down on Rilke and the hieratic boys just now. I don't deny his

---

*E.M. Halliday, *John Berryman and the Thirties* (Amherst: University of Massa-chusetts, 1987)

sensitivity and his marvellous melody, or Valéry's vivacity –
incomparable exc w Stendhal's whom he passionately admired.
But it is necessary to get down into the arena and kick around.'
This creed coarsened and warped into the one he enunciated in
his last years, most signally in his *Paris Review* interview of
1970:

> My idea is this: the artist is extremely lucky who is presented with
> the worst possible ordeal which will not actually kill him. At that
> point he's in business. Beethoven's deafness, Goya's deafness, Milton's
> blindness, that kind of thing.

Kicking around isn't enough; the artist has to let in the lions.
Mercifully, this brutal and degenerate idea hasn't been so very
influential, though it has turned people against Berryman's own
practice in poetry.

This, I would argue, is quite separate. The intensity of lan-
guage comes out of intensity of thought and feeling – but to
summon down vicissitudes of experience is a masochistic irrel-
evance. It is making a cult of chance. But before Berryman
formulated this, in the late 1950s and early 1960s, he wrote
poems of a kind of perverse and molecular joy, fighting off the
continual wish to die; little crumbs of pleasure, solidarity and
elegance:

> and Henry was happy & beside him with excitement.
> Beside himself, his possibilities;
> salaaming hours of a half-blind morning
> while the rainy lepers salaamed back,
> smiles & a passion of their & his eyes flew
> in feelings not ever accorded solely to oneself.

Very little of the poetry of the post-war era has addressed itself
so frankly to the question of 'Why we are here', and none so
credibly as this.

ROBERT LOWELL'S PROSE

'His most confident writing, perhaps, is autobiographical.' This is Robert Lowell, not on Lowell, but on Hawthorne, and yet it might be at least as true of himself. Autobiography, he said in 1976, was the thread that strung together his life's work, and an autobiography was one of the two prose books Lowell actually contemplated in his lifetime. In 1955, he went to his publisher Robert Giroux and asked for a contract for such a book, as a spur to writing it. He worked on it for the next two years, but progress was slow, and it was never completed. The largest part of it – still invariably called, demeaningly, a 'prose fragment' – appeared in *Life Studies* in 1959 as '91 Revere Street'. Now, two further pieces from the manuscript, 'Antebellum Boston' and 'Near the Unbalanced Aquarium', are published in their entirety for the first time. They are so good, so pre-eminently what Lowell is good at, and their period, the late 1950s, is so clearly the best period of Lowell's prose (which seems to be five years ahead of the poetry, whose time came in the early 1960s), that one might have wished for a more permissive editing policy for the *Collected Prose*, more 'jumble or jungle', some of the chips of 'waste marble' – surely they exist – as well as 'the figure'.

The more so, as much of the other writing, the critical writing, is just such 'waste marble' and 'jumble'. The second of Lowell's projected prose books was to be called *A Moment in American Poetry*, but its proposed contents went beyond 'the generation of Eliot, Frost and William Carlos Williams', to take in subjects some of whom, as Giroux observes in his introduction, with plaintive reasonableness, were not Americans, and others not poets. Apart from his inability to complete either of his prose books, there are other suggestions that Lowell lacked true commitment to the medium. On the subject of his autobiographical writing, he told Frederick Seidel in the *Paris Review* (the interview is reprinted here): 'I found it got awfully tedious working out transitions and putting in things that didn't seem very important but were necessary to the prose continuity'.

Review of Robert Lowell, *Collected Prose*, ed. Robert Giroux
(London: Faber and Faber, 1987)

As a critic, Lowell has not a fraction of the gifts of his friend and class-mate Randall Jarrell, to whom, in his essays and reviews, he is forever referring and deferring: on Eliot, on Williams, on Frost, on Ransom, on Jarrell himself, 'so bewilderingly gifted that it is impossible to comment on him without the humiliating thought that he himself could do it better'. Lowell's criticism is short, limited in its occasions, violently evaluative, and, as his Hawthorne sentence suggests, unconfident. Even his stance of not doing 'the standard analytical essay' won't quite protect him: Jarrell wasn't exactly the standard analyst either. One might adapt Lowell's stricture on Wallace Stevens – in 1947, in Lowell's strenuous period – and say: 'there seems to be something in the critic [poet] that protects itself by asserting that it is not making too much of an effort'.

Apart from Dylan Thomas and (I think) Stevens, all of Lowell's review-subjects were personally well known to him already: they were friends and contemporaries (Jarrell, Bishop, Berryman, Kunitz), a former student (Plath), but most often they were his elders and teachers: Tate and Ransom, Eliot, Frost, Williams, Ford. He didn't write more than one or two reviews in a year – each of them was, as Robert Giroux says, an occasion – and his last pieces of that kind were on 77 *Dream Songs* in 1964 and *Ariel* in 1966. But even though they are personal occasions, there is little of the tone of 'O world, I am sorry for you,/ You do not know these four people', of Pound's poem 'Causa'. They are neither revealingly private, nor convincingly addressed to a public; there is something ceremonial, almost sacramental about them. In an illuminating phrase on Yvor Winters, he speaks of him not being 'adequately praised', and it seems to me it is this 'adequate praise' (a dubious, stiff, almost paradoxical notion) that he is most often giving. Lowell is not a proselytizer, not an unraveller; he seems to keep a constant distance between himself and his subjects; his reviews are not discoveries.

His quick responses to new books or poets seem particularly cluttered and uncertain; here, he compares most unfavourably with Jarrell, when he writes about Bishop or Berryman. The much-quoted sentence about Berryman, 'This great Pierrot's universe is more tearful and funny than we can easily bear', the final sentence in the review, is a lot less convincing in context ('hazardous, imperfect book', 'relentless indulgence') and conforms to a pattern of final sentences that are little eulogistic curls. Again, on Bishop, who was to be for him the contemporary he most admired, his first response is choked with comparisons: 'In this, and in her marvelous command of shifting speech tones, Bishop resembles Robert Frost. In her bare objective language, she also reminds one at times of William Carlos Williams; but it is obvious that her most important model is Marianne Moore.' Compared to Jarrell, he is unenthusiastic and wooden, not easily fervent or cool, sometimes even without the ability to make himself believed. As Lowell himself admits, he quotes badly, either too much or not at all, with 'no gift for the authoritative and lucid comment that somehow makes a quotation sail'. Though his subjects are all important and survive, one rarely gets the impression that they were important to him at the time of writing (as against, say, Heaney's criticism). In the early reviews, he is dutiful and circumspect, and later – he stopped writing them. (One would have liked to read him on late Bishop, or on European writing, Flaubert and Pasternak – whose names crop up most frequently – or Montale, mentioned in the introduction to *Imitations* as having 'long amazed' him, but not again.)

Written, then, out of personal acquaintance and devotion, the reviews really come into their own when the personal or the human is allowed primacy, often in a second shot at a subject, in pieces that recollect or grieve. Lowell's best short prose form is the free personal memoir. After reading him on Ransom's poems, to read him on his 'den' or the layout of his garden is a revelation: 'His rather repellent and unwayward rows of flowers seemed laid out by tape measure and colour chart.' Rather than dwelling exclusively on the poems of *Goodbye, Earth*, Lowell discusses its photograph of I. A. Richards climbing in the Swiss Alps. His short, very funny piece, 'Visiting the Tates', word for word the best in the book, gives an objective correlative of the Tate poem (if not of Tate himself):

> a tar-black cabinet with huge earlobe-like handles. It was his own workmanship. I had supposed that crafts were repeatable skills and

belonged to the pedestrian boredom of manual-training classes. However, something warped, fissured, strained, and terrific about this cabinet suggested that it would be Tate's last.

As well as this boisterous and puzzled insolence, it also manages infinitely subtle and musical sentences, like this one, again on décor: 'A reproduced sketch of Leonardo's *Virgin of the Rocks* balanced an engraving of Stonewall Jackson.' The balance extends further than that, though: to reproduced and virgin, rocks and stone, virgin and stonewall; and to the 'o's of Leonardo and Stonewall, and the 'x's of Rocks and Jackson.

The circumstantial everywhere out-performs the purely literary. Quoting another critic on 'the greatest modern master of the comma' seems even more arid when set against his own mystified, youthful admiration of William Carlos Williams: 'I was surprised that Williams used commas, and that my three or four methods of adjusting his lines to uniform typewriter spaces failed. I supposed he had gone on to some bolder and still more mature system.' Wherever Lowell himself can be present, or where there are physical circumstances to be described, or far-off events to be related, his gifts seem to blossom: humour, candour, warmth, attention. The best of Lowell always comes out of years of presence and study: *For Lizzie and Harriet*, his retrospective book of 1973 with its settings of Maine, Boston and New York, is far better than its instant, up-to-the-minute twin, *The Dolphin*, about England. He needs time, research, preparation, revision.

It is in the autobiographical pieces that the virtues of Lowell's style, and of his eye and ear, are most evident and free-standing: the sardonic epithets, 'interestingly costly', 'lethal ferns' or 'intense moves back to Boston', all coming out of a loosened awareness of his mother's near-hysterical snobbery. At times, the epithets queue up to make points: 'All was hushed, vexed and ajar', or 'To be a boy at Brimmer was to be small, denied and weak.' There are no fewer than nine of them in succession, describing his father's 'rhinoceros hide' armchair, a piece of equipment eminently comparable in monstrosity and symbolic weight to Tate's cabinet. This is 'the style that made writing impossible', that Lowell mentions in another context: it is all concentration, all epiphany, all climax. It seems that to drag it from its intense absorption of one object, circumstance or episode to another would kill it. Here, it seems, is style forever wanting to stop and bury itself in a kind of articulate hysteria.

WELDON KEES

Weldon Kees (1914–?55) has remained a name to conjure with, though it's thirty-three years since he disappeared – car found abandoned on the approach to the Golden Gate Bridge; never seen again – and the one book to his name, *The Collected Poems of Weldon Kees*, edited by Donald Justice (University of Nebraska Press), was first published almost as long ago, and is sometimes available, sometimes not. It has, though, endured, and will endure. There is another name, indissolubly linked to Kees's: 'Robinson', the hero of four manifestly autobiographical, defiantly external poems, a kind of *ur*-Henry, dapper, melancholy and doomed:

> Robinson on a roof above the Heights; the boats
> Mourn like the lost. Water is slate, far down.
> Through sounds of ice cubes dropped in glass, an osteopath,
> Dressed for the links, describes an old Intourist tour.
> – Here's where old Gibbons jumped from, Robinson.
>
> ('Aspects of Robinson')

Kees writes what one might call grotesque brochure style: dandyish trappings, promotional clarity and a view of frightful abysses of sadness, cruelty and despair. His poems resound from a black hole in the drawing-room, or they are found outlined in police chalk on the floor. From the rigid 1950s, a contemporary, no question. To any British publisher who took him on, a reward in Heaven, and perhaps even in Britain first.

ELIZABETH BISHOP
Prose

If Molière is right, and everything that isn't verse is prose, and everything that isn't prose is verse, then, with *The Collected Prose* of Elizabeth Bishop (companion-volume to *The Complete Poems*, out last year, from the same publisher), we shall have seen all we shall ever get to see of this wonderful author's work. The two books, in their peach and chlorine jackets, with watercolours by Bishop on the covers look well together, and they are well matched in size, both coming in at just under 300 pages. If the excellence of the *Prose* is quite unsurprising (as unsurprising as that the author was referred to as 'the Bishop' when a schoolgirl by her companions; or that 'we all knew with no doubt whatsoever that she was a genius'), then it should only be observed that it is not a separate excellence from that of the poems.

The virtues of the prose are the virtues of the poems: observation, wit, decorum, a sinuous intelligence, and above all what Randall Jarrell called her 'moral attractiveness' – no abuse, no indiscretion, no protests. If this sounds prim, it isn't: it's only an indication of how far things have gone the other way. Here is Jarrell again:

> It is odd how pleasant and sympathetic her poems are, in these days when many a poet had rather walk down children like Mr Hyde than weep over them like Swinburne, and when many a poem is gruesome occupational therapy for a poet who stays legally innocuous by means of it.

The prose is odd and pleasant and sympathetic in much the same way. The subjects are largely those familiar from the poems: her family, her native Nova Scotia, life by the shores of the Atlantic, in Massachusetts and Brazil, paintings, human portraits and 'questions of travel'. The *aller-et-retour* form of many of the poems is discernible in some of the prose, in 'To the Botequim and Back' and 'A Trip to Vigia'. (Interestingly, Bishop admits

Review of Elizabeth Bishop, *The Collected Prose* (London: Chatto and Windus, 1984)

elsewhere, 'I am superstitious about going "back" to places, anyway: they have changed; you have changed; even the weather may have changed.') Sometimes, there are detailed correspondences between the poems and the prose: it is the same scene from childhood in 'The Country Mouse' and 'In the Waiting Room'. Or correspondences of genre: the realistically elaborated story 'The Sea and its Shore' is charmed from its hypothetical premiss in just the same way as 'The Man-Moth' from its newspaper misprint. Both are abstract fantasies indebted, it seems to me, to Kafka. Or again, one might identify two distinct styles in Bishop, in her prose as in her poems: a loose, probing, 'spoken' style, and a stately 'high style', literary, fixed, almost artificial, hinting at Victorian prose and at Defoe, and exemplified here in the story 'In Prison'. These similarities and others make the division of Bishop's prose into the two categories 'Memory' and 'Stories' rather factitious: after all, no such division is made among her poems.

If one imagined a square with admiration and sympathy, amusement and dignity as its four corners, the whole of Elizabeth Bishop's work would be situated inside it. Take for instance the account of only her second meeting with Marianne Moore, an outing – at Miss Bishop's inspired suggestion – to the circus at Madison Square Garden. Miss Moore was carrying

> two huge brown paper bags, full of something. I was given one of these. They contained, she told me, stale brown bread for the elephants, because stale brown bread was one of the things they liked best to eat. (I later suspected that they might like stale white bread just as much but that Marianne had been thinking of their health.)

In a way, the scene is 'a gift', just as the remarkable Miss Moore and her mother are 'a gift', but how easy it would have been to collapse it into sentimental farce. Instead, all the parties involved, and not least the elephants, whose wishes are solicitously though never intrusively guessed at, are treated with the utmost respect – a smiling respect, though, not stiffness or stuffiness. Elizabeth Bishop marries generosity of spirit with generosity of style ('one of the things', 'just as much'): how well her memoir earns its title – itself an acknowledged and admired borrowing from Miss Moore – 'Efforts of Affection'.

It is this kind of tact and attention – one should perhaps call it grace – that is maintained throughout this collection, and makes it so delightful and rewarding. Whenever it really matters to her, Elizabeth Bishop has the ability to procure for herself the reader's utter, unreserved belief, most obviously when she is writing, as a child, about her childhood. This, just as fraught with difficulties as the type of scene with Miss Moore, is managed with equal assurance. It is, I think, because Bishop is always so committed to the moment and the scene she is describing, and that she is free from any ulterior purpose, that she is both so engaging and so trustworthy. Her naturalness, self-possession and fun *are* those of a child: 'My grandmother settled herself on a log to talk to her friends, and I went wading in the river with mine.' There is so much more I would like to say about her: her ingenuity, her freakishness, her tendency to personify objects and places (another sign of generosity, for she doesn't do the opposite and reify people in the way, say, Dickens does), the wonderfully candid way she allows her self to be scrutinized and laughed at, just as she, in her writing, laughs and scrutinizes. The freedom of her manner: 'he gave me his name and asked me to print it; here it is: Manoel Benicio de Loyola, "diamond-hunter of Curralinho".' The way virtue and virtuosity seem to be inextricably bound up in her work: Miss Mamie in 'Mercedes Hospital' who 'has the local reputation of a saint'; the naive painter Gregorio Valdes whom she encourages; the blue-and-white bandstand in the plaza which is hideous, 'but because it was so small it didn't spoil the effect at all'; the shy poet Ruy (and his even shyer son) who knows no English and admires T. S. Eliot, whom everyone knows, and for whom Bishop and her friend are unable to do anything, not even to buy him a cup of coffee; the grey-green mildew in the rainy season in Rio which will, Bishop knows, sooner or later attack the portrait of her 'Uncle Neddy' but which she still loves. I have helplessly and purposely left out of my account all mention of Elizabeth Bishop's masterpiece 'In the Village' which concludes this book, which, even without it, would be wholly admirable. If only there were another to come!

ELIZABETH BISHOP
Letters

Elizabeth Bishop (1911–1979) is the best-loved poet in America, and has been for some years. Such dissimilar poets as Anthony Hecht and John Ashbery unite in proclaiming their devotion to her work. Typically, an American writing student will have read one or two anthologies, some randomly chosen volume published in the last six months, and – Elizabeth Bishop. This huge volume of her letters – one fifth of the total, selected by her friend and publisher, Robert Giroux – doubles her output at a stroke, but without impairing its quality. No one who has *The Complete Poems* and *The Collected Prose* (and everyone should!) will want to be without it for long.

In her lifetime, she was the poets' poet: her noisier and more eye-catchingly self-destructive male colleagues, Lowell, Jarrell, Berryman, all admired her and fell over themselves to commend her cool, elusive and home-made ('But aren't we all?') poems. But if they would be astonished by her pre-eminence over them now, so, still more, would she, who lived almost half of her working life outside the US, didn't teach, gave no readings, didn't engage in poe-business until her last years, and, as she wrote to Lowell: 'always felt that I've written poetry more by *not* writing it than writing it.'

She was a traveller from conviction, and from necessity. Like the sandpiper in her poem of that name, she ranged up and down the Atlantic coastline, from Nova Scotia where she grew up, to Brazil where she arrived on a cruise and ended up staying 15 years. Being, as she said, 'elsewhere' was essential to her. In the States, she preferred the unregarded corners of Key West and Maine. With the material she collected in these places, she bought herself privacy and space.

Once, in an uncharacteristic moment of *guignol*, she said to Robert Lowell: 'when you write my epitaph, you must say I was the loneliest person who ever lived.' Lonely but far from unsocial, in fact with a gift for intimacy, keeping friends for 30, 40, 50 years. Her letters are like wonderful conversation (as the

Review of Elizabeth Bishop, *One Art: Letters Selected and Edited by Robert Giroux* (London: Chatto and Windus, 1994)

poems are too): entertaining, communicative, vocal, solicitous, affectionate, generous; what they aren't (except very rarely) is personal: the subjectivity is always directed outwards.

The particular virtue of Elizabeth Bishop is the balance between the self and the world, between the eye (or 'I') and what it sees. Her contemporaries invited the reader into their souls, had no secrets, cultivated extreme individuality and extreme experience; she (while just as unhappy and unstable as they, an orphan at two, a borderline alcoholic, two long lesbian relationships ending in the suicide and insanity of companions) practised decorum and wit, was recessive, fugitive, kept pointing to a world beyond herself, in what now seems a brilliantly and heroically diversionary defensive strategy, a form of camouflage or display. What she offered her correspondents and her readers was not herself – fearing or deprecating the gift – but the world, which has rarely seemed more fascinating or beautiful than in her descriptions of it.

Line for line, her writing must have more colour, amusement and brilliance (literally: effulgence, rainbows, iridescence) in it than anyone's, whether it's the blue skin of her toucan bathing, 'as if he had blue jeans on under the feathers', or some Carolina hillbillies:

> *almost* like *Tobacco Road*. One little girl comes in every morning to help us clean; her name is *Walterine*, her father is a moonshiner. She is 14 and very pretty and is going to get married this winter to a boy of 16. She has eight brothers and sisters . . .

These letters communicate the joy of experiencing the world through Bishop's eyes, and very little of the ghastliness, though there is no doubt at all that she felt that too. 'Most things are for the worst,' she merely observes.

Most writers pluck or strum or bang, Bishop (and I can only think of Kafka who proceeds in anything like the same way) arranges impressions into complicated chords, full of revised, contradictory, accumulated notions. Elements of 'design' or 'meaning' seem almost frivolous, compared to these precisely chaotic chords. It is what finally makes her such a tremendously inspiriting writer:

> Lota was away in Rio and I was all alone with the servants and the

toucan (who had a sore foot) & the cat (who was being wormed) and the *roaring* waterfall. I feel as if I'd undergone a sort of Robinson Crusoe experience. Also I kept reading Coleridge's letters – just couldn't stop – and *his* weather got worse and worse & his health more and more excruciating, until when he had 'flying irregular gout', had got drenched one more time and his finances were beyond hope, I could scarcely believe that I was dry, had no symptoms of anything at all, and was at least solvent enough to send you this very small memento. I feel as if I could scarcely be said to exist, beside C. You must read him, though . . .

FRANK O'HARA

Frank O'Hara was the life and soul of the New York school of poets. He was born in 1926 and died in 1966, in what is usually described as a 'freak accident', when a beach buggy reversed into him on the resort of Fire Island. How this fact – if it is a fact – ever swam into my consciousness, I have no idea, but its scatty and tenacious detail is somehow typical of this poet who worked in the art world, whose friends were painters and ballet-dancers, and whose breezy poems were composed – another 'fact' – in his lunch hours on typewriters he would ask to try out in typewriter shops.

In the generation since his death, the survival of his poetry has become assured. A monumental canvas-bound *Collected Poems* – more like an art book or Mount Rushmore than a volume of poetry – was issued in 1971 (its editors were unable to refrain from noting how astounded, even embarrassed O'Hara would have been by its scale and splendour). In 1974, there was a *Selected* edited by his friend Donald Allen, the odd copy of which fetched up in English bookshops; this is the book which Carcanet have taken on, and is now under review. His most famous book, the City Lights volume *Lunch Poems*, has been reprinting steadily since 1964. (It was translated into German soon after by Rolf Dieter Brinkmann: *Mittagessengedichte* had a huge impact on German poetry of the late 1960s and 1970s.) Last but not least are the anthologies, where O'Hara is such an appealing presence; Moore and Hall each allow him four poems, Ellman and Vendler eight. I can't imagine anyone reading 'A Step Away from Them' or 'The Day Lady Died' or 'Ave Maria' and remaining indifferent to the enormous and uncomplicated freshness of those poems. It is probably still the best way to read O'Hara, to come upon him unsuspecting, in an anthology; I suppose because that replicates the crowd experience, the surprise and delight that the poems are so often about. Anthologies are cities and O'Hara was after all a city poet.

Much though I like O'Hara, and though I've had these

Review of Frank O'Hara, *Selected Poems*, ed. Donald Allen
(Manchester: Carcanet, 1991)

Selected Poems for fourteen years, it's not a book I care for, and I almost wish Carcanet hadn't taken it on. (All they've brought to it are a few remarks of John Ashbery's on the jacket, but they were so acute I wished he could have been more involved.) It isn't an introduction, isn't a 'best of' and it isn't everything. O'Hara is not really a poet you select from: it goes against his own poetic, which you might describe as 'bulk inclusion'. I could imagine taking down his *Collected* – though unfortunately I don't own one – and consulting it almost randomly like a medical dictionary, *Bibelstechen* or *sors virgiliana*, the way you consult any compendious, varied and pertinent work of prophetic pretensions. As it is, I carry around his *Lunch Poems*, which are the size and weight of a medium sandwich. The *Selected Poems* is betwixt and between. This new English hardback edition is expensive and smart, although not comically intimidating – without the monumental 'sprawl' of the American *Collected* which made it so unforgettable and provocative. The chosen poems are in chronological order, but are undated. They make up about a third of O'Hara's oeuvre, but they exceed by far too many the thirty or forty poems on which his reputation rests. For a selection, there is simply far too much dead wood.

In particular, Donald Allen has over-represented O'Hara's early work. Half the book goes on things written before 1956, and only a quarter is left for poems from 1959 and after, which make up O'Hara's best and most characteristic work. Early O'Hara is practically unreadable. I mean, you read it but nothing happens. It is as arid and as much 'practising' as, say, early Berryman. Occasionally it even sounds like early Berryman, as in 'A Sonnet for Jane Freilicher':

> bring me that breath more dear than Fabergé
> your secret puissance Operator loan
> to pretty Jane whose paintings like a stone
> are massive true and silently risqué

(The main difference between this and early Berryman is that O'Hara is laughing at himself; whether that makes it any better I wouldn't know.) The lines are unusual because, to use the current jargon, they are in 'form' – they rhyme, and how! – but they would not be the only O'Hara exhibits in a museum of poetic awfulness, 1945–55.

Bad poetry is far more instructive about the practice of its time than good poetry. Most early O'Hara, whether written in pseudo-stanzas (his word 'optometrical' suggests itself) or slabs (he has a poem called 'Blocks') of free verse, gives one a sense of almost helpless proliferation. The poem is the victim of a hypertrophic and overweening grammar. It looks furiously like sense, except that there has been some substitution giving one the wrong verbs and adverbs and nouns, and leaving only correct prepositions in place. It is both wild and mechanical, and it is fast – fast bad writing is always more fun than slow – and it is purposeless. The response it demands from the reader is not 'this is good (or bad)', nor 'why is this good (or bad)?' but 'why is this the way it is?' This is what you rack your brains over as you read:

> O the glassy towns are fucked by yaks
> Slowly bleeding a quiet filigree on the leaves of that souvenir
> of a bird chastely crossing the boulevard of falling stars
> cold in the dull heavens
> drowned in flesh,
>   it's the night like a love it all cruisy and nelly
> fingered fan of boskage fronds the white smile of sleeps.
>
>   ('Easter')

or this:

> Lepers nest on the surly cats of glistening delirium,
> feet of fire drowning in the attitude of relinquishing foreheads
> remember always the barriers so cupiditously defended,
> no spume breezy enough for the tempestuous sabers
> sent reeling into the charades of fears of the nubile
>
>   ('Invincibility')

Such passages read like literal translations from – maybe – Spanish, copied by surrealists with bad memories. The poems are impenetrable surfaces, carapaces the poet hides behind, saying to himself 'What is this stuff? Do *you* get it?' At the same time, it would be quite wrong to say O'Hara is unpromising or untalented: he displays the talents of others, the pyrite glitter of French poetry, the smoothness of Stevens, Surrealism. This is the dominant period style. Nowadays you need a machete to read it.

O'Hara's conversion can't be dated precisely. In the midst of all that showy tangle there are passages that are pleasing and original, deft endings and wonderful and outrageous similes, things like 'as ill at ease as sea-food' and 'the leaves falling/ like angels who've been discharged for sodomy.' At all stages of his career he wrote short clear poems that simply command one's assent: 'Autobiographia Literaria', 'Poem (The eager note on my door)', 'The Critic', 'Les Etiquettes Jaunes'. There are growing signs of an argument with himself: 'To a Poet'

> I am sober and industrious
> and would be plain and plainer
> for a little while
>   until my rococo
> self is more assured of its
> distinction.

and in 'My Heart':

> I want my feet to be bare,
> I want my face to be shaven, and my heart –
> you can't plan on the heart, but
> the better part of it, my poetry, is open.

In 1956 he wrote 'A Step Away from Them' in short lines and simple sentences, eating lunch, looking at building workers and thinking about Jackson Pollock. The collisions between sentences, on which this new poetry is founded, are still apt to be crude at times –

> I stop for a cheeseburger at JULIET'S
> CORNER. Giulietta Masina, wife of
> Federico Fellini, è bell' attrice.

– but O'Hara is on his way. By 1959, practically everything he wrote is considerable and original and looks set to last – for at least another generation anyway.

O'Hara's discovery – apart from the paratactic sentences – was the simultaneous or double subject of himself and New York City. That was what he came out from behind his carapace to write: the poetry of the open-eyed, open-minded, open-

hearted urbanite; cheerful diversions; the protocols of a con-
sciousness as quick and dazzling, unpredictable and unconnected
as neon lights and street noise and traffic. His lunchtime gander-
ings seemed to convert time – and many of the poems give the
time – straightforwardly into objects, stimuli, electrical pulses
of thought. As Ashbery says, he had 'a concept of the poem as
a chronicle of the creative act which produced it.' The poem
starts as simply and naturally as a door opening or a bell ringing:
'It is 12:10 in New York and I am wondering', 'It is 12:20 in
New York a Friday.' O'Hara is about as life-affirming as poetry
gets: nothing less like 'melancholy disciplined by metre'
(Brodsky) or 'lamentosa letteratura' (Montale) can be imagined.
The optimism and gaiety of it all is heightened for us, thirty
years later, by our perception that the New York O'Hara was
writing about was a kind of El Dorado, like Swinging London,
the New York of jazz and good paintings and black and white
movies, New York before muggers and drugs and racial tension
and homelessness and insider dealing. No one now feels as good
about their city, their lives and their times as O'Hara. We read
him with a sentimental feeling in our hearts for the good old
days of the avant-garde. But O'Hara has seen us coming, and
pokes fun at us:

> Ah Jean Dubuffet
> when you think of him
> doing his military service in the Eiffel Tower
> as a meteorologist
> in 1922
> you know how wonderful the 20th century
> can be
>
> ('Naphtha')

Ah Frank O'Hara, when you think of him working for MOMA
organizing exhibitions in the early 1960s, etc.

American poetry is a sectarian affair; it was strange to read
Donald Hall, in the *Review*'s poetry symposium, saying it
wasn't. Of the 'academic' crowd I most know about, Lowell and
Berryman and Jarrell, no one has anything to say on O'Hara. It
seems a great pity, and it leaves me at a loss: that Jarrell, the
other poet of enthusiasm, one might say, and such a catholic
critic, and, like O'Hara, an admirer of the dancer Tanaquil

Leclercq to boot, never considered him; or Berryman, emerging, like O'Hara, from poetic murk into the living American language; or Lowell, who trod the same midtown pavements and cultivated 'unrealism' in a book called *Notebook*. If only one's friends got along with each other!

That 'official' neglect, taken with his own rather breathless manner, tends to make one think there was something rather undiscriminating, almost foolish about O'Hara, retailing his enthusiasms, going from one moment of exaltation to the next. But, as 'Naphtha' shows, he was highly self-aware. In addition to his capacity for delight, he had an ironic intelligence, referring to his ' "I do this I do that" poems', and in 'Post the Lake Poets Ballad', giving this wonderfully dry and clever anatomy of himself:

> I think of myself
> as a cheerful type who pretends to
> be hurt to get a little depth into
>   things that interest me
>
> and I've even given that up
> lately with the stream of events
> going so fast and the movingly
>   alternating with the amusingly

The protestation of cheerfulness and the send-up of 'depth' are followed by a half-serious point about the pace of events: how can anyone be anything, least of all keep up any pose, when things are so quick to change. O'Hara's attitudes, his preference for brevity, variety and unpredictability, are, he argues, forced on him by modern life. He may not be able to indulge the same long-held emotions as the Lake Poets, but that doesn't make him an airhead.

O'Hara's best poems, seemingly so jumbled and aleatory, are actually, I would argue, quite tough, pretty organized and very difficult to imitate successfully. The endless syntactical meanderings of his youth stand him in good stead in such rhetorical and argumentative poems as 'Ave Maria' or the superb 'Answer to Voznesensky & Evtushenko' (sic), an unlikely aesthetico-patriotic outburst in response, no doubt, to considerable provocation:

> We are tired of your tiresome imitations of Mayakovsky
> we are tired
>   of your dreary tourist ideas of our Negro selves
> our selves are in far worse condition than the obviousness
> of your color sense
>   your general sense of Poughkeepsie is
> a gaucherie no American poet would be guilty of in Tiflis

Rhetoric, pride, invention and vocabulary are all splendidly marshalled in the aid of a crushing and all too plausible argument. I would like to quote all thirty-odd lines of 'The Day Lady Died', O'Hara's elegy for Billie Holiday and many people's favourite poem of his, but I will content myself with the beginning and end:

> It is 12:20 in New York a Friday
> three days after Bastille day, yes
> it is 1959 and I go get a shoeshine
> because I will get off the 4:19 in Easthampton
> at 7:15 and then go straight to dinner
> and I don't know the people who will feed me

There follow nineteen lines of 'I do this I do that' as O'Hara goes to the bank, buys himself lunch, buys books and cigarettes and liquor for friends, and 'a NEW YORK POST with her face on it', and then:

> I am sweating a lot by now and thinking of
> leaning on the john door in the 5 SPOT
> while she whispered a song along the keyboard
> to Mal Waldron and everyone and I stopped breathing

For all that it appears to be a loose collocation of things of little importance, this is a classic elegy with a classic elegy's undertow – Bishop's 'North Haven', Lowell's 'Alfred Corning Clark' – of 'why am I alive when you/he/she are dead?' The coyly merry beginning turns out to be the commemoration of an historic day. The divers purchases for friends all amount to less than the whispered song to Mal Waldron. His present and his plans for the future only end up in the past, the 'muggy street' is a prelude to 'stopped breathing'. 'The Day Lady Died' is a poem about not knowing people – not the people who will feed O'Hara, not his bank teller 'Miss Stillwagon (first name Linda I once heard)', not the friends he tries so hard to please by buying them things, and most of all not Lady, who has died. The poem's one moment of unanimity is at the finish, a tribute to the singer and a premonition of death, hers and everyone else's. It is a great poem, and he wrote others as great or nearly so. Perhaps in a hundred years someone will make a career by proving that O'Hara, like Byron, revised. But please not yet.

C. K. WILLIAMS

The American poet C. K. Williams is now practically synony-
mous with the very long poetic line of his devising, the line in
which he has written his most recent book, *Flesh and Blood*,
and the two books that preceded it, *Tar* and *With Ignorance*
(both of which are included in their entirety in *Poems
1963–1983*, along with most of the shorter-lined poems from
his first two books). I will talk about the line later, but suffice
it to say for the moment that the poetry Williams has written
using it has as much scope and truthfulness as any American
poetry since Lowell and Berryman.

There are no doubt theses to be written, proving that long-
lined and short-lined Williams are basically the same commodity,
and no doubt the poet himself has a keen sense of the continuity
of his work, but the reader of *Poems 1963–1983* will surely see it
as a book of two halves, in which distinctiveness and excellence –
some would even say competence and readability – are confined
to the second. A more severe poet – or a vainer, more deceitful
one – might well have omitted the first part of the book alto-
gether. The poems taken from Williams's first two volumes bring
to mind John Berryman's deprecating comment on his own early
work: 'I wrote mostly about death.' They are poems written as
for the microphone, hot roars of anguish and protest, unformed,
unpunctuated, almost – and aspiringly – unverbal, written in
the thin, paltry, generalizing diction of such things. They are
tinged with the surrealism that swept through American poetry
in the 1960s. They themselves stampede through conjurations
of sexual horror and indignity to their patly colloquial final
phrases: 'please stop me', 'no more please no more/ I mean it'
or 'I'm so lonely/ god so/ broken'. For all their fever and fervour,
they leave the reader cold. The garish vocabulary, the caprices
of surrealism, the recurring 'genitals' ('she is hauling his genitals
out, basket/ after basket/ and mangling all of it in the crusher')
are merely bland and deadening.

What is interesting about these poems is not the poems them-

Review of C. K. Williams, *Poems 1963–1983* and *Flesh and Blood*
(Newcastle upon Tyne: Bloodaxe, 1988)

selves, but the fact of their existence, and what has brought them into being: not any feeling for words, or even, actually, images, but the twin springs of horror and compassion, the one every bit as violent as the other. There is a poem which begins, 'I'd like every girl in the world to have a poem/ I've written for her'. There is a poem-sequence addressed to Anne Frank. There is a poem called 'Bringing It Home', with the lines:

> a room all the way across america
> and a girl in the room and the plastic fattening her breasts
> starting to sag o god
> she thinks they're going o god o god
> I would do anything to help her
> I would take all of her secret pain onto myself if she'd let me
> my best darling.

Another begins – and this is Williams's real subject over these two first books – 'There is a world somewhere else that is unendurable.' At this stage, neither are his poems in that world, nor do they properly relate it.

From the first lines of *With Ignorance,* the world is – perforce – endurable, it is here, and so is the poem, that will help us endure it: 'The men working on the building going up here have got these great,/ little motorized wheel-barrows that're supposed to be for lugging bricks and mortar/ but that they seem to spend most of their time barrel-assing up the street in,/ racing each other or trying to con the local secretaries into taking rides in the bucket.' Perhaps not since *Life Studies* has a poet so transformed his prospects and perspectives. Things previously unimaginable are suddenly admissible in these long lines: men working, bricks and mortar, the external scene brightly and understandingly put over. And from this, autobiographical recollection, a puzzling incident, and an elusive but shimmering conclusion about labour follow on. The volatile craving to empathize of the early books has been replaced by a kind of Bellovian fellow-feeling: 'he was beautiful', Williams says of the carpenter he remembers; 'the dear chin', of a Rabbi whom the Nazis tormented, 'the beauty' of an old drunk, looking across the street at a man 'like lovers'.

If the fourteen poems of *With Ignorance* and the seventeen in

Tar have any serious drawback, it is that the elements in them
of story and portraiture are so strong that they rapidly become
over-familiar to the reader. On a re-reading, the poems immedi-
ately leap up to greet the reader with character and plot, while
moralizing and reflecting passages are a little apt to lurk in the
shadows. These poems yield up an alarming amount to résumé:
'Tar' is about a new roof being laid on Williams's house on the
day of Three-Mile Island; 'Neglect' describes two people in a
rural bus-station and the decaying countryside around; 'The
Color of Time' is a Proustian piece about the fears of an ado-
lescent boy. Moreover, in those of the poems that connect two
discrete subjects, the hinge is rarely subtle or hidden. Berryman
offers an unfathomably wild and erudite mind; with Lowell
there is the feeling that the words have collusively found their
own inspired arrangements; but with Williams there never seems
to be any chance of finding the poem anywhere but in the place
where you remember having left it. He has profusion, but he is
orderly and patient with it. His two-page poem 'Waking Jed'
is proof of that. His implicit trust is not in the single blinding
flash of insight, which nothing precedes or succeeds, but in a
series of four or five patient sweeps; not in the clinching phrase,
but in modification, rebuttal, improved accuracy. He has made
himself – perhaps somewhat surprisingly, considering the way
he began – a reliable poet, rather than a fascinating one. Still,
pieces like 'From My Window', 'Flight', 'Neglect' or 'On
Learning of a Friend's Illness' are outstanding by any standards,
and it is perfectly possible that time will show that, in some
obscure corner of themselves – like the bacon in Dickens – they
have their own means for survival.

Whether or not Williams felt himself caught in the toils of
the short-story-as-poem, he has given it the slip most elegantly
and cleverly in his most recent and best volume to date, *Flesh and
Blood* (first published in 1987 in the United States). This, too,
is composed in the long line, now curling unerringly for up to
a line and a half (a full line, justified at both ends; and a part
of one, indented, beneath), for twenty or twenty-five syllables,
or, say, a hundred microns: but now each poem may contain
only eight of them; and there are two on a page, as with Lowell's
sonnets, or Berryman's Dream Songs in his *Selected*. The effect

is an extraordinary combination of disciplined compression, and
Williams's now fully assured, luxuriant exfoliation. The mind is
flattered by matter and urgency, while the eye is soothed by
space. The form is perhaps more spacious than the couplet, and
it makes a far more interesting impression on the page. The
poems are beautifully punctuated, with most of the lines end-
stopped; and many of the lines are so managed that they seem
to end twice: 'She answers the bothersome telephone, takes the
message, forgets the mes-/ sage, forgets who called/'. Scrupulous
rhetorical control is demanded for such a form, and Williams
seems to bring it off quite effortlessly, without the little strainings
and paddings ('born and born', 'sorrow and sorrow') in the
earlier books. A poem may be one sentence ('Repression'), or it
may be seven ('Love: Petulance'), but in either case it will be
for a reason, and it will be well managed, clear and easy to
follow.

The subjects are the by-now familiar gallery of hobos and
winos, children and old people, lovers and invalids; the settings,
typically, public places, on holiday, in parks, on pavements and
metro-stations. Little sequences have been put together – I par-
ticularly like the one on 'Reading' – and also a set of metaphor-
essays, entitled 'Vehicles', on abstractions such as 'Conscience'
and 'Forgetting'. These last, extended similes in a Rilkean
manner, benefit especially from the dissolution of the earlier,
baggier forms of *Tar* and *With Ignorance*: they are no longer
outperformed by narrative. Finally, there is a sequence of
eighteen of these eight-liners in memory of Williams's friend,
the poet and biographer of Whitman, Paul Zweig. Every aspect
of Williams's writing is represented here, sincerity of feeling,
plasticity of recollection, ardour of thought, all sifted and quali-
fied in the tides of the long lines.

Clearly C. K. Williams is an important poet. For over a dozen
years he has written like himself, he has matter and a manner,
and has refined them both. One might see a Williams poem
happening on the street and there are not many poets of whom
that could be said. If some of his earlier long-lined pieces had a
somewhat posturing ('my friend Dave') garrulousness about
them, and had arguments with himself that – Yeats to the con-
trary – remained firmly arguments with himself, he has come

through that to sound, in *Flesh and Blood*, likeable, mature and even-tempered. The only defects he has are those of his virtues: his determined ordinariness, an unwillingness to let something go, a certain predictability. A word is rarely stretched in a C. K. Williams poem, rarely finds itself in an unaccustomed context, is rarely memorable. But then – unlike the generation preceding his, the Lowell and Berryman generation – he doesn't write as though nothing mattered beyond words.

RILKE
Poetry and Letters

Rilke may well be the apotheosis of the German language: the poet in whom its persuasions, abstracts and music are most triumphantly effective. The best exponent of its inflections, genders, moods, word-order and latencies; who writes in 'the language of word-kernels' for which it is so particularly well-suited. To an extraordinary degree, the miracles of Rilke are the common features of German: the image-fostering capitalization of nouns; the suppleness of word-order and the strictness of declension and conjugation; the permissible drift of a word from one part of speech to another; the way a word can be assembled, disassembled, reassembled, dissembled; and, throughout, the utter transparency and naturalness of it all. When he wrote – and there were times when he couldn't – he wrote cleanly, fluently and rapidly. He wrote fair copy. He tore up the page where his pen had slipped. It was, as he said, describing the way the first lines of the first Elegy came to him on the wind at Duino, like taking dictation. German underwrote him. Stefan Zweig was surely right in saying translation could produce no more than a colourless shadow of Rilke. In custom-driven English, his translators have tried to hide in the extraordinary, the stilted, the obscure, the calculatedly dazzling – all enemies of Rilke.

Since his death in 1926, every decade has had its translators of Rilke: Sidney Keyes, Leishman and Spender, C. F. MacIntyre, Randall Jarrell, W. D. Snodgrass, Robert Bly. Now, the American translator Stephen Mitchell has put forward the first consistently readable versions of Rilke that I have seen; the first that can be read on their own, without requiring toning up or down by others; the first not to depend on mirrors, pulleys and trust. An English reader can now see something of Rilke for the first time.

Review of Rainer Maria Rilke, *The Selected Poetry of Rainer Maria Rilke*, trans. and ed. Stephen Mitchell (London: Picador, 1987), *The Notebooks of Malte Laurids Brigge*, trans. Stephen Mitchell (London: Picador, 1987), *Selected Letters 1902–1926*, trans. R. F. C. Hull (London: Quartet, 1988), Rainer Maria Rilke and Stefan Zweig, *Briefe und Dokumente*, ed. Donald A. Prater (Frankfurt: Insel, 1987)

This is not to say, of course, that Mitchell's solutions are in every instance to be preferred to those of his predecessors: Leishman and Spender score some fine magniloquent hits in the *Elegies*. But a compilation of Rilke translations would be half made up of Mitchell's, if not more.

To begin with, he passes the negative tests: he writes English, he is accurate, clear and seemly. He avoids poetizing, the writing of ten deadly lines in the attempt to write a deathless one. His watchwords are sense and tautness, though he is not afraid to expand a phrase or clause that is too compact. 'For there is no place where we can remain', he says, for 'Denn Bleiben ist nirgends'. (Leishman and Spender have 'For staying is nowhere.') The result is that the sound of Rilke's thinking becomes audible for the first time; that he is heard pleading, reasoning, improvising even, a man to men, scooping up arguments and instances wherever he can; and there is an end to the pompous darkness that had previously appeared to be an essential adjunct to Rilke in English, and there is an end too to the whole misprision of Rilke as a weaver of unfathomable opacities round a few untranslatable concepts. The conscientious infelicities of earlier translations stand revealed as quite groundless as well, as Mitchell is mostly more accurate into the bargain.

The Rilke he is most comfortable with – and whom he is most generous in representing – is the late Rilke of the *Elegies*, the *Sonnets*, and the elusive flotsam stuff that washed up afterwards. Half this selection is devoted to work published after 1923 (and Mitchell has gone on to translate, in a volume so far only available in the United States, all the *Sonnets to Orpheus*, complete with those Rilke decided were surplus to requirements). Against that, his choices from the *Neue Gedichte* of 1907 and 1908, while sound – 'The Panther', 'Portrait of My Father as a Young Man', 'Self-Portrait, 1906', 'Orpheus. Eurydice. Hermes' and 'The Flamingos' are all included – are a little mean. As he was about to embark on them, in 1903, Rilke wrote: 'Mir ist, als hätte ich immer so geschaffen: das Gesicht im Anschauen ferner Dinge, die Hände allein.' ('It seems to me that I have always written in this way: my regard fixed on some faraway object, my hands by themselves.') Over the next twenty years, the emphasis shifted from the hands to the mysteries

contemplated; or, to use another distinction from the program-
matic poem 'Wendung' ('Turning-Point') also included by
Mitchell, from 'work of the eyes' to 'heart-work'. My own
preference, or that of my time in life, is still for the work of the
hands (and eyes): the *Neue Gedichte*, 'exercise-poems', tasks
devised in emulation of the continual labour of Rilke's 'Master'
Rodin; not deep, but effortlessly well-made poems, rhymed and
musical iambics with a keen, almost metallic presence:

> Auf einmal kreischt ein Neid durch die Volière;
> sie aber haben sich erstaunt gestreckt
> und schreiten einzeln ins Imaginäre.

> A shriek of envy shakes the parrot cage;
> but *they* stretch out, astonished, and one by one
> stride into their imaginary world

Compared to that, how quiet (*kleinlaut*), how lacking in majesty,
how marginal almost, is the ending of the *Duino Elegies*:

> Und wir, die an ein *steigendes* Glück
> denken, empfänden die Rührung,
> die uns beinah bestürzt,
> wenn ein Glückliches *fällt*.

> And we, who have always thought
> of happiness as *rising*, would feel
> the emotion that almost overwhelms us
> whenever a happy thing *falls*.

Even in the *Elegies*, though, Rilke may often be seen writing
with his hands as well as his heart. His use of similes, for
instance, is surprisingly practical, even humdrum: the loss of
self 'wie die Hitze von einem/ heißen Gericht' (even more so in
Mitchell: 'like steam from a dish/ of hot food'); consolation
'clean and disenchanted and shut as a post-office on Sunday'.
How much strength Rilke draws from these, with his parabolist's
intentness on *meaning*. And there is the wonderful intelligence
of his sudden reversals of cause and effect, of chronology: 'that
man with the broken nose, unforgettable as a suddenly raised
fist'; a scene with the Rodins, at which Madame 'began to push
all the things about on the table, so that it looked as though
the meal were already over'. There is a sublime economy and

functionality about such writing, and Rilke never lost it. It corroborates the most startling, sympathetic and provocative witness in Donald Prater's recent biography of the poet: 'The painter and writer Hermann Burte, who met him now for the first time, recalled how much more down-to-earth, rational and orderly a person he was than he has often been depicted.'

In the United States, Stephen Mitchell's new version of *The Notebooks of Malte Laurids Brigge* received as many plaudits as his treatment of the poems, but I am not quite so taken with it. The prose translation actually seems more tense and stiff, to grip the original more fearfully and clingingly than was the case with the poems. It would appear to be one more indication that the novel – even this one of Rilke's – is a more timebound form, that Mitchell, happily unvarnished in the poetry, suddenly seems uncertain whether to distress his prose for antiquity or not. Prose Rilke sometimes eludes him, especially – another 'animal that never was', like the unicorn – his humour.

> Dieses ausgezeichnete Hôtel ist sehr alt, schon zu König Chlodwigs Zeiten starb man darin in einigen Betten. Jetzt wird in 559 Betten gestorben. Natürlich fabrikmäßig. Bei so enormer Produktion ist der einzelne Tod nicht so gut ausgeführt, aber darauf kommt es auch nicht an.

The passage has an eccentricity, a dandyish, macabre, disdainful humour (in the 'man' form, in the passives) that do not emerge in Mitchell's version of it:

> This excellent hotel is very ancient; already in the time of King Clovis people were dying here, in a few beds. Now there are 559 beds to die in. Like a factory, of course. With production so enormous, each individual death is not made very carefully; but that isn't important.

One can't tell from the deadpan English, but it might have been Des Esseintes, leafing through a morbid Baedeker. Mitchell's translation looks best – as the quotation again shows – as an interlinear version; his decision to choose some half-dozen passages from *Malte* and include them in the *Selected Poetry* with the German facing makes sense. In any case, the novel is something of an anthology already. Its Parisian scenes link it to the city literature of the turn of the century – Hamsun, Strindberg, Emmanuel Bove. There are times you think you have

blundered into Kafka: the scene with the neighbour Nikolai
Kuzmitch, or the bizarre, somewhat masochistic fantasy about
being a lid on a tin:

> Indeed, there is something almost ideal about being patiently and
> gently turned and coming to rest evenly on the small projecting rim,
> and feeling its interlocking edge inside you, elastic and just as sharp
> as your own edge is when you are lying along.

But then what does one make of Malte's Danish memories, or
his chronicling of French history? I can't help thinking that
a real novelist like Hamsun would have realized that Malte's
aristocratic background (in best Gothic style) is mostly to do
with his author's vanity – Hamsun's own very earliest books
were about secret aristos – and that it is a rather over-literal
vestige of what is more properly a metaphor: Malte's aristocracy
resides securely in his nerve-ends.

Selected Letters 1902–1926 is a pretty supine piece of pub-
lishing, being a straight reprint of a book that first appeared
over forty years ago. A short modern blurb pays tribute to
Rilke's friendship with Cézanne. (A nonsense. Rilke's *Letters on
Cézanne* were written a year after Cézanne's death, during
October 1907, the month of the artist's retrospective exhibition
in Paris; and they show the poet as a lover of form, a brilliant
colourist, and an occasionally perfervid and unrealistic admirer
of Cézanne, whom he describes as curt, inarticulate and
enraged.) The translator's introduction by R. F. C. Hull com-
plains, in a gentlemanly way, at the hagiographical mission of
Rilke's executors, who held back passages and letters that
informed on Rilke the man. While this was once the case, it is
less so now, after the publication of further selections and prob-
ably dozens of individual correspondences. To trot out, in 1988,
as a *Selected Letters*, this old book produced under wartime
conditions – and containing, just to give one example, not even
any of Rilke's letters to his *publisher* – is quite staggering.

One thing that Quartet have run to is the commissioning of
a briskly centrifugal introduction by John Bayley, in which he
tries to make a case for Rilke as 'a great European genius,
probably the last of the breed'. I think Bayley could not be more
wrong. Practically any genius alive at the time of the First World

War – and any Austrian genius in particular – would have a stronger claim. To have been born in Prague and died in Switzerland, to have written in German and lived in Paris, and to have been called, by turns, Rainer or René, does not make one a European; to have visited Spain and Scandinavia, and to have thought of oneself for many years as a Russian *manqué*, doesn't either – and, in fact, it puts up the first counter-argument: namely, that Rilke was simply too wide-ranging in his travels, that he had neither a particular place nor a particular direction in which to go from it.

For even the designation 'European' implies constraints as well as freedom. Rilke was too set on invulnerability, too fearful of extending himself, to be a European. When his hosts' dog died, he complained; ideally, he would have forbidden it. He was without either loyalty or acceptance. He lived in Paris to be alone. The stars by which he sailed were randomness and self-interest: the chance invitations of patrons and the ruthlessness of Number One. The best image of Rilke I have seen is in one of his own letters – not selected, as it happens – where the poet has strayed into the *Oktoberfest* (Horváth country!), and walks around carrying a peacock feather; while the crowds around him use similar feathers to tickle and tease one another, the poet feels his own is far too proud to be used in such a way, and instead he just looks at it. It is a quite infernal image of pride and alienation. Rilke felt qualmed and doubtful about using the plural (in *Malte*). How could he be a European? He was a man out of time and a man out of place. Who could claim Rilke as a fellow-citizen or a contemporary? Was there an Age of Rilke, and if so, where should it be located? His own plans for further study specifically excluded 'the history of art or any other histories'. Confusing early and late paintings, he spoke instead of the expression of the Mona Lisa 'on that particular day'. On a particular day in August, he sought out part of a garden that seemed to him less like summer: autumn was his favourite season. What price Rilke as part of something bigger, deregulated, *sans frontières*? He noted, in 1914, 'the excellent news from the Russian front'. Would you buy a spindly beard and peasant blouse from René Osipovitch?

Nor was he any more constant in his personal attachments.

His letters to his discontinued wife – and that means even those passed for publication in the saintly 1930s – are often quite reptilian: crass, devious and wounding ('a sobering experience for his wife Clara', Bayley concedes). He writes to *her* of how he spoke to the womanizing Rodin 'of Northern people, of women who do not want to hold the man fast, of possibilities of loving without deception'. I think it was this kind of thing, and not anything to do with 'the spirit of that [pre-war] civilisation' that led John Berryman to call him a 'jerk', or, strictly speaking, a '*jerk*'. Even his gallantries have something unpleasantly indirect about them: 'And then (if I were rich) I should give you my favourite dog so that he might look at you and be near you.' And then, quickly, as if even that were too much: 'But I am poor.' Rilke cannot be called European because he never committed himself to anything beyond himself and his poetry.

Inevitably, this also appears from Donald Prater's little volume of letters and documents exchanged by and relating to Rilke and Stefan Zweig, another off the Insel assembly line of Rilkeana, and the very model of how such things ought to be. At first, the subject would seem a rather unpromising one: the relationship, somehow carried on over twenty-odd years, between Zweig, the man of letters, with his capacity for kindness and lionization, and the poet five years his senior, and with little aptitude for either commodity – when it was offered by a male colleague, at any rate. Most of the time, the two were apart – there were only two periods during which they saw one another with any regularity. They didn't collaborate on anything together, started no movements, signed no manifestos, left no mark: and yet their story is absolutely riveting.

Thomas Mann couldn't have produced a sharper contrast: worker Zweig happy with (literary) life as he found it, eagerly promoting and introducing, humming and buzzing about; and queenly Rilke living his own rarefied existence to his own specifications, guarding his own privacy (finding he could do it for himself better than Clara could do it for him), unchummy and blandly discouraging, yet somehow crumbling (rather than melting) with pleasure at Zweig's undaunted advances. His posture of refusal, though of course sincere, is often hilarious:

not reading reviews because he feels they are 'personal letters addressed to other people' and thus of no concern to himself; or thanking Zweig for a copy of his collection of youthful poems, by telling him it would always have a special place in his – i.e., Zweig's – heart.

But the story never descends into undignified farce (as the three-way correspondence between Tsvetayeva, Pasternak and Rilke did), because, in spite of the inequality of the correspondents, a nice balance is somehow preserved. If Rilke keeps his freedom then Zweig holds on to his integrity. The reviews he wrote of some of Rilke's books – even if the poet refused to read them – are surprisingly sharp. Zweig held fast to his preference for the earliest Rilke; his judgments throughout are independent and often penetrating. It is quite a shock to read that Rilke's features are 'without significance' and his manner is 'chattering'. Zweig's observation that Rilke had 'sacrificed one half of himself, in order to exist completely with the other' is one of the most balanced and pithy things that has been said of him.

Later, especially in the two obituaries Zweig wrote, time and fame rather get the better of judgment, and a sentimental note creeps in. Still, for most of the book, he does a good job of personifying a friendly collegiality and thus, ironically, one of the most awkward, thankless and inimical presences in Rilke's life: trying to fix up readings for Rilke in Vienna; getting him out of any more arduous or unhealthy activity in the war than archiving (a particularly amusing interlude, with the Austrian authorities falling over themselves to make things as pleasant as possible for Rilke); organizing André Gide and Romain Rolland to try to recover Rilke's possessions in Paris, which had been auctioned off during the war for his unpaid rent, all three of them far more exercised on the subject than the expropriated poet. It is attractive in Zweig that he seems never entirely to have realized quite how tightly Rilke's frontiers were drawn: he asks him once to write in to the satirical magazine *Simplicissimus* to protest at an obscene caricature of a former benefactress, Ellen Key. It is hard to imagine anything less likely than Rilke's complying with such a request. No such letter from the poet is known, is the editor's mild comment.

RILKE
Life and Uncollected Poems

Fame, Rilke says somewhere, is the sum of misunderstandings that collect around a person, and, whatever else, Rilke – who liked to be misunderstood, and for whom every kind of human dealing was a form of misunderstanding anyway – is famous. In his lively and detailed new biography, Ralph Freedman refers to 'Rilke's stardom'. At first I quarrelled with the phrase, but on reflection it seems absolutely right.

More than Cavafy or Neruda or Mandelstam or anyone I can think of, Rilke is the pre-eminent international poet, and has been, I would say, since 1945, some twenty years after his death. Truly, to English and American readers and writers – and most probably for those of other nations too, though I can't speak for them – he is the 'significant other'. He is challenged only by Whitman and Dickinson as the best embodiment of 'the poet', and by no one in our century. He is read by people who read no other German poetry, perhaps no other poetry at all. The story of how he wrote the *Duino Elegies*, hearing the first lines dictated to him by the wind on the terrace of the castle of Duino near Trieste, in January of 1912, and only completed them – wrestled them to the ground – in three hurricane days fully ten years later, in his tower at Muzot in Switzerland, is probably as well known to English readers as the story of Coleridge waking from a laudanum dream to write 'Kubla Khan' until interrupted by the person from Porlock. A myth of completion to set alongside a myth of incompleteness.

The phenomenon of Rilke's standing only really makes sense against the backdrop of the global village and cablevision and net-surfing. What other period but one of easy access and nodding acquaintance would try and make him over or believe it had succeeded? For the fact is that Rilke wrote in German – I know he wrote some early poems in Russian, and three

Review of Ralph Freedman, *Life of a Poet: Rainer Maria Rilke* (New York: Farrar, Straus and Giroux, 1996) and Rainer Maria Rilke, *Uncollected Poems*, selected and translated by Edward Snow (New York: North Point Press, 1996)

mediocre late books in French – and that he is as inextricably (if less tragically) bound up with German as Heine or Celan. When Stephen Mitchell's translations were published – and they are better than anything I thought I'd see in English – Denis Donoghue remarked, 'It is easy to believe that if Rilke had written in English, he would have written in this English.' But this strikes me not only as untrue – what translation has the valency and the plenitude and the control of the original? – but nonsensical even as a speculation. It is simply unimaginable that Rilke could have written in a language that denied him his coinages and his subjunctives ('schriee' in the first line of the *Elegies*; 'stürbe' at the beginning of *Malte*; and thousands of others less prominently placed), his messing with prepositions, his deep puns and re-routing of word-roots, the plasticity of upper-case nouns, his noble tintinnabulations, his dubious and unforgettable slogans ('Denn Bleiben ist nirgends', 'Hiersein ist herrlich'), the kind of reverse animations that all underlie and make possible his perverse imagistic metaphysics. As the Irishman said to the man who stopped him for directions, 'I wouldn't start from here', but this is where English has to start with Rilke, with impossibility (quite a Rilkean proposition, actually). It's not something one hears often, because of Rilke's English reputation, but it's worth saying.

The bare bones of Rilke's life are as follows: he was born in 1875 in Prague to a snobbish mother disappointed with life and with her husband, a minor railway official. After going to military schools in Austria, he began writing, first in Prague, later on in Munich and Berlin, surviving as a reviewer and playwright, and virtually publishing himself. He had the most important relationship of his life with Lou Andreas-Salome, the wife of a Persian scholar and later a disciple of Freud's: she was successively lover, mother and confidante to him. When he broke with her, he quickly married the sculptress Clara Westhoff and lived with her in Worpswede, a North German artists' colony. Straight after the birth of a daughter, Ruth, in 1901, he took off for Paris, to write a monograph on the great French sculptor Auguste Rodin (Clara's former teacher): subsequently, he became his secretary. Influenced by the atmosphere of incessant work around Rodin, he set himself daily exercise poems which

he published as the *New Poems* of 1907 and 1908. Many of
his best-known pieces are there: 'The Panther', 'Self-Portrait,
1906', 'Archaic Torso of Apollo'. He also began writing a novel,
The Notebooks of Malte Laurids Brigge, a psychically and
emotionally draining task, but an extraordinary and still insuf-
ficiently appreciated achievement. Gradually falling in with a
titled and moneyed Continental set, including Marie von Thurn
und Taxis and the actress Eleonora Duse, he largely gave up his
independence and became a wandering house-guest: Rilke the
social and sexual butterfly has emerged ever more strongly over
the last couple of decades, giving the lie to the myth of the
austere and unworldly poet. After the war, he moved to Switzer-
land, where he completed the *Duino Elegies* and wrote the sixty-
odd *Sonnets to Orpheus* inside a few days in February 1922.
Towards the end of his life, he fell into a more French orbit,
admiring and translating Paul Valery. He died of leukaemia in
1926, the illness first heralded – though of course not caused,
as the legend would have it – when he pricked his finger on a
rose thorn.

The two books under review, part of an obviously undimin-
ished fascination and pursuit, represent two ways of coming at
Rilke: the one through the life, the other by translating the
poems. Both, obviously, end at one remove: the one with dates
and places and people and events, the other with English. One
amplifies what is unacceptable or – not too strong a word –
repulsive about Rilke, the other struggles to convey what is
great about him. Both seem to me liable to diminish Rilke –
though I'm sure that isn't the intention – because a man's
behaviour and way of life don't require the filter of translation.
Both alter the balance in the same way, so that, having read
them, one is less prepared to say: yes, but it was worth it for
the poetry. Rather, the poetry seems more and more like a
disreputable and self-serving attempt to defend the indefensible.

There is something incredibly unedifying about Rilke's life
and character, so much so that his biographers put themselves
in jeopardy. This, after all, is the man who was called 'a *jerk*'
by the American poet John Berryman and, a little more wittily,
'the greatest lesbian poet since Sappho' by W. H. Auden. The
point of both taunts, I think, is a chronic lack of commitment

in Rilke: the combination of lifelong dependence on others – for hospitality, money, love – and extreme selfishness: the simultaneous contradictory impulses to be adored and alone, connected and adrift; the always wanting to have it all ways. (Auden's remark is directed at the fakery of Rilke, not at lesbians; as a good homosexual, he was married to one himself.) And so there is the pattern of Rilke's life: the prissy peregrinations through Europe (newly arrived in Spain, he hankered after Scandinavia, Berlin and German spa-towns – a kind of perpetual allo-fixation); brief passionate flare-ups with actresses and titled ladies, and long epistolary retreats; ecstatic arrivals in new places followed by disillusionment and panic departure; running up debts in life that he tried to discharge in art; his indeterminate positioning towards and courtship of the avant-garde and the establishment, the aristocracy and the masses, Germany and France; what he was pleased to call 'an interior marriage' and fatherhood, both suspended; 'Doctor Serafico' to one patroness and Don Juan to some others; a flirtation – even at the age of forty – with the idea of going to university; a vegetarian not averse to 'a most unvegetarian restaurant named Boeuf à la Mode': in short, someone so fluid and two-faced that, as he once noted, 'I had become improbable, even to myself'.

It is the hardest thing to read all this and not blame the messenger, but of course the irritant is Rilke and not Mr Freedman, and, apart from the choice of subject, there is not much one can fault him for. Indeed, he keeps quite an acerbic tongue in his head: on Rilke's 'extremely realistic and breathtakingly sentimental and melodramatic' plays; on letters 'exuding oily didacticism', 'hyperbolically flattering' or 'of extraordinary length to ... a nineteen-year-old acquaintance'; a 'disarmingly obtuse' observer, 'conditioned by a tourist's myopia; on behaviour that is 'shabby' and 'like a vagrant in an adolescent dream', following which, 'characteristically, Rilke became promptly invisible'. He notes the way 'moral fervour and self-recognition manifested themselves in poetry' – rather than elsewhere – and observes 'Rilke's pattern of living through failure as part of a process that turns denial into poetic art'. He quotes Rilke's victims – most of whom later wrote dewy-eyed books about him – calling him 'an adventurer of the soul' and 'a trickster of misery'. His worst weapon, particularly puncturing to Rilke, is slang: 'Paris had been a bust', 'The Worpswede monograph had not played well', and a failed seduction 'squelched all desire to work'. Still I think that by going into as much detail as he does, he makes a rod for his own back: Donald Prater's biography of the poet, *A Ringing Glass*, published only ten years ago, seemed to keep the Pandora's box of Rilke under closer control, and unleash the reader's repugnance less often. He wondered, too, about the wisdom and the need for a life of Rilke: it seems people no longer wonder.

Uncollected Poems is Edward Snow's fourth book of Rilke translations: he has previously done *The Book of Images* and the two volumes of *New Poems*. The new book covers Rilke's German output between 1909 and 1926, excepting of course the *Duino Elegies* and the *Sonnets to Orpheus*; basically, they are the poems he wrote between completing his novel (and arguably his very greatest work) *The Notebooks of Malte Laurids Brigge* and his death. These poems are not new to English readers: Stephen Mitchell and Michael Hamburger (in a volume called *An Unofficial Rilke*) have both offered only slightly shorter selections from the same period. Included are well-known favourites like 'The Great Night', 'Left Exposed on the Mountains of the Heart', 'Antistrophes', an 'Elegy' to Marina Tsvetayeva and Rilke's last poem, 'Come, you last thing'. There is an astonishingly vitriolic poem to Rilke's mother that I had overlooked previously, 'Ah misery, my mother tears me down'. Mr Snow is generally extremely faithful and reluctant to part from his original:

> May my spirit be like rock
> and the shepherd's task seem possible,
> the way he browns and moves and with practised stone-throw
> mends his flock, wherever it strays.
>
> ('The Spanish Trilogy')

He has no music, little sense of diction, and makes no attempt at rhyme. At their worst, his versions strike me as peculiar without being possible ('But need it be: "lament"? Why not: "younger jubilation down below"?'); at their best, useful trots to the facing German. He claims in his introduction that these poems, had Rilke put them out in a volume, would be one of the great books of the century, which I think is a little hyperbolic: but they are absolutely characteristic – Rilke working in his set vocabulary with his set tricks on his set preoccupations, with an extremely small paraphrasable content. Of course, they *are* impossible. The last line of a crucial eight-line poem called 'Narcissus' goes: 'und hob sich auf und konnte nicht mehr sein' playing perhaps five or six ways with the German verb 'aufheben' (which also appears in the first line). There is no way that Edward Snow's line 'and self-annulled and could exist no more' can begin to do justice to that sort of polyvalent ghost.

GOTTFRIED BENN

At the age of eighteen, Gottfried Benn submitted some poems to a Berlin newspaper, and, as he reminisced in a lecture of 1951, they were returned, marked:

> 'G.B. – agreeable in feeling, weak in expression. Do try us again some time.' That was a long time ago, and now, you see, after decades of labour, they have included me among the so-called Expressionist poets, while the feeling in my work is generally described as disagreeable.

The period of 'agreeable feeling' was short and of little consequence: only a few such poems have survived to be reprinted in Volume Two of the centennial edition of his complete works, which replaces Dieter Wellershoff's four-volume edition of 1961. At the same time, the publishers have also commissioned a biography by Hans Egon Holthusen, a distinguished writer, Germanist and friend of the poet in his later years. The two volumes of Benn's poetry – the first comprising the 'collected' poems of 1956, the *Auswahl letzter Hand*, and the second containing published, unpublished and fragmentary work – will be followed, in 1987 and 1988, by the prose in two volumes, and, in 1989, by a final volume containing 'dialogische Formen' and a general index.

Benn first made his name in 1912, with the five poems of the cycle 'Morgue', written in an hour, published in a week, and notorious ever since for their bleak aestheticism, their macabre juxtapositions, their reduction of human life to a bizarre and pitiful spectacle of no content or significance. Even now – and perhaps for all perpetuity – this is the work for which Benn is best known. Despite the rejection slip cited in the lecture, despite the *trouvailles* of Volume Two, Benn's work begins with 'Kleine Aster', an envoi to a flower, playfully stitched into a corpse by a medical student (such as Benn himself was):

Review of Gottfried Benn, *Sämtliche Werke*, ed. Gerhard Schuster (Stuttgart: Klett-Cotta, 2 vols., 1986), and Hans Egon Holthusen, *Gottfried Benn: Leben Werk Widerspruch 1886–1922* (Stuttgart: Klett-Cotta, 1986)

Trinke dich satt in deiner Vase!
Ruhe sanft,
kleine Aster!

Drink your bellyful in your vase!
Rest easy,
little aster!
[reviewer's translation]

Under these circumstances, flesh is even less than grass.

In fact, though, the position of 'Kleine Aster' is not as unassailable as perhaps it seems. In an appendix, Gerhard Schuster, the editor of this new edition, quotes from the correspondence of 1955 and 1956 between Benn and his publishers, concerning the arrangements for what in the end turned into his collected poems. Both sides were cautious, Benn for instance proposing at one stage that a few 'programmatically beautiful' poems be set at the front of the book, 'perhaps in a different type-face'. This is not cowardice or the wish to deceive (which would be completely out of character), but the understandable anxiety of a man near the end of a lifetime of writing. When the book was published, it was for his seventieth birthday; within a few weeks, it had to stand as his monument. For most of his life, Benn had been, if not reviled, then at least seen as an eccentric or marginal figure. Already in 1913, he had remarked that 'art is a matter of some fifty people or so, of whom at least thirty are round the bend'. He had had to suppress poems from his 'selected' of 1936, and even so found himself the subject of vicious attacks from literary critics among the S.S. It was his last publication for twelve years. 'Undesirable then, undesirable again now' – the *Statische Gedichte* of 1948 had to be published in Switzerland, and an anodyne selection they were too: he complained that the Swiss had made him look like a 'sanfter Heinrich', a 'soppy Simon'. Now, approaching death and classic status *aequo pede*, Benn's deliberations on his latest self-presentation were conditioned not by self-doubt but by doubt about this newest generation of Germans.

All his life, the noises Benn makes about his poems are modest, sceptical, disparaging. His *Gesammelte Schriften* of 1922 end

with an Epilogue that can hardly have been calculated to sell
the book to its readers:

> So now these collected works are published, one volume, two
> hundred pages, how paltry, one would have to be ashamed of it if
> one were still alive. Not a document worth mentioning; I would be
> amazed if anyone were to read it; I feel quite remote from them, I
> throw them over my shoulder like Deucalion and his stones; maybe
> their distortions will turn into human beings, but whatever happens,
> I don't care for them.

Of his whole career, he says: 'At best, you were a character
cameo, an eccentric, a specialist – you didn't get any big parts
to fill an evening with', and, in the last words of the first
volume of his works, he wonders whether 'Großartiges und
Geschlossenes', anything 'magnificent and completed', is feasible
in modern times. But the thing about these dismissals is that
they are without any real, specific, independent doubt. The
nihilism they represent is a constant, even an innate quality. It
should not be taken for disavowal, renunciation, 'agonizing
reappraisal', least of all for any kind of argument with himself.
Benn's poetry is not homogeneous, not even consistent, but it is
not divided against itself. A Benn poem – whatever direction it
goes in – has an air of unanimity. In another late lecture, Benn
says: 'No question, the modern poem is monological, it is a
poem without belief, without hope, it is a poem consisting
of words, which you arrange in a fascinating way.' However
mundane, however approximate, that attribute 'fascination' is
still the best word for Benn, both his effects and his objectives.
He uses it again when he says:

> An affinity with words is a primary quality, it can't be learned. You
> can learn tight-rope walking, funambulism, high-wire acts, walking
> on nails, but a fascinating way with words, you either have it or you
> don't.

Benn's severe gloom, his habitual dejection, are, I would say,
one aspect of his fascination. It is a mood, a tone, equanimity,
indifference, exhaustion, a kind of dandyism, a matter of words,
a pretext for vocabulary. It might be noted that not only his
clinical medical terms, but also his English and French
Fremdwörter, many of them used in critical places like endings

or titles, almost all convey depression, negation, failure: 'après-lude', 'à bas', 'l'heure bleue', 'finish', 'Long, long ago'. In the letters, there are *Mischwörter*, things like 'Downheit' and 'ausge-powert', parts of a supralingual language of melancholy. In anyone else, they would signal depression: but in Benn, they are also style and fascination, a style he describes as 'Krisenstil, hybrid und final', a crisis-style, hybrid and terminal – one that was, nevertheless, sustained and varied for almost fifty years.

Looking back at 'Kleine Aster' and the other poems of 1912, it is hard to see in them the beginning of an *oeuvre*: anywhere for them to go, any way in which they might be expanded, any sense of unfulfilled potential. There is in them a scientific awareness of the indestructibility of matter, of the whole of a life being the merest part of a mute cycle: 'earth calls' from around a hospital deathbed, a gold tooth is taken from a corpse by a morgue attendant, and buys an evening in a dance-hall. Given a synoptic nihilism like this, where is there to go? What mysteries? 'Morgue II', quite properly dropped by Benn (and therefore now in Volume Two), is a rather routine variorum of prankish rearrangements of corpses. There is a brief spell of interest in the other parts of the cycle, in the dance-hall; a move from operating tables to café tables, from the death industry backwards (or forwards) to the pleasure industry of 'Nacht-café', 'Englisches Café', 'Kurkonzert'; morbidity re-appears briefly as *morbidezza*:

> Eine entkleidet ihre Hände.
> Die sind weich, weiβ, groβ,
> Wie aus Fleisch von einem Schoβ.
> ('Dirnen')
> One strips off her hands.
> They're soft, white, large,
> As though made of flesh from her belly.

But the implantation of the aster also anticipates a more durable and substantial theme. In the 1913 poem 'Untergrundbahn' (Holthusen comments usefully on the distracting irrelevance of some of Benn's early titles), there are the lines (in Michael Hamburger's translation):

Ein armer Hirnhund, schwer mit Gott behangen.
Ich bin der Stirn so satt. Oh, ein Gerüste
von Blütenkolben löste sanft sie ab
und schwölle mit und schauerte und triefte.

A wretched braindog, laden down with God.
My forehead wearies me. Oh that a frame
of clustered blooms would gently take its place,
to swell in unison and stream and shudder.

Those longing subjunctives are echoed in the name of the hero
of Benn's 1916 prose-pieces *Gehirne* (Brains): Werff Rönne, an
imperative followed by a subjunctive, urging dissolution, the
melt-down of consciousness. For the next period, the brain and
consciousness (that 'sentry between blood and claw' of 'Icarus')
will be Benn's enemy: opening out into expressionistic travel-
posters, hymns to preconsciousness and community, to the dion-
ysiac realms of the Mediterranean; poems evoking the
quaternary decline of the human race, poems to oblivion and
pure form.

Form, for most of the 1920s, was synonymous with the eight-
line stanza: a Mediterranean shape, but with primitive heaviness
and lassitude in the rhymes, sentences yoked together by
commas, short, noun-heavy lines, almost asyntactical, with caes-
uras of staggering indifference. Again, not arguing a case – there
are no verbs to do it with – but throwing out noun-projectiles,
gnostic shards, *Stichwörter*, in a frenetic chant. Tone is almost
indescribable, there are too many possibilities: Spenglerian
gloom, cultural cynicism, melancholy sonorities in 'a' and 'au',
but all of it quite hypnotic in effect. The critic Max Rychner
describes it: 'Every word an allusion, making the strings vibrate
in a precisely calculated rhythmic curve, no depiction, nothing *in
extenso*, written for cognoscenti, for whom each word has its
own nimbus.' One of the most excessive poems of the time –
though not in octaves – is 'Prolog 1920':

> Individual-Ich: abgetakelt,
> Psychologie: zum Kotzen,
> Entwicklungsprinzip: der Hund bleibt am Ofen,
> Kausalgenese: wer will das wissen,
> Ergebnis: réponse payée!!

Individual ego: washed up,
psychology: makes you puke,
development principle: sleeping dogs,
aetiology: who cares,
sum total: réponse payée!!

The lines systematically, economically and ferociously take apart contemporary intellectual structures, not by argument, but by energetic branding and labelling. What is propounded instead is a kind of fluid, dissociated, primordial existence: 'Totalisation', 'Orphische Zellen', 'thalassale Regression', 'trunken zerebral', is how the famous catch-phrases and slogan-words go. One is reminded of Benn's own crisis as a psychiatrist – a modern collapse as crucial as that of Hofmannsthal's Lord Chandos – when he lost all interest in individual cases. His character Rönne is called 'Flagellant der Einzeldinge', 'the flagellant of individual phenomena'. In his letters, Benn discusses his 'aversion to impressions', he refuses Frau Hindemith's offer of an outing, saying he found nature 'exaggerated', and sunshine 'tiring', he is offended, injured almost, when another friend springs a social evening on him.

The emphases shifted with the years, became less exotic, less dionysiac, more melancholic; there is more solitude, more of the redemption of pure form, the 'hour' of creation, and stress on spiritual distinction. Where the solution, or anyway the yearning, had been for luxuriance, pre- or post-consciousness, polysyllables and place-names, it was now transformed into something more stoical, austere and simple:

es gibt nur zwei Dinge: die Leere
und das gezeichnete Ich.

('Nur Zwei Dinge', 1953)

This pairing, 'emptiness and the marked self', is Benn's subject in the poems of his last decade. The titles of his books of the 1950s tell their own story: *Fragmente*, *Destillationen*, *Aprèslude*. These poems are his most moving; they have a Chinese asceticism and sorrow; they use the music of simple words, in basic quatrains; they arise from the daily conditions of Benn's life, a walk, an evening in a bar, a gift of flowers, a book he has been reading. Some others are in free form, so-called *Sprech-*

gedichte, the poet musing aloud, his own thoughts, or on lives that interest him: La Duse, Chopin, Clemenceau, Rembrandt (in Hamburger's translation):

> Ah – Hulstkamp –
> Wärmezentrum,
> Farbenmittelpunkt,
> mein Schattenbraun –
> Bartstoppelfluidum um Herz und Auge –

> Ah – Hulstkamp –
> midpoint of warmth,
> centre of colours,
> my shadow brown –
> aura of unshaved bristle round heart and eye –

Sometimes their Anglo-Saxon flatness is such that many English poems in the same genre look positively vibrant by comparison, late Lowell, say, or Larkin. Occasionally, they muster a little indignant humour, the last vestiges of decades of rage and denial: 'Kleiner Kulturspiegel' or 'Radio' for instance, both in Volume Two, along with many other of the late poems. In general, though, they show an old man, dignified, sonorous, surrounded by impenetrable griefs: he is quoted in the Notes, saying 'The intellect always has the departed in its train, the intellect must remain cold, otherwise it would become familiar.' That never befell Benn.

What seems to me more suggestive of Benn's nature and purpose than anything else, and more transportable, are two idyllic periods in his life, one in each of the two world wars. He has written, inimitably, about both:

> What I produced in the way of literature, apart from 'Morgue', which appeared with A. R. Meyer in 1912, I wrote in the spring of 1916 in Brussels. I was a doctor in a hospital for prostitutes, lived in a confiscated house, eleven rooms, just me and my orderly, few duties, allowed to wear civvies, had no responsibilities, no ties, barely understood the language; I walked the streets, strange faces; a peculiar spring, three months, quite unique, what if not a day passed without the shelling at the Yser, life swung in an orbit of silence and forlornness, I lived on the margins where existence dies and the self begins. I often think back on those weeks; they were life, they'll not return, everything else was trash.

The second passage, less dense, more descriptive, more soberly written, comes from a prose piece called 'Block II, Room 66', the address of Benn and his second wife for a year towards the end of the Second World War (translated by E. B. Ashton):

> Nothing dreamier than barracks! Room 66 faces the drill ground; before it grow three small rowan trees, their berries without purple, the leaves as though stained from brown tears. It is late August; the swallows still fly, but already are massed for the great passage. A battalion band rehearses in a corner, the sun sparkling on trumpets and percussives as they play, 'Die Himmel rühmen', and 'Ich schiess den Hirsch im wilden Forst.' It is the fifth year of war, and here is a completely secluded world, a kind of béguinage. The shouts of command are external; inwardly all things are muffled and still.

Both passages describe peace-in-war, a behind-the-lines exist-ence that seems positively idyllic: 'they were life', and 'a kind of béguinage'. But there is more to them than Benn's good fortune in finding himself out of the way; or confirmation of his provocative witticism that the army (which he rejoined in 1935) was 'the aristocratic form of emigration'. They show him thriving in anomalous, withdrawn, insensitive, somehow inex-pressive (as opposed to Berlin, where he lived, practised and wrote) locations. In each case, he was provided with a little work – in Landsberg, he was busy with statistics on suicides in the army – but this too seemed bizarre, decorative, and left him at liberty. Uprooted, he flourished. Perhaps the fact of the army is also relevant: in its hierarchical, gleaming structure, he was more blissfully private and opaque than ever, truly at home, masked by a spurious (albeit real) function, furtive and pro-ductive. Somehow, both situations were turned by him into intensifications of his life in Berlin, instead of its opposite: small ground-floor flat, small practice (skin and venereal specialist), humble view on a yard full of washing, and even a few chickens (not his own) pecking about in it. Occasional cut flowers. Rare visitors (and only if announced previously). The two situations seem to me endlessly suggestive of Benn: the massive military carapace, well run, imposing, neglected, and behind it, Valéry's poet in a lab-coat, in and out of uniform, the only intelligent life, attending to the leaves on rowan trees.

In his – to my mind, outstanding – monograph on Benn,

Walter Lennig (like Holthusen, a former associate of the poet) writes of a life so bizarrely straightforward and without incident that the lives of Rilke and George look positively sensational by comparison. In the 1920 Expressionist anthology, *Menschheits-dämmerung*, Benn's note on himself runs as follows: 'Born 1886 and grew up in villages in the province of Brandenburg. Past life unimportant, unimportant existence as doctor in Berlin.' It takes either courage or exasperation or both to begin a biography on this footing, as Holthusen does. It is an admission, straight away, that he will not be able to count on the co-operation, even the interest, or the sympathy, of his subject.

Benn's recalcitrance, his stern posthumous resistance, is impressive and awkward: Holthusen is generous in documenting it. A biography of Benn, he says, 'has to be written against the grain', against the anti-biographical, anti-narrative course of Benn's thinking. It has to put up with the subject's jeering too: 'Herkunft, Lebenslauf – Unsinn!', 'Background, C.V. – rubbish!' and more sophisticated jokes like this: 'Most of them come from Jüterborg or Königsberg, and they usually wind up in some Black Forest or other.' Where there is evidence from Benn, this itself becomes a problem: who would care to hear another version, let alone an independent one, after hearing from Benn himself? When Benn writes, 'went to America, vaccinated the steerage', what else is there to say? The biographer is up against a man whose aesthetic is 'Ausdruck und Stoffvernichtung', 'expression and the destruction of subject-matter'.

Holthusen is unable, or more likely unwilling, to impose a proper biography-style narrative pattern on his subject. What *Gottfried Benn: Leben Werk Widerspruch 1886–1922* pursues is not the regular melancholy imperceptible chronological flow of a biography, but a series of tangents, local expansions of date of birth, ancestry, social character of German pastors (Benn came from a long line of them; Holthusen himself is a *Pastorensohn*), school, university in Marburg, science and medicine at the turn of the century, Expressionism and avant-garde art, Rönne and Brussels, the case of the British spy Edith Cavell (Benn was the doctor present at her shooting), the publication of the *Gesammelte Schriften* and the death of Benn's first wife. The information is given clearly, not always in close formation, and not always in order, but the approach is congenial to Holt-husen, who quotes generously from various sources, evaluating the evidence, and sends detail skittering after detail. In the only really absurd example of this last trait, a discussion of 1920s Berlin produces the name and dates of Christopher Isherwood, the date of his novel *Goodbye to Berlin* (1939) and the date of the American film *Cabaret* (1972), 'starring Liza Minnelli'. But this is only to cavil at the misapplication of learning that, for most of the book, is left at the service of its subject. Holt-husen's literary judgments, delivered sometimes in a swinging, Bennian style, are mostly very acute: as when he describes Benn's language on family matters as 'floskelhaft', 'formulaic', or finds a piece on Benn's childhood 'both laconic and rhapsodic – he *hymns* his childhood in prose'. If there is any serious criticism of the book, it is that Holthusen never really opposes any tend-ency of his own to those of Benn; it remains less a biography than an annotated anthology. But it is still a work that, once completed, will surely be detailed, sympathetic and perceptive.

GEORG TRAKL

If the non-specialist reader knows anything about Georg Trakl, he probably knows about his death: a drug overdose after the battle of Grodek in 1914. And if he knows anything of his life, it may well fit into the four words, 'Drugs Alcohol Little Sister', of the title of a poem by John Berryman. The impression is of a 'typically Germanic' mixture of bleakness and luridness; a frail, self-imperilled, insatiable nature; and a poetry dwelling obsessively on death and decay, narrowly and culpably pathognomic.

It is the Germans who make a virtue of efficiency and diligence (*Tüchtigkeit*); yet its opposite, an almost total inability to live (*Lebensuntauglichkeit*), is even harder for the more accommodating English to accept: especially when it is allied as it is with Trakl, to an unwavering seriousness and unknown depths – of feeling, of belief, of psychosis. Trakl once threatened to kill himself unless he was given credit by a sweet-shop owner. The same complicated helplessness is displayed throughout his life. As a small boy, he walked into a pond until only his hat remained visible above the surface. At seventeen he was found by his family, lying on a sofa, in a chloroform-induced blackout. It seems likely that he committed incest with his sister Gretl, and internal evidence from the poems suggests that his mother caught them in the act. In later life, he tried repeatedly to find work and live normally; but his attempts lasted mostly just for a few days. Even in his own ominously chosen profession of pharmacist, it is reported, his fear of the customers made him sweat through six shirts in a morning. When in 1914 he found an anonymous patron (in Wittgenstein), he was quite unable to go to the bank and pick up his money.

Physical impressions of Trakl centre on the frozen rigidity of his features, his quiet, monotonous voice, and the evil, metallic, criminal glitter of his eyes – 'Funkelnd-Böse', as even his late,

Review of Frank Graziano, ed., *Georg Trakl: A Profile* (Manchester: Carcanet, 1983), and Richard Detsch, *Georg Trakl's Poetry* (Philadelphia: Pennsylvania State University Press, 1983)

close friend, Ludwig von Ficker, the editor of *Der Brenner*, conceded. There is something wolfish about Trakl's face – malice, avidity, suddenness, contempt – and his poems contain several such self-identifications: 'And he passed his days in a dark pit, lied and stole and hid himself – a flaming wolf – from the white face of his mother' ('Dream and Derangement') and in 'Passion' it is between wolves that a suggested incest occurs:

> Zwei Wölfe im finsteren Wald
> Mischten wir unser Blut in steinerner Umarmung
> Und die Sterne unseres Geschlechts fielen auf uns.
>
> (Two wolves in the dark wood
> We mingled our blood in a stone embrace
> And the stars of our breed fell on us.)

In Michael Hamburger's introduction to *Georg Trakl: A Profile*, this dangerous and alien figure is domesticated until he seems to be just another black sheep of German literature, under Hamburger's tutelary crook. Hamburger's is a dignified, withdrawn, almost Olympian performance in which he denies that biographical inferences can be drawn from the poems, and claims that 'Trakl's dominant aspiration was to lose himself'. This may well be so, but surely the aspiration of his readers is to find him among the constant recurrences of figures and scenes, their compulsive resumptions and variations? To refuse to countenance incest is, if nothing else, unprofitable: the Trakl-critic Walther Killy, quoted in Richard Detsch's *Georg Trakl's Poetry: Towards a Union of Opposites*, sees incest as 'die stellvertretend erlittene Unordnung ... die zur grossen, metaphysisch gerichteten Unruhe wird' ('a representative affliction ... which is expanded into a grand, metaphysical disorder'). And Detsch's own close reading of a handful of poems, with the added witness of Heidegger, Jung, Novalis, Goethe and others, succeeds in making compelling sense of what, without such a reading, would remain vague, random and imponderable.

With the help of early drafts – Trakl constantly rewrote his own poems, often cutting them down by two-thirds or more – Detsch is able to clarify the 'intermingling of roles', and produce a satisfying account of the difficult late poem 'Passion': an adumbrated movement from 'incest – the boy and his sister', to 'death

– Orpheus and Eurydice', to 'expiation and transformation – Christ and the penitent woman'. Detsch then produces accounts of alchemical writings analysed by Jung, and finds that they have in common with Trakl 'the production of a unisexual being who is both the offspring of the incestuous pair and the result of their own fusion into one person, their own achievement of wholeness'. (The phrase, '*ein* Geschlecht', both 'one sex' and 'one kin', in 'Abendländisches Lied' is, he notes, the only use of italic emphasis in all of Trakl's writing.) This being in turn is the dead or unborn child who occurs frequently in Trakl; it is Elis ('O Elis, how long you have been dead'), it is a conductor of dead souls, a psychopomp: 'As in "Passion", almost all of Trakl's human figures seem to be dead and yet continue to act as though they were alive in some way. His is the poetry of the living dead.'

This is lurid, heady stuff, but not the less true for that. Nor are its conclusions all that different from Hamburger's; for instance, that the dead are 'more vivid, more full of life than the living', or that a poem is 'an allegory of the relation between innocence and death'. The main difference is that Detsch gives a detailed and credible account of how such conclusions were reached. This difference is most plainly demonstrated in his excellent chapter on 'Trakl's Symbolic Style', and the almost incredible proliferation of uncertainty in Trakl's work: the use of verbs to blur contours; the 'frequent impersonalization of human figures through the nominal use of indefinite neuter singular adjectives'; the juxtaposition of unrelated observations, so that a poem of four quatrains can – and does – consist of sixteen unconnected sentences; the 'absolute use of metaphors', in which there is no basis for comparison; the disconcerting use of the words 'perhaps', 'or' and 'but'. Against this, Hamburger advances the sentence, 'Trakl's ambiguities are not deliberate or cerebral.' Possibly not, but they are absolutely pervasive. Richard Detsch's idea that they further the cause of unity by eroding concreteness and individuation seems just, and it is only one of many such ideas in a clever, sympathetic study.

By contrast, *Georg Trakl: A Profile* is a disappointing book. The bulk of it was published by Cape in 1968, as *Selected Poems*, with a parallel text. This has now had one poem, 'Music in the Mirabel', added to it, and Michael Hamburger's 'Dejection' comes in for Robert Grenier's 'Melancholy'. Christopher Middleton's blunder in 'Western Song', 'O the ancient sound of the little home' (for 'Heimchen', a cricket) has been corrected (but then, in the newly added 'Music in the Mirabel', Michael Hamburger has misread 'Feuerschein' as 'Feuerstein', giving him 'A flint lights up inside the room'). Firmly on the debit side is the fact that the originals are not reprinted. This is a bad loss, because, as Hamburger admits in his introduction, 'Trakl's long lines do not translate well into English', because English lacks the inflections of German, and because 'Trakl's adjectives carry much more weight than English usage allows.' He might have added, I think, that the generalizing latinity of English is a disadvantage: for 'schwarze Verwesung' there is 'black corruption', for 'herbstliche Träumerei' there is 'autumnal reverie' and for 'Untergang' the reversible 'Decline'. The translations are rarely better than lame trots, with a paucity of rhythmic excitement, an absence of grace and clarity in the phrasing, a loss of the unique, echo-less tone of the originals. They are cautious and inhibited, acting under duress. 'Trumpets' is a success, and there are vivid passages in 'Childhood' and 'Helian', but spontaneous-sounding phrasing is conspicuously rare – like this line of Middleton's 'To One Who Died Young': 'You walk and talk together under elms by the green riverside.' The appendix of five translations by an American poet, the late James Wright, is a lesson to the others in its naturalness:

> In the farmyard the white moon of autumn shines.
> Fantastic shadows fall from the eaves of the roof.
> A silence is living in the empty windows;
> Now from it the rats emerge softly
> And skitter here and there, squeaking.

Compare this to Grenier's version:

> In the courtyard the autumn moon shines white.
> From the roof's edge wild shadows drop.
> A silence lives in empty windows,
> Easily up into which leap the rats
> And flit hissing here and there –

Surely a different approach might have been tried out in the sixteen years since *Selected Poems*? One stumbles through these, with little pleasure for the most part, only – *pace* Hamburger – briefly electrified by the many occurrences of the word 'sister'.

The rest of this *Profile* is made up of Trakl's prose-poems and a selection from his letters, with a commentary. Here, the matter of translation becomes quite grave. Agreed, Trakl is one of the most difficult of authors, but surely Frank Graziano (or someone) should have cast an eye over these versions. Roderick Iverson, the translator of the prose-poems, has a cavalier way with articles and with singulars and plurals that is generally at variance with the original; his 'Dream and Derangement' misses out two whole sentences; he renders 'Gestalt' by 'complex' or 'complexity' ('his own bloody complexity rose before him, towering stiffly from the rubbish' instead of 'he saw his own bleeding form, stiff with rubbish'). Sometimes, Iverson just has no idea of the meaning and makes an impressionistic guess: 'he raped the quiet child, and, reflected in the afterglow, saw that profound darkness, his own face'. What Trakl wrote is 'in her beaming face he recognized his own deranged features': it is a family resemblance, not a mystical 'afterglow'. As well as count- less inelegances and approximations, there are a score of serious mistakes. With the letters, the problem is slightly different: neither translations nor commentary, both by Siegfried Mandel, quite succeed in making the break with German. The whole section is informed by a kind of grimly resolute pretentiousness and enthusiasm that can do Trakl no good at all, with their talk of images 'wrought in his inner smithy' and the like.

This publication, of which much might have been expected, and on which much depends, is inept, contradictory and dis- creditable. Michael Hamburger's coolly abstemious introduction is opposed by the printing of a picture of Gretl, by the experience of reading the poems and by Mandel's talk of Trakl's 'suc- cumbing to tabus'. It is a pity that valuable work like that of Richard Detsch should thus be isolated still further from a community of interested and informed readers. To say nothing of Trakl himself, whose cold, undelighting, unhuman speech, with its small, select and poisoned vocabulary, is like no other in German, let alone English. It has been called visionary, and indeed, one of the translators has mistakenly put 'visionary' for

'Schauender', but it is realism, albeit of a reality that has yet to
come into being:

> Dornige Wildnis umgürtet die Stadt.
> Von blutenden Stufen jagt der Mond
> Die erschrockenen Frauen.
> Wilde Wölfe brachen durchs Tor.

> (Thorny wilderness girdles the town about.
> From bloody doorsteps the moon
> Chases terrified women.
> Wild wolves have poured through the gates.)

BERTOLT BRECHT
Life

I have never read a life like John Fuegi's of Brecht. Revisionism doesn't begin to describe it. This is dartboard stuff, effigy abuse, voodoo biography. If Fuegi could get inside the Dorotheenfried-hof, uproot Brecht's jagged scalene headstone, dig through six feet of Brandenburg sand and a zinc coffin, and do something to the remains involving chicken heads, inverted crosses and black candles, I don't doubt that he would. In an epigraph over his preface – the first words in the book, effectively – he quotes an oblique little exchange from *Waiting for Godot*:

> Estragon: All the dead voices.
> Vladimir: To be dead is not enough for them.

I suppose this must be meant as a nod to Elisabeth Hauptmann, Margarete Steffin, Ruth Berlau, and the other oppressed and occluded members of 'Brecht & Co', but because Brecht himself is so much at the centre of the book, and it is Fuegi's hatred for *him* that drives it, I can't help but relate it to B.B. himself. 'To be dead is not enough.' And so Brecht, almost forty years dead, hopelessly, perhaps irredeemably unpopular, but still, mercifully, unignorable, gets another savaging.

It isn't that I would have *nihil nisi bonum*. But a balanced, pro-Brecht book, giving equal space to the poetry, the plays, the ideas and the life, would be infinitely more valuable than this kicking, especially in the Anglo-Saxon world, where, with a few rare exceptions – Tynan, John Willett and a handful of others – Brecht has always gone over badly. Two visits to London in the Thirties were pretty unavailing; the only dramatic success in six years' exile in the States was not on Broadway or in Hollywood, but the cigar-smoking stone-walling in front of the House Un-American Activities Committee in Washington; and in one of the last things he wrote, days before his death (in 1956), a note to his Berliner Ensemble on their forthcoming visit to London, he was unillusioned, even prophetic about what awaited him there: 'the English have long dreaded German art

Review of John Fuegi, *The Life and Lies of Bertolt Brecht*
(London: Harper Collins, 1994)

(literature, painting and music) as sure to be dreadfully ponderous, slow, involved and pedestrian.'

Xenophobia, philistinism, censoriousness, priggishness have always been offered in loose handfuls by the English to foreign writers. Fuegi, who is described as 'British-born', no doubt thinks he is killing two (if not three) birds with one stone, when imparting such nuggets of information as the following in his nastily telescoped sentences: 'When *Threepenny* opened in Paris, not only did it do splendidly at the box office, but it also won the endorsement of both the young Jean-Paul Sartre and Simone de Beauvoir, with Sartre (whose life is strikingly similar to that of Brecht) learning the catchy tunes by heart.' As an approach, this is about as discriminating as the ducking-stool, and will no doubt draw similar circles of admirers.

To call this book one-eyed would be an overstatement. If Brecht had ever in his life helped an old lady across the road (doubtful, but still), don't look for an account of the circumstance in Fuegi; but if someone somewhere had accused him of eating babies, it would be there in the index: 'babies, B.B. eater of'. Things are used only inasmuch as they damage Brecht, and with the express purpose of doing so. There are various objections to this approach. First, six hundred pages of animus is overdoing it some: it is, to put it no higher, rather undramatic and lacking in variety. The pamphlet form might have served Fuegi better. Secondly, a biography, a vita, is a rather strange vehicle for such loathing. Every so often – actually, all the time – he suspends the narrative to give Brecht another wigging, and then resumes. Thirdly, this doesn't actually do what it is supposed to do – namely, persuade the reader of the rightness of its case. That the reader will unquestioningly believe what he is told, and, if told it enough times, may even carry on on Fuegi's behalf, telling his friends, 'That Brecht was a nasty piece of work, and he didn't even write his own plays,' assumes a rather naive view of reading. It also doesn't allow for fairness, the English equivalent of dialectic. Fourth, it wastes its time and the reader's on a lot of aunt sallies: Brecht the lifelong Communist, Brecht the fair dealer and feminist, Brecht the bold anti-Nazi, Brecht the solitary genius, Brecht the selfless promoter of others' works, Brecht the champion of alternative or under-

ground theatre. So far as I know, no one now believes that
Brecht was these things, and surely not many ever did. And yet
Fuegi goes around stamping on them in his big boots. His book
is full of detail and research, but on a larger level, it told me
nothing I didn't know, and, needless to say, I couldn't hear
Brecht in it. It's only the counsel for the prosecution that ever
gets to speak.

Fuegi was for 18 years managing editor of something called
the International Brecht Society, but now he writes with the zeal
of the unconverted. Any page, paragraph or even (one sometimes
thinks) sentence not slamming Brecht is a waste of space. It
begins with the book's title and jacket. I'd actually been reading
it for a couple of days before taking them in, at which point the
title made me giggle, the near-subliminal variant on 'Life and
Works' or 'Life and Times', but finally so impatiently, almost
neurotically declarative. And then the typography: Fuegi's name
in white, in a round, solid typeface, the title by contrast in
jagged, dripping Kung Fu characters, the first five words in
white, but 'Bertolt' and 'Brecht', bigger and finally enormous,
and red! That in conjunction with one of his 1927 photographs,
wearing a large leather coat with a knotted belt, one arm thrown
over the back of his chair, the other hand holding a cigar (what's
he about to do with it?), deep-set eyes and a torturer's personal
smile: the very image for Fuegi to pin his Brecht = Hitler line.

Obviously Fuegi is extremely knowledgeable about Brecht,
but all his knowledge is in the service of a rabid hatred. His
book is six hundred pages of loathing, indignation, will-to-
assassinate. It is difficult to read such a book, even more difficult
not to become desensitized while reading it, to go on responding
to its venom and absurdity all the way through – is it possible
he relents for a time during the last East German years?

But before I became utterly punchdrunk, while I was still
able to respond, it seemed to me his techniques were those of
propaganda: everything done to serve a – transparent – inten-
tion. There is the sentence as mugging: 'Bright, bold and delicate
in his appreciation of the arts, while being at the same time
apparently helpless in doing everyday tasks, he appealed to both
young men and young women.' There are the warped lists:
'Brecht, Ulbricht and his successor, Erich Honecker'; 'Stalin,

Brecht, and the East German Government'. There are the fitted-up pairings and outrageous comparisons: 'Bébé, like Nero'; 'like the Berlin wine salesman Joachim von Ribbentrop, Brecht'; 'Stalin's and Brecht's systems of control'; even 'the jacket . . . that would soon be associated with Brecht and Mao'. There is loads of sex, all of it intended to be discreditable, whether it be Brecht's youthful (alleged) homosexuality or later homophobia, his multiple partners or his flaccidity and 'urinary tract ailments' late in life. There is the subtle widening of focus, to take in something irrelevant but lingeringly poisonous like 'dreamily beautiful Dachau'. There is the tabloid-style use of detail or intensives to taint, magnify or belittle, as in '300 tons of *pure* gold a year' (my italic); and also the tabloid-style reverse, the undifferentiated, intellectually aimless but rallying rehearsal of certain 'facts': '31 and enormously wealthy', 'increasingly wealthy', 'now wealthy and with real estate values driven radically down in the depression', 'in 1932, such was his success that a country estate was virtually an obligation', and so forth. There is the vindictive pursuit of a course of particulars, without any suggestion that a variation or difference in them would be enough to cause leniency to operate:

> As the violently aroused audience finally began to file out of the theatre, Bert told Bie that they could now go off alone together at least for a time, and she hobbled through the street in her tight dress. Brecht did not propose that they take a taxi to their destination, the Café Fahrig. Brecht had brought along a bottle of now-warm champagne that he had been given earlier by one of his admirers. He was incensed when the waiter charged a corking fee. They sat for two hours over the bottle, and then Brecht accompanied Bie on the long hobble back to her aunt's in the Schwanthalerstrasse. He dropped her off and was gone.

If there is anything funnier than the tight-fisted and terminally ungallant Brecht, it is surely the fuming, violently aroused Fuegi, remorselessly tracking the couple through their evening together; but one should ask oneself if it would have made the blindest bit of difference to his curmudgeonliness if Bie's skirts had been looser, the champagne had been cold, Brecht had urbanely tipped the waiter and the two had had it away at her aunt's. The answer, obviously, is no. Always first there is Fuegi's rancour.

Fuegi's besetting rage at Brecht regularly leads him into inconsistency. All his leitmotifs – money, for instance – are stunningly badly handled. Another obsession is with Brecht's wardrobe and particularly his spectacles, but I defy any reader to say whether it is because they are cheap or expensive or cheap-looking. He simply has it in for Brecht, and it shows: 'If he had made a lot of money from *Threepenny*, it did not look to her as if he had invested any of it into clothes: his suit was shabby, and his hair poked out from under a cap that he never bothered to take off. No sooner had he arrived than he was gone again.' Then why should he have taken his cap off? But that's Brecht in this book: he stays only long enough for Fuegi to parade his violent dislike for him – or for someone else, in this case, Margarete Steffin, to fall in love with him, a circumstance Fuegi leaves himself at a loss to explain.

Sometimes, when Fuegi does get it right, he is so elaborately vindictive that the effect is funny: 'Before the master was up Brecht's pretty maid, Mari "Peppi" Hold, took out the ashes and relit the stoves, brought in the milk and the newspaper, and put on water to boil for his tea. She brought him the newspaper in his bedroom, opened the drapes, and every few days brought him hot shaving water.' I could only write 'Oo!' in the margin at that.

Equally vindictive, equally ineffective, is the two- or occasionally threefold use of certain witnesses and material; for instance and ironically, the tag that Brecht, 'ever the literary ecologist', recycled material. There are vulgar jingles, 'sex for text', practically delirious alliteration like 'sickening sycophancy', semiconscious word-play – 'Eisenstein's case was a warning of what was to come as the arts were brought under Stalin's steel heel' – and mindless near-nonsense like 'discreet marital indiscretions'.

A corresponding poverty of epithets makes itself felt, all manner of people and things being classed as 'famous' and anything from the breasts of Marieluise Fleisser to the Finnish countryside to old Danish copper pots being described as 'lovely', usually because they stand in some sort of victim-relation to Brecht. And then there is plain, fearless – because there is nothing to be feared – bullying, totalitarian coarseness,

Brecht 'emptying his gonads', or his women being 'pushed, pulled, and periodically fucked into providing him with the life-style that Brecht felt was essential if he, the great master, was to publish "his" masterworks on the needs of the poor'.

This isn't just low-grade, malicious and badly handled: it's not new and not important. Along the way, as hapless and omnivorous in his fury as Erysichthon, Fuegi quotes familiar statements that make his book redundant: for instance, Auden's remark about having known three great poets who were 'prize sonsofbitches'. (Or that's how the remark was always relayed to me; it appears here, apparently gentrified by Charles Monteith, as: 'Auden said to me . . . that of the literary men he had known only three struck him as positively evil: Robert Frost, Yeats and Brecht!') Paul Tillich saying: 'We have two and one-half Communist representatives on the council. The half is Bert Brecht.' And Eric Bentley and Lotte Lenya lament Brecht's lack of decency and manners. It would be one thing to introduce such material for the first time, or even to come round to sharing such a point of view: but to believe it from the outset and stuff it behind the dripping cover is something else. The real drama, the only drama, is the palace revolution in John Fuegi's mind some time in the last thirty years, and we're not made a party to that.

Halfway through, I felt I had to bale out for a while, and read Klaus Völker's 1976 life of Brecht, to try and preserve my responses. After Fuegi, it did seem bland, undetailed and occasionally servile (what wouldn't?) – but you could also hear Brecht in it, and that was just so much more interesting. Fuegi, either wilfully, or because of limited capacity, tends only to tell half the story. Repeatedly – but then everything in the book is repeated – he makes little connections between Brecht and Hitler: 'When Fritz Kortner directed Dorothy Thompson's *Another Sun* in 1939, he shouted at her, as she put it, "like a crazed gorilla, his face purple, his eyes bulging". Brecht, Viertel and Kortner, opposed as they were in theory to Adolf Hitler, repeatedly used an apoplectic style of directing in the American theatre.' (Note the contrived seep from the descriptiveness of the first sentence into the second, and the planting of that '1939', as though Brecht and the others were in the business of invading Poland.)

Twenty years before Fuegi, Völker pointed out that Brecht liked having a good shout in the theatre (especially at technical incompetence); that he would call people Nazis very readily; and that, where possible, he avoided unplanned 'scenes', for 'Ruhe gehört zum Regieführen wie alles andere' ('calm, like everything else, is a part of directing'), the kind of mildly provocative Brecht sentence Fuegi has no ear for. Such remarks as the 'nice little dictatorship' he needed to set up to get his 1935 American debut on the right lines, or – of Stalin's victims – 'the more innocent they are, the more they deserve to die' may contain more wit than judgment, but they are meant as provocations, and Fuegi falls for every one of them with reflex outrage. I much prefer Völker's response, which is to speak of 'shock sentences' and to comment on Brecht's 'passionate injustice' when faced by stupidity and narrow-mindedness (not that Brecht couldn't on occasion be stupid and narrow-minded himself).

The longer one spends over Fuegi (with or without the palliative of Völker), the more unsatisfactory he appears. Time and again, he pulls out, as though his case had been made. He harps on and on about Brecht's wealth and his diddling of publishers (Völker quotes Brecht quoting Ramsay Macdonald to the effect that while all contracts are sacred, none lasts for ever), but he gives very few figures. It should have been the backbone of his book, but accountancy interests him less than moralizing. Brecht's meanness is a primary quality, and not interesting per se: some people just are mean. His need for money, though, and presumably for far more than he could ever spend, interests me – though unfortunately not Fuegi. Insecurity, to measure his success, out of an arithmetical cast of mind? No word from Fuegi.

On the other hand, Fuegi is forever accusing and hanging Brecht for faithlessness: but why did he keep the one promise in his life he did keep, his 1940 agreement never to harm the Soviet Union by anything he wrote or said? Fuegi doesn't say. And again, Brecht is accused of chasing big productions of his plays (nothing that much wrong with that, one might think);

but then he lets slip something about an all-black production of the *Threepenny Opera* in California. What about that?

A small amount of the book's effort goes into establishing or rehabilitating the reputations of Hauptmann, Steffin and Berlau, Brecht's principal cohorts (pictured on the back cover). But if Fuegi had been properly serious about this, he would have made them, or one or two of them, the subject of a book, not the done-to-death-and-beyond Brecht. Secondly, though the case for these sexually and literarily exploited women as the originators of much of Brecht's dramatic work in particular is very strong – and again, not new – Fuegi makes it badly. The fact that Hauptmann contributed translations from English, French or Chinese (via Arthur Waley) does nothing for the claim that she was an original writer; quoting her as saying, 'up until '33 I either wrote or wrote down most of the poems,' isn't a great piece of evidence; and describing a poem by Steffin as 'one of the many that Steffin wrote capturing his style precisely' isn't exactly impressive either. Nor does Fuegi do much to individuate them. Each makes the plays she is involved with centre on a 'strong female character'. Well, thanks for nothing.

In the end, this is not just a nasty book, but an obtuse one. If one wants a description of the Sirens' song, one would ask Odysseus, who had himself chained to the mast to be able to hear it, and not one of his earplugged oarsmen. But that's what Fuegi is. He doesn't hear Brecht, and doesn't let his readers either. References to Brecht's wit, charm, irony and playfulness come about every hundred pages, and, from Fuegi, don't sound terribly convincing anyway. (Brecht in Fuegi's translations, as often in English, is charmless, witless, generally voiceless: it might have been done deliberately.) Ironically, then, Fuegi is repeatedly drawn into descriptions of Brecht the Singing Seducer. These become, like much else in the book, unintentionally comic. Brecht picks up a guitar and sings one of his ballads, and people are all over him. But not John Fuegi. No.

BERTOLT BRECHT
Letters, Poems and Songs

Poor B.B. His granddaughter is detained at Heathrow and all but turned back when she comes to give a recital of his songs. A new production of a Brecht play actually sells itself as – I forget the adverb – 'unBrechtian'. A *Times* profile, rather well-meaning, comes up with a variant of the Schleswig-Holstein story, by saying that Brecht had only ever truly been admired by one Englishman, and that was Kenneth Tynan, and he was dead.

These are dark times. Under the circumstances, with so many voices calling for his dismissal from the pantheon, it seems gallant of the publishers Methuen to go on bringing out Brecht's work in ample succession, from the splendid editing-and-translating team of John Willett and Ralph Manheim – particularly as the books under review are somewhat specialized. Brecht was not one of the great letter-writers, and the volume of *Poems and Songs from the Plays* is no more than a supplement to the indispensable *Poems 1913–1956*. Nevertheless, both books are fine productions, readable and informative from red end-paper to red end-paper.

Overall, Brecht's correspondence is neither particularly intimate nor especially literary. One of the few references to books is that to Rilke's novel *The Notebooks of Malte Laurids Brigge*, which crops up only because Brecht sent a copy to his publishers because he liked the typeface, and thought his *Threepenny Novel* might be set the same way. It is a manufacturer's or an industrialist's touch rather than an artist's: a rival firm with a good blueprint or a nice design feature. This is typical of the correspondence, which is busy, fretful and above all practical. They are working letters, written either with a particular tangible objective in mind, or else to keep communications open. For large stretches one may think of them as being not by Brecht at all but by a small part of him, his internal secretariat. They

Review of Bertolt Brecht, *Letters 1913–1956*, ed. John Willett, trans. Ralph Manheim (London: Methuen, 1990), and *Poems and Songs from the Plays*, ed. and trans. John Willett (London: Methuen, 1990)

might all be signed 'pp B.B.' Of their kind, they are also
extremely good letters, letters one would love to have working
for oneself, letters to agents and theatres and publishers and tax
authorities. They are a most effective representation of Brecht,
his strong will, his attention to detail, his economy of means
occasionally overwhelmed by his argumentativeness and love of
company. Reading them, one realizes to what an extraordinary
extent business did have to be conducted by letter in his life.
He spent his middle years, from thirty-five to fifty, in exile, first
inching up Scandinavia, then – by way of the trans-Siberian
railway and a Swedish freighter across the Pacific – in California.
Skovsbostrand, Helsinki, Santa Monica: they were the years of
his peak achievements, and in them he was denied the support
of theatres and institutions, and was left to scratch around at
one remove at least from his true creativity: to get a Danish
proverb instated as the title of the Danish *Threepenny Novel*;
to organize divisions of labour among discontented American
translators, unaware of one another's existence; to obtain hard
currency payments from the Soviet Union in the 1930s for
contributions to the international periodical *Das Wort*.

Brecht was one of the great literary collaborators of all time.
While he managed to keep a kind of *Arbeitsgruppe Brecht*
(mainly women) going through all the years of his exile, there
were other friends (mainly men) from whom he was apart.
Consequently, perhaps the most characteristic and certainly the
most winning form in these *Letters* is the invitation, an open
one to be sure, but needing the factitious glamour of an occasion
or purpose. Brecht is like an exiled Circe, pleading and wheed-
ling and conjuring visitors from more attractive spots than his
own. Here his powerful charm becomes apparent, his gifts for
friendship and persuasion. Not even Garrison Keillor can have
done as much for Denmark as Brecht. To George Grosz:

> Summer is coming, the water is warming up. It will soon be time for
> your annual trip to Europe, friend. Arise, embark. Room and board
> here cost four crowns (two marks forty). A small Ford from olden
> days makes life easier. Nowhere will you be closer to your homeland.

To Erwin Piscator:

> Why don't you discuss it with me on the green island of Fyn over a

cigar or two? You could swim and drive around in my old Ford.
There are newspapers and books, and you'll have a pleasant room.
The programme changes twice a week at the two cinemas and they
show nice American films. Of course we could work together too.

To Walter Benjamin:

> How's your health? How about a trip to the northland? The chess
> board lies orphaned; every half hour a tremor of remembrance runs
> through it; that was when you made your moves.

At other times, in slightly more formal circumstances, Brecht's
frustrated gregariousness takes the form of organizing rather
nonsensical little gangs, like something called the 'Diderot
Society' in 1937 – 'only productive people' – for which Brecht
sent out what amount to chain letters to celebrities saying bring
a friend. This is something that actually inheres in all Brecht's
correspondence, a cajoling browbeating, a lining up of people
on his side, a marshalling of translators, keeping track of Ruth
Berlau's mood-swings while she was in New York and he in
California. In inverse relation to his actual remoteness and help-
lessness was a surge of manipulativeness and a quixotic frenzy
to control.

The tone of the letters is mostly hasty, reasonable and neutral.
One may go through pages and pages without finding any
pleasing or arresting turn of phrase. It should be pointed out
that the present volume is a large selection from a German
edition which will shortly be superseded by the new 'Frank-
furt' edition of Brecht, which will certainly contain more
business letters – previously edited out by the East Germans –
and possibly more intimate correspondence. It is striking that,
apart from two to an uncle, there are no letters to Brecht's
family, and apart from those to Ruth Berlau and his wife Helene
Weigel, no letters of love here. Even then, it's often a case, as
he says to Berlau at one point, of 'Please take these dry-as-dust
lines as lines of love.' Brecht seems to have kept a special tone
for George Grosz. He seems younger, more cynical, more effer-
vescent there than elsewhere – 'The Lord of the Straw Hats to
the Lord of the Skyscrapers' – and also, occasionally, more
genuine: 'Remember me to your wife and if you have a sad
moment one of these days, drop me a few lines, they're sure to

reach me in a sad moment.' Generally, Brecht specializes in a brisk, studiedly cool and objective tone, playing down any feelings of danger or despair. The flight to Finland ('changing countries oftener than our shoes' in the poem 'To Those Born Later') is described with positively British nonchalance: 'Things weren't looking so rosy any more in this part of the world, so we decided to move to Helsingfors.' Altogether, the letters-of-arrival-in-a-new-place stand out: the Finnish ones for their superb dignity, and American ones for their mixture of gratitude and waspish irony. One could only wish that this last had survived into his final years as more than a private resource: the letters in which he defers to the artistic judgment of Ulbricht and his party hacks are horrible:

> I wish to thank you and the comrades for making possible the production of Dessau's opera [which was pulled]. In doing so you have demonstrated the republic's great comradely understanding for the difficulties besetting artists in the present phase of reconstruction.

Everything in one aches to read this ironically, as a linguistic experiment, but it isn't. It is formal kowtowing and self-criticism in the approved manner. Brecht maintained his belief in the GDR more than most who lived there, but took refuge, as they did, in silence, cunning and jokes in safe company. It was a sad split between the public and the private man, who consoled himself by writing tragic riven poems, dissident whispers like 'Der Radwechsel', 'Changing the Wheel':

> I sit by the roadside.
> The driver changes the wheel.
> I do not like the place I have come from.
> I do not like the place I am going to.
> Why with impatience do I
> Watch him changing the wheel?

Poems and Songs from the Plays takes one back to the other end of Brecht's career, his green beginnings as a writer of poems as joyful and delirious and carnal as Rimbaud's: the Baal poems, 'Bidi im Herbst', 'Über die Anstrengung', or 'Oh, ihr Zeiten meiner Jugend' (in *Poems 1913–1956*, translated by John Willett):

O Gekreisch der schnarrenden Gitarren!
Ach, du himmlisch aufgeblähter Hals!
Hosen, die von Schmutz und Liebe starren!
Und in schleimig grünen Nächten: welch Gebalz!

Oh the harsh snarl of guitar strings roaring!
Heavenly distensions of our throats!
Trousers stiff with dirt and love! Such whoring!
Long green slimy nights: we were like stoats.

Brecht arrived fully formed from an unholy union between Kipling and Rimbaud, with Villon standing at the crib. From the very beginning, he had a formidable technical gift, new matter and an extraordinary range from song to speech, from chugging ballads – he accompanied himself on the guitar to his own melodies – to lofty, biblical, irregular rhetoric. The poems here enact that variety. Perhaps the most remarkable thing about the songs is their double life: cold fusion when sung to Weill or Eisler or Dessau, but full of literary poise and subtlety when read on the page. Take certainly his most famous song, 'Die Moritat von Mackie Messer', 'The Crimes of Mac the Knife' as it is presented here by Willett. The whole thing is a sustained equivocation between man and shark, simple and balanced and hinged like a shark's jaw, down to details in the fourth verse:

An 'nem schönen, blauen Sonntag
Liegt ein toter Mann am Strand
Und ein Mensch geht um die Ecke
Den man Mackie Messer nennt.

Is the blue of 'blauen Sonntag' sky or sea? Is 'am Strand' 'on the shore' or is it the street in London? Brecht's verse is full of such finesse and ornamentation. It seems bizarre to connect him with Pound, but there is as much logopoeia in Brecht as in anyone. The poem 'Lied von der belebenden Wirkung des Geldes' – a flowery, dactyllic title, rather brutally rendered as 'Song of the Stimulating Impact of Cash' – begins:

Niedrig gilt das Geld auf dieser Erden
Und doch ist sie, wenn es mangelt, kalt
Und sie kann sehr gastlich werden
Plötzlich durch des Gelds Gewalt.

> People keep on saying cash is sordid
> Yet this world's a cold place if you're short.
> Not so once you can afford it
> And have ample cash support.

The 'gilt' (counts for) / 'Geld' (money) play in the first line is daring and delicious; the inversion, the archaic 'Erden' (earth) and the further play between that and 'gastlich' (hospitable) – a guest on this earth – give the quatrain a biblical solemnity; 'gastlich' in particular is astounding, a word of epicurean relish and abundance. The English version, one has to say, is padded and uninteresting. Its obviousness and functionalism – neither a feature of the original – go some way towards explaining Brecht's poor standing in England. It is not that Brecht is a boring and preachy writer, it's because he's a poet and untranslatable. The cavalier in him, the pleasure of a word placed to perfection and absurdly fine, the inessentials that are everything – it is these that have failed to survive.

Willett has very reasonably set himself to match the form: he has his eyes on the length of the line, and the rhyme at the end of it, and in the great majority of the poems here, his little flat sign in the notes indicates that he has achieved parity. It is in itself an astonishing achievement, and one for which I have all the respect in the world. Furthermore, the best versions here are the short-lined, punchy, heavily rhyming forms: 'The Legend of the Dead Soldier', 'The New Cannon Song', 'Song to Inaugurate the National Deposit Bank'. There are praiseworthy efforts to re-enrich the language: 'In winter time the coolies need warm clothing'; 'First they shoot up like a comet/ Then tail off like comets falling'; even – though not everyone will like this – 'You must muster for the march' (but that is what Brecht is actually like). In another form of compensation, a very strong line occasionally contrives to give the impression of rhyme – even though it doesn't: 'Food is fuel, cash makes you randy.' (An irrational phenomenon first noticed by John Berryman, who used it in the *Dream Songs*.) For all that, there is no English in the book to touch the plangent 'Benares Song', written in English 'for Brecht' (wonderful preposition, that!) by Elisabeth Hauptmann, one of his collaborators:

There is no whisky in this town
There is no bar to sit us down
Oh!
Where is the telephone?
Is there no telephone?
Oh, sir, God damn it:
No!

PAUL CELAN

Paul Celan was born in 1920 as Paul Antschel, to German-speaking Jewish parents in Czernowitz, the capital of the Bukovina: 'a posthumously born *Kakanier*,' he once said of himself (the city and province of his birth had been ceded to Romania in 1918, when the Habsburg Empire was broken up). His upbringing reflected the family's Jewish traditions, but also the deep love of German literature and culture that was often found, especially in Jewish populations, in the Eastern marches of Austria-Hungary (think of the Galician, Joseph Roth). In Celan's case, this came to him from his mother: German was, in every sense, his mother-tongue. Already as a boy, he loved poetry, first Goethe and Schiller, then Hölderlin, Heine, Trakl, Kafka and in particular Rilke. He spoke German, Hebrew, Romanian and some Yiddish and was obviously an exceptional linguist, later translating poetry from Russian, English, French and Italian. And yet, when he came to write, he had no real alternative to German: 'Poetry – that is the fateful uniqueness of language,' he wrote. Only slightly younger Jewish writers like Yehuda Amichai and Dan Pagis – a fellow Bukovinan – emigrated to Israel and wrote their poetry in Hebrew: Celan couldn't. It is what gives his poetry its desperate distinction. 'There is nothing in the world,' Celan said, 'for which a poet will give up writing, not even when he is a Jew, and the language of his poems is German.'

In 1938 he went as a student to France – still thinking to study medicine – but he returned home the following year committed to literature and philology. When the war started, Czernowitz was occupied first by Russian troops and then by the Germans and their Romanian allies. The Antschels were put in a ghetto and got out of it, but in the summer of 1942 his parents were picked up and taken to a Nazi labour camp in Transnistria – one of the bleak, almost nonce names of South-

Review of John Felstiner, *Paul Celan: Poet, Survivor, Jew* (New Haven: Yale University Press, 1995), and Paul Celan, *Breathturn*, trans. Pierre Joris (Sun & Moon, 1995)

Eastern Europe. Celan himself was fortuitously absent. His father died there, after a few months, of typhoid fever, and his mother was murdered – shot in the neck – by the Germans for being unfit to work. 'These killings, especially that of his mother, were to remain the core experiences of his life,' writes Pierre Joris in a biographical note. Celan himself did forced labour. When the Russians retook the Bukovina, he went back to Czernowitz. In 1945, having anagrammatized himself to Paul Celan, he was in Bucharest, where an early version of his most celebrated poem, 'Todesfuge', came out in a friend's Romanian translation: it was his first publication. In 1947 he went west to Vienna. The following year he settled in Paris, where he worked as a translator and taught – German – at the Ecole Normale Supérieure. He married the graphic artist Gisèle de Lestrange in 1952; they had a son, Eric (having lost another in infancy), and lived in Paris and Normandy, Celan teaching and publishing poems. He visited Germany fairly frequently for professional reasons, giving readings and receiving awards, and in 1969 paid a short but intense visit to Israel. In April 1970, he drowned himself in the Seine.

Celan published six substantial volumes of poetry in his lifetime, of which *Atemwende* (*Breathturn*) was the fifth; three more appeared posthumously. A selection from these posthumous books, called *Last Poems* and published by North Point in 1986, was made by Katharine Washburn and Margret Guillemin. Michael Hamburger has published translations from Celan in increasing volume since a 1972 *Selected* from Penguin; *Poems of Paul Celan*, containing work from every one of Celan's nine volumes, is published by Anvil and Persea. All the English editions – except the old Penguin – have parallel texts. All of them too, I think, make some appeal to Celan's own activity as a translator – Shakespeare's sonnets, Emily Dickinson, Mandelstam, Blok, Yesenin, Apollinaire, Valéry, Supervielle, Ungaretti – to validate their own efforts. A scholarly edition of Celan, obviously an exceptionally difficult and delicate undertaking, has been underway in Germany for some years. In the meantime he is surely the most written about poet of our time – over three thousand items, Pierre Joris reckons.

John Felstiner's book is of inestimable value to anyone

wanting to read Celan with understanding. It provides a sort of triple deal, giving a rudimentary narrative of the life, and combining this with translations and brilliant readings of maybe four or five dozen poems, the two acceptance speeches of 1958 (the City of Bremen Literature Prize) and 1960 (the Georg Büchner Prize), and the 1959 prose piece 'Conversation in the Mountains'. When Felstiner ends: 'From first to last his poems stand' – a crucial verb in Celan – and follows that with four pages of lines from Celan's poems, with their dates, from 1938 to 1970, it is like getting a dramatis personae; and when the reader feels, at each line or fragment, a pang of recognition, orientation and emotion, it is a tribute to what Felstiner has achieved in mediating and explicating these urgent and often enigmatic writings.

To anyone raised on Anglo-American biographies of the sort that know everything about their subject and will say anything, Felstiner's propriety and lack of intrusiveness come as quite a shock. His gentle approach seems to push Celan back into a more dignified past: it is strange to think he died just two years before John Berryman, whose hospitalizations, marriages, alcoholism and so on are all common knowledge – not least because Berryman wrote about them himself. As Hamburger says, Celan 'had hardly any use for realism of a kind that merely imitates and reproduces, for what Northrop Frye has called "the low mimetic"'. He never wrote anything like Berryman's 'I didn't & I didn't. Sharp the Spanish blade' and the corollary is that we aren't now being told what Celan liked for breakfast. We don't know with what feelings or even exactly when he went to his death, nor can we picture the scene on 27 June 1942 when his parents were taken away. In part, it is Celan's difficulty and delicacy that continue to protect him from any intrusiveness. A poem in *Breathturn* begins, 'Temple-pincers, eyed by your cheekbone'. Felstiner conjectures it might be about shock therapy. But it's good not to know, or rather not to be told for sure – and all these dark and heavy biographical facts are left to accrue to the benefit of the poems (and out of range of the trivialization and inquisition of biography). It is striking, too, how people who knew Celan talk about him in terms that are reminiscent of his own poems. At times, their statements show a mastery of one of his own favourite forms, paradox: his style of reading aloud, with 'a cold heat'; the poet Henri Michaux's laconic Möbius-ism 'we spoke so as not to have to speak'; or Emmanuel Lévinas's Dickinsonian remark that Celan's poems testified to his – stunning phrase – 'Insomnia in the bed of Being'. Clearly, no one is about to write a knock-down-drag-out biography of Paul Celan; in fact Felstiner's book is the nearest there has yet been to anything of the kind.

Still, it is not biography that is the motor for *Poet, Survivor, Jew*, but translation. Translation in the service of comprehension, not as its own end (it makes, I think, all the difference in the world). Thus, Felstiner comes to a poem, offers his English version of it, explaining his priorities and choices, rejoicing in his successes and lamenting his failures, the impossibilities and the imponderables, gives the background to the poem – the imagery, the experience behind it, Celan's reading, inaccessible allusions and bits of word-play – and goes on. In a sense, the translation is the least conspicuous part of the process; it seems to abolish itself, it is just the vector that delivers the poem. I kept thinking what a roundabout way of doing things this was, how much more straightforward and strictly focused if the whole thing had been kept to German, as poem plus elucidation – but actually it works like a charm. (And it does bring in an English readership: Felstiner's book assumes no German on the reader's part, while managing to make it continually available – perhaps the single most wonderful thing about what he does.) As he observes in his Introduction, 'to grow attentive, especially in translating, is to activate these poems.' Primarily, then, the translating is for Felstiner's own benefit: it keeps him honest and up to the mark, it leaves him all the time exposed (as Celan said, 'poetry exposes itself'), and the continual friction between the languages gives him energy and material. It remains a weird undertaking, this parallel action – a phantom operation, a powerplant with dummy fuel rods. In the context of his book, however, it makes sense: his enthusiasm, scholarship and literary sensitivity enrich these rods. It is crucial that we get not just the translations – inadequate, depleted and impossible as they almost invariably are with a poet like Celan, embedded in that 'fateful uniqueness of language' – but a sense of the things that need to be added to make them live. And for that, Felstiner deserves enormous credit.

On their own, the translations can indeed look a little odd. One has been done as a Dickinson pastiche. The most famous one, the version of 'Deathfugue' that Daniel Weissbort used in his anthology, *The Poetry of Survival*, where I first saw it, goes, as Weissbort describes it, 'at certain crucial points, *back* into German, in an almost sacramental completion of the translational circle'. Fugally and incrementally, Felstiner incorporates the original, so that the last two and a half lines are exactly as Celan wrote them:

a man lives in the house your goldenes Haar Margarete
he looses his hounds on us grants us a grave in the air
he plays with his vipers and daydreams der Tod ist ein Meister aus
    Deutschland

dein goldenes Haar Margarete
dein aschenes Haar Sulamith

(Since they have been translated earlier on in the poem, there can be no possibility of not understanding them.) It is a way of acknowledging – and in a translation! – the untranslatability of Celan. How can the within/without, first/third-person ambivalence of 'Deutschland' be rendered by the unfreighted and external 'Germany' (with its distinct root of 'Aleman-' for 'Teutsch', all cosy and Western)? What seems at first like a pointless stunt is in fact only doing in a performative way – and only here, in this of all Celan's poems, 'the *Guernica* of postwar European poetry', Felstiner calls it – what Felstiner does throughout *Poet, Survivor, Jew*, which is to bring the German within reach of the English reader.

More striking, and more valuable than his translations, are the readings (of the necessary microscopic acuity) to which Felstiner subjects Celan's poems. One of his odder words for Celan is 'reliable' – reminding me of Heaney's sloes 'bitter and dependable', and then in turn of Celan's almonds – and he uses it only once, but it stays with the reader, so that by the end of a book expounding (Katharine Washburn's words) 'small poems, speaking little, saying everything', – reliability has come to seem anything but a minor virtue. It is here that Felstiner's book

becomes incomparably, almost unimaginably – and finally sus-
piciously, even counter-productively – richer than reading
someone's English versions of the poems, or even the originals
unassisted. Take 'Tenebrae', a transparently great poem in any
language, not 'hard' but with a howling, desolating coldness to
it: 'Nah sind wir, Herr,/ nahe und greifbar.// Gegriffen schon,
Herr,/ ineinander verkrallt, als wär/ der Leib eines jeden von
uns/ dein Leib, Herr.// Bete, Herr,/ bete zu uns,/ wir sind nah.'
This is ferocious, terrifying in its insistence, and not a letter –
the 'e' in 'nahe' – out of place. Michael Hamburger's version
goes:

> We are near, Lord,
> near and at hand.
> Handled already, Lord,
> clawed and clawing as though
> the body of each of us were
> your body, Lord.
>
> Pray, Lord,
> pray to us,
> we are near.

Felstiner has it:

> Near are we, Lord,
> near and graspable.
>
> Grasped already, Lord,
> clawed into each other, as if
> each of our bodies were
> your body, Lord.
>
> Pray, Lord,
> pray to us,
> we are near.

The fifth line is inelegant, and he loses the thudding *ds* and
the gathering movement of 'at hand' to 'handled'; then again,
'handled' is really not adequate for 'gegriffen', and Hamburger
saves a little more of Celan's terrifying dactylic metre. But where
Felstiner really scores is in his sourcing of the poem in Scripture
and theology, and, still more, of its fourth line, 'ineinander
verkrallt' to the German translation of *The Final Solution* by

Gerald Reitlinger, which Celan had been reading and which describes a cluster of Jews pressed against the gas chamber door, 'even in death clawed into each other'. Here and elsewhere, Felstiner shows Celan as a harsh and knowing poet, and any idea of him as advancing Jewish-Christian or Jewish-German reconciliation is not only half-baked but deliberately, even viciously untrue.

In this instance, the reader might perhaps have intuited what was behind Celan's phrase, but elsewhere Felstiner shows things that are off the charts. At the time of Celan's third book, *Sprachgitter (Speech Grille)*, he and his wife visited her mother who had retired to a nunnery and spoke to them, literally, through a grille. Near the end of the long poem 'Engführung', variously 'Straitening' or 'Stretto' in translation, is a little stanza: 'Chöre, damals, die/ Psalmen. Ho, ho-/ sianna.' ('Choirs, back then, the/ Psalms. Ho, ho-/ sanna.') It's not a problem to translate – a lot of Celan isn't – but it's numbing to read, without the help of Felstiner: ' "Hosanna" shouts welcome and praise, like the glorious *Osanna in excelsis* in Bach's B Minor Mass. But in Psalms the Hebrew term means "Save [us] please!" (118:25). "Ho, ho-/ sanna" reduces to a stammer or derisive laughter, with echoes of the German marching song "For we are Hitler's brown-clad host – Huzza, ho-ho!"' A late poem called 'Frankfurt, September' is about the Book Fair – Freud and Kafka, both published by Fischer, as was Celan, still – but who would know it: 'The simulate-/ jackdaw/ breakfasts.// The glottal stop/ sings.' In German, the two *k*s in 'Kehlkopfverschlusslaut' ('glottal stop') signal Kafka, as does the jackdaw, 'kafka' in Czech. A poem written after Celan's visit to Jerusalem goes, in its entirety: 'Ich trink Wein aus zwei Gläsern/ und zackere an/ der Konigszäsur/ wie Jener/ am Pindar.// Gott gibt die Stimmgabel ab/ als einer der kleinen/ Gerechten,// aus der Lostrommel fällt/ unser Deut.' Here, the Washburn/Guillemin translation ends: 'God turns over the tuning-fork/ alone of the small/ just ones,// from the fate-engine falls/ our measure.' From that the reader gets the usual vaguely and comfortingly doomy feeling, but they've got the verb wrong, the 'alone' construction wrong, and have approximated the ending. Not only does Felstiner offer a much better translation –

I drink wine from two glasses
and plough away at
the king's caesura
like that one
at Pindar.

God turns in his tuning-fork
as one among the least
of the Just

the lottery drum spills
our two bits

– he also offers a page of outstanding commentary, relating the poem to Celan's quandary about whether to remain in France or go and live in Jerusalem (hence the two glasses, the caesura and the tuning-fork, and the inspired 'two bits' at the end). Felstiner ends: 'With God diminished, the lovers' fate falls to chance. A lottery spills out *unser Deut* – our "doit", a coin not worth a farthing, implying *Deutsch* as well as *Deutung* ("interpretation" – our "cents" of things?). My "two bits" gets only a little of that.' This is extremely persuasive, but also so enlivening and so much fun it makes the reader want to chance his own arm: what about 'turning in your tuning-fork' (*die Stimmgabel abgeben*) as something you do when you no longer have a voice, or vote (*die Stimme abgeben*), or even as a version of *den Löffel abgeben*, to 'turn in your spoon', slang for 'die'?

My only reservation about Felstiner is that he succeeds too well. Being guided by him through Celan is an experience that is nothing like what I have when I read Celan on my own, and must surely boggle the minds of readers who can approach him only through translation. And to me there's something wrong about that: these things shouldn't be so utterly distinct. A commentary ought to be an extension or a deepening of a reading, not, essentially, the recovery, revelation, or possibly invention of a poem (although I hasten to add that I follow and believe John Felstiner wherever he goes). By the same token, a translation should be able to do more than just slide the words and punctuation across the page, losing practically everything en route and still leaving the reader utterly baffled as most Celan

translations inevitably and unapologetically do. Celan provides
the terrain – we are talking about his words – but the
authority, the creativity, the freedom and the space all belong
to the exegetes: they are the ones who are giving him to us.
With other poets, these things are shared out in some measure:
the poet does more work on himself, the reader can do more, the
translator does more. With Celan's extremely idiosyncratic,
compressed, meta-linguistic poetry, there is even a case for
saying there is no point in translating him at all. The syllogism
which proposes that, since Celan is just as strange in German
and to German, he might as well be translated into English or
anything else – and he used to do translations himself too – is
just nonsense. His words are defined by – they exist in – their
relation to German, their separation from German. Even the
very lightest translation – just a sort of Englishing-over, one coat
with a camel-hair brush – takes him away. And what sort of
translating is that anyway? A translator wants, at some point,
to make a difference, to be something other than an autopilot.
But how can one aspire to 'make a difference' with Celan? The
temerity! Even Joseph Brodsky's argument in favour of 'bad
translations' – they won't mislead the reader by any qualities of
their own, but will leave his intuition to engage with the original
– doesn't work, because all translations of almost anything by
Celan are bound to be 'bad', and intuition – or, in Michael
Hamburger's phrase, 'the gesture of the poem as a whole' – is
all we have to go on anyway. The only possible translation, it
seems to me, is the kind practised by John Felstiner in the last
two lines of 'Deathfugue' (elsewhere, too, he speaks movingly
about his success in replicating a break between stanzas). I really
think an English reader might as well sit down with the original
text and a dictionary, and look up every single word.

'Ganz und gar nicht hermetisch', Celan famously inscribed a
book for Michael Hamburger: 'absolutely not hermetic'. That
insistence – which utterly fails to square with most people's
experience of reading him – finds an explanation in Felstiner:
'if his poetry was seen as magically sealed off from under-
standing, that would relieve its readers of responsibility.' That
is in part a serious argument. When Celan read at a Hölderlin
celebration shortly before his death, one of the attending aca-

demics reported that 'philologists precisely informed . . . on particular obscurities in Hölderlin shook their heads, rejecting the man up there and his word.' That obscurity is of our choosing, it is we who make it so. Celan's is of a different order; in Felstiner's words, he 'was not dealing in a universal currency, like Yeats's Byzantium, Pound's Cathay, Eliot's Augustine and Lowell's Ahab, to which we all (we're told) have access.' It's a good point, and we need, as Celan says, to listen our way in with our mouths. But beyond the Jewish themes and buried history in the poems, there are other, more recalcitrant difficulties. 'Attention . . . the natural prayer of the soul' (Celan quoting from Malebranche) – a tag that the translations like to pass on to their readers in lieu of instructions for use – often isn't enough. Even Felstiner says at one point: 'It was all very well for Celan in 1961 to advise someone, "Read! Just keep reading, understanding comes of itself."' Celan's dealings with postwar Germany were unbearably and continually wounding: the reviews, the way that 'Todesfuge' was taught in schools, the accusation of plagiarism from Claire Goll. Writing was partly revenge – on 'those football players' of the Gruppe 47 who took him up and called him hermetic, on that 'something rotten in the state of the D-Mark', as he exquisitely said. His two acceptance speeches, for all their hesitancy, were subliminal – and sublime – instances of 'Publikumsbeschimpfung' (Handke's title), 'insulting the audience'. And then the poems, designed, I would almost say, to compel but not to be read, tying down armies of Germanists.

Celan perfected a style of writing that was able to absorb unprecedented quantities of reality: so much so that the poems don't require to be read so much as reconstituted. But they have become – and I wonder whether Celan intended this – ideal objects of exploration and explanation, 'gestures' so complicated that they can't possibly be copied, only described. These descriptions, then, are for me the most worthwhile part of Celan translations: in essence, that is the case with Felstiner. Pierre Joris sandwiches his loyally stiff versions between a brilliant Introduction and some helpful and appealingly modest notes; and the Washburn/Guillemin *Last Poems*, with fallible translation (Celan's magical verb 'stand' – 'survive' or 'endure', harking back to Rilke's 'überstehn ist alles' – given four times as 'was' in one poem, 'Kolbenschlag' translated as 'stroke of the piston' when I think a blow with the butt of a rifle is meant) and a perfumed Introduction, still has gorgeous quotes in it: 'We are digging the pit of Babel' from Kafka, and the amazingly Kafkaesque sentence, from Schönberg on Webern, 'Though the brevity of these pieces is a persuasive advocate for them, on the other hand that very brevity itself requires an advocate,' which one would be glad to see anywhere. I suppose in the end a translation should sound as though it understood, even in some sense compassed an original; it is 'catching' something and throwing it on to the reader. And I suppose no translator of Celan would have the hubris to say he had caught or could compass Celan: all he is doing is standing in very little light, and waiting to catch something of unknown dimensions.

I'm not sure how important Celan is to poetry in English. I think the American 'deep image' school, writing short poems with a small vocabulary, may think they are doing something comparable. But I don't understand how people with a basically uncomplicated relationship to their own blameless language can think they are learning from Celan. 'What a game!' he once said, of poetry.

ANNA AKHMATOVA

Russian poetry is different, as Fitzgerald once said of the rich. It has another dimension of intensity, of public speech, of moral hygiene, of tragedy. The English poet speaks for himself and cultivates his oddity in a corner of the language; the Russian is ordinary and speaks for everyone. This function of poetry, its familiarity and importance, its conspicuous place at the head of an alternative hierarchy, resists translation into English more than the words themselves – they arrive with an echo, and perhaps sound hollow to our ears. In England, poetry is a mews off Grub Street; in Russia, it is celestial, half-Parnassus and half-Hollywood.

Perhaps only American poetry can begin to compare with it. John Berryman summons 'the worst possible ordeal that will not actually kill him'; Akhmatova asserts that 'Shakespeare's plays – the sensational atrocities, passions, duels – are child's play compared to the life of each one of us'. Robert Lowell makes his 'manic statement/ telling off the state and president' and Pasternak tells Stalin on the telephone that he wanted to talk to him about life and death. All are on the Richter Scale, with their exorbitance and risk.

The difference is that the Americans were brinkmen: calculating, perhaps bored; their success or failure mattered only to themselves. It is impossible to imagine *them* saying (as Akhmatova said): 'The Nobel is not enough.' And if they had said it, it would have been a demand for a rise. For the Russians, poetry was not a career, and they toughed it out, none more than Akhmatova: the only game in town.

There was a golden age of Russian poetry, but that was in the early nineteenth century, and, like most golden ages (in fact, it seems axiomatic) it travels badly: Pushkin in translation seems like a lesser Byron rather than a later Shakespeare. Akhmatova became an expert on Pushkin, and uses his words, sparingly as saffron, as epigraphs for some of her own work.

She was, believe it or not, part of the silver age of Russian

Review of *The Complete Poems of Anna Akhmatova*, trans. Judith Hemschemeyer (Edinburgh: Zephyr/Canongate, 1990)

poetry: herself, Pasternak, Mandelstam and Tsvetayeva were born in consecutive years, from 1889 to 1892. They are beyond question the most gifted group of poets of the century. Akhmatova, the first of them, was also the last; she died in 1966. Isaiah Berlin writes: 'The widespread worship of her memory in the Soviet Union today, both as an artist and as an unsurrendering human being, has, so far as I know, no parallel.'

The pupil and protégé of her last years, Joseph Brodsky, offers the best description of Akhmatova's poetry (in an essay, 'The Keening Muse', included in his *Less Than One*). She is 'the kind of poet that simply "happens"', without apprenticeship or discernible development, unlike anyone else and impossible to imitate. He calls her 'blatantly non-avant-garde', 'a poet of strict metres, exact rhymes and short sentences'.

Of these three qualities, only the third can be relied upon to survive in translation; metre and rhyme (the great majority of Akhmatova's poems consist of three or four rhymed quatrains) have to be imagined. Even so, it is enough. Judith Hemschemeyer's versions are the best I have seen; they have dignity and pace, and are part way rhymed. Above all, her mission to translate all of Akhmatova – for which she taught herself Russian, though working from literal versions, like many translators – proves to have been inspired. This great lilac brick of a book, with 800 poems (some mere scraps of only two or three wonderful lines), a hundred photographs, Berlin's memoir of his amazing nocturnal meeting with Akhmatova in 1945, all annotated and introduced, is a stupendous bargain.

Akhmatova at 20 wrote poems in which she was flawless, interesting and herself. Brodsky comments on the 'terrific novelistic quality' of her love poems, and I was captivated especially by her second book *Rosary* (1914); those poems were recited in order by her admirers, round a room. Each one is a moment of great physical and psychological clarity: a room or street, an encounter, an exchange of words or gestures, and often some bitter twist at the end. Love can be 'calculating and malicious', a nightingale sings 'poisonously', in a Victorian image of sexual taint, there is the smell of tobacco in dishevelled braids.

A romantic and fêted and beautiful youth was misleading and left Akhmatova unprepared, one would have thought, for the future: her first husband, the poet Gumilyov, shot in 1921, two unsatisfactory remarriages, the imprisonment of her son under Stalin, deaths and betrayals and chicaneries. But no, the proportions of bitterness and passion in her work were reversed, her poetic resources dealt magnificently with what was thrown at her. At 30 she described herself as old and wrote about her losses. She compared her life to a train rushing off the tracks or – that other miracle of Soviet engineering – a re-routed river. Poetry, she said superbly, grows from 'rubbish'.

The appalling drama of her life – Shakespearean, as she said – is traced and surmounted by the poems. Seamlessly, a girl's love-poems become the tough lamentations of a survivor. At times I thought I was reading something thousands of years old; the Romans or the ancient Chinese would have understood Akhmatova. We are lucky to have this account of her in English.

JOSEPH BRODSKY

Joseph Brodsky was, in the line of Baudelaire, a *flâneur*. His presence in a place always struck me as a magnificent gift, and I used to think of him turning up incognito and unannounced in a city somewhere – be it London or Istanbul or Lisbon or Venice – an autodidact and globe-trotter, as though these weren't distinct things, but basically aspects of one: the poet. A 'spend-thrift talker', in Robert Lowell's phrase, he was bewilderingly well read and *au fait*, generous, unsnobbish, stern, funny, modest and doctrinaire. I didn't share what seemed to me his over-valuation of Auden and Milosz and Walcott; for his part, I expect he would have disagreed with me over Lowell (too scruffy, too unhealthily personal), Enzensberger and Brecht (both tainted as 'men of the Left'). Mostly, though, our pan-theons satisfyingly overlapped: Benn and Rilke; Szymborska and (I trust) Herbert; Montale and Cavafy. In prose too, he was much better read than most poets.

And yet it would be utterly mistaken to think of Brodsky as some kind of bookman: someone pleased to soar on literary subjects, but a swan or albatross on dry land. If books had a special position for him, it was because in the course of an uncommonly large life (*ein bewegtes Leben*, a travelled or tra-vailed life), they were the best thing he had experienced, the thing most worth putting his trust in, the thing – in the most maximalist pieces in *On Grief and Reason*, such as 'An Immodest Proposal' or 'Letter to a President' – that came closest to being a religion. The word of such a man on literature and on literacy is worth more than anyone else's – and not least because of his life.

He was born in what he might have called 'Theningrad' in 1940. He left school at fifteen, began to write at eighteen, taught himself English and Polish, and, when still a very young man, impressed Anna Akhmatova. He did literary work, translating the English Metaphysicals among others. In 1964, he was accused of 'parasitism' – the judge, I remember from David

Review of Joseph Brodsky, *So Forth* and *On Grief and Reason*
(London: Hamish Hamilton, 1996)

Remnick's piece in the *New Yorker*, referred to 'velvet trousers' – and was sentenced to internal exile in the far north of the USSR. In 1972, he was put on a plane to Vienna, where he was met by his idol, W. H. Auden. The following year Penguin published his *Selected Poems*, translated by George Kline, and with an introduction by Auden, who pointed out that these poems strikingly combined modernity with the traditional virtues of metre and rhyme. He moved to the United States, first to Ann Arbor, Michigan, later to New York City, where he taught at Columbia; for the last ten years or so, he divided his time between New York and Mount Holyoke College, Massachusetts. In 1987, he won the Nobel Prize for literature. He published five compendious books of poems in English, rather jumbled together, I get the impression, from Russian volumes that appeared, sometimes substantially earlier, from the Chekhov Publishing Corporation; two books of essays, almost entirely written in Brodsky's energetic, personal and wonderfully audible English; a play; and a prose book about Venice, where he is buried. When he died last January, he left a wife, Maria, and a young daughter, Anna – having been once married previously in Russia, with a son. The books under review had just left his hands.

It is hard to think of a man, as it were, surviving such a life, but to Brodsky it was no big deal. Looking just now at his long poem 'Lullaby of Cape Cod', almost those very words leap up at me: 'It's strange to think of surviving, but that's what happened.' He didn't talk or write about his vicissitudes, hating nothing more than larmoyance and display. In *On Grief and Reason*, he declares that the poet 'is never, in the final analysis, a victim'. In 1967, recently returned from Archangel and his first marriage over, he began a poem: 'Refusing to catalogue all of one's woes/ is a very broad gesture in pedants.' With another broad and characteristically burlesquing gesture, he describes his exile, again in 'Lullaby of Cape Cod':

> Like a despotic Sheik, who can be untrue
> to his vast seraglio and multiple desires
> only with a harem altogether new,
> varied and numerous, I have switched Empires.

Not for him the 'balalaika strummings' of nostalgia derided by another exile, Joseph Roth – whom Brodsky admired, and from whose birthplace, Brody, he claimed, I don't know how seriously or warrantably, his surname was derived. His translation and subsequent professionalization – or professorization – in America became: 'the function/ to which I'd been appointed was to wear out/ the patience of the ingenuous local youth'. This in a poem misnamed with a heroic shrug 'In the Lake District' – the Great Lakes, of course, nothing to do with Wordsworth and the 'Pond Poets', as Byron liked to call them. In a poem written on his fortieth birthday, 'May 24, 1980', he wrote, with a Byronic swagger:

> Twice have drowned, thrice let knives rake my nitty-gritty.
> Quit the country that bore and nursed me.
> Those who forgot me would make a city.

Christopher Reid, reviewing *To Urania* in the *London Review of Books*, jibbed at that 'nitty-gritty', but it's not there just as a bit of misuse or obscurantism. It's part of the 'tall', clownish idiom of the poem – the stoic's refusal to flinch or blink, or so much as to dignify the affliction (in this case, probably open-heart surgery) with its proper, emotive name. The swinging hyperbole of the poem, as so often in Brodsky, works as understatement. Things are talked down by being talked up; if you exaggerate something, it can't be that big. It is a strange procedure, both blunt and profound, that serves to assert the independence and the incorruptibility of the poet's mind. It seems to me it would have been ridiculously easy for someone like Brodsky to have wound up in thrall to his own biography, to have traded on misery and displacement and the loss of his native tongue; but that didn't happen. The bigger the life, the more powerfully and determinedly he opposed it in his work. Exile was not fate but opportunity, not an impact crater but a launch-pad. In his essay 'The Condition We Call Exile', or alternatively, in a typically derisive pun, 'Acorns Aweigh', he describes the life of the exiled writer as 'tragicomedy'. In almost anyone else, the work would have been like jetsam on the tide of the life: not Brodsky, with his inveterate dignity – which he was careful always to send up, so that it never had the limitations or the boring stylization of dignity – and his immeasurable pride. Nor was it only adversity to which he responded with such blithe doughtiness. Even in a moment of triumph – his Nobel Prize acceptance speech – he Kipling-ishly abstracts himself from a situation that appears to him momentary, contingent, almost not real: 'And as far as this room is concerned, I think it was empty just a couple of hours ago, and it will be empty again a couple of hours hence. Our presence in it, mine especially, is quite incidental from its walls' point of view.'

I am not sure which came first with Brodsky: the modesty or the metaphysics of absence. Success is a chimera, so is fame – 'On any street of any city in the world at any time of night or day there are more people who haven't heard of you than those who have'; all that has a chance of existing or maintaining its existence is writing:

> This won't be heard up North, nor where hot sands hug cactus.
> I don't know anymore what earth will nurse my carcass.
> Scratch on, my pen: let's mark the white the way it marks us.
>
> ('The Fifth Anniversary')

This is how many of the poems end, with script, or with the sound of speech or the blank of silence. A cameo self-assertion at the vanishing-point. More or less direct – 'And the clearer the song is heard,/ the smaller the bird' ('In England'), 'now a line scrawled in haste and rhyming' ('In Front of Casa Marcello'), ' "Bust," it will utter in the tongue of ruins/ and of contracting muscles. "Bust. Bust. Bust." ' ('The Bust of Tiberius') – or more or less oblique – 'A cod stands at the door' ('Lullaby of Cape Cod'), 'all the better for you not to notice when my talk stops,/ as Red Riding Hood didn't mutter to her gray partner' ('Afterword'), 'If anything blackens, it's just the letters, / like the tracks of some rabbit, preserved by a wonder' ('Lines on the Winter Campaign, 1980'). These endings, not 'big' even when they're cosmic – 'In the provinces, too, nobody's getting laid,/ as through the galaxy' ('Homage to Chekhov') – often have a kind of crumpled bathos to them. If they show anything at all, it's something in the nature of a remainder, a sediment, a plus or minus constant. And from that in turn, you come to understand that the poems are basically sums, great lists of like or unlike items – the apples and pears of arithmetic – converted to their particular emotional-ontological valency, totted up and 'solved'. In his essay 'A Cat's Meow' in *On Grief and Reason*, Brodsky writes: 'Ideally, perhaps, the animate and the inanimate should swap places.' This is what happens in his poems. The person, the poet, is atomized, centrifuged, dispersed, while his inanimate surroundings are spun into an increasingly concrete aura, a genie, that comes to stand in for him. The poems are very heavily, almost thickly furnished, but the things in them are not disjunct. They turn into the characteristic 'Brodsky' atmosphere, corroded by metaphysics or metamorphics, and leave their residue at the end:

> Being itself the essence of all things,
> solitude teaches essentials. How gratefully the skin
> receives the leathery coolness of its chair.
> Meanwhile, my arm, off in the dark somewhere,
> goes wooden in sympathetic brotherhood
> with the chair's listless arm of oaken wood.
> A glowing oaken grain
> covers the tiny bones of the joints. And the brain
> knocks like the glass's ice cube tinkling.
>
> ('Lullaby of Cape Cod')

Little wonder the poem becomes 'the soft song of the cod' – fishes in Brodsky always stand in for *homo sapiens* by retro-evolution, while the more highly evolved birds are replacement bards ('Thrushes chirp within the hairdo of the cypress' in 'Letters to a Roman Friend' and *passim*).

What makes a Brodsky poem so immediately distinctive is its materiality, all those things you stub your toe on as you read. There's nothing easier than to draw up a list of his characteristic properties, overcoats, shirts, street-lights, Steinways, the sea, house-fronts, windows, body parts, furniture, statues, colon-nades, the weather. Amalgamate these, you think, and you would get 90 per cent of the poems. And it's true, there is a persistent, even an indefatigable notation, cognition, registering going on, a turning of things into words, an eye talking to an ear. Rather surprisingly for a supremacist poet, I think Brodsky had the equipment to have been a wonderful novelist; he had the abundance, he could do people, settings, incidents, as his non-critical prose in 'Collector's Item' (in *On Grief and Reason*) or *Watermark* shows. But it's important to remember that we aren't talking about photographic realism, that things don't appear in Brodsky's poems as they appear in life, still less because they appeared in his life. A poem of his is always an alternative, an abstraction, a set of calculations, even the baggiest of them. To put it another way, for all his modesty and clutter, Brodsky isn't an empirical English type of poet.

Perhaps that's why Christopher Reid and, following him, Craig Raine, didn't get on with him. His metaphors tend not to be visually accurate – or visually exhaustible: 'Sunk in raw twilight, the pupil blinks but gulps/ the memory-numbing pills of opaque streetlamps' ('December in Florence'). Unlikeness and exaggeration are more important to the image than resemblance and plausibility. It is recklessly out of scale; the cartoonishly avid eye – a mouth – fills, but at the same time empties as it swallows what's before it ('memory-numbing'). It owes more to persistence of thought, and difficulty of thought, than to mere looking. (How many people would you have to set in front of a row of lamp-posts before they came up with tranquillizers?) Also, the image is kinetic, it galvanizes, it has an effect; it isn't decorative, and it doesn't necessarily harmonize with what follows or goes before. After a time, therefore, you realize that what you are reading Brodsky for is not his list of perquisites, charming and atmospheric though they are, but for whatever strenuous and unpredictable things happen to them in the poems, when 'the head combines/ its existence with that of a hand' in its project of turning the world inside out, disanimating the self and reanimating things, so that they can cease to be – you forget at a certain point that you are looking at streetlamps, as you wouldn't in a Martian poem, in spite of its $x = y$ formula – or, perhaps better, so that the self can cease to be, so that all you are left with is a residue of words. Martianism affects to enrich the world, adding a clever self to whatever's in view. Brodsky, who writes 'to regard yourself/ as the hub of even a negligible universe,/ [is] unbearable and indecent', does the opposite: he subtracts himself.

All the verbal underpinning that's then required to prevent the world from collapsing in on itself, or the words from prematurely saying 'Uncle', makes for poems characterized by untidiness, torque and diseconomy; 'A bard of/ trash, extra thoughts, broken lines' is Brodsky's self-characterization in his 'Roman Elegies'. A moody, whimsical and driven voice relays its brilliantly resourceful semi-detached observations, sometimes staccato, sometimes in an explanatory curve:

> Two in the afternoon. A postman's silhouette
> takes on sharp definition in a hallway only
> to become an instant later a silhouette again.
> A bell, as it tolls in the fog,
> merely repeats the procedure.
> So you automatically glance around
> in your own direction – like a random stroller
> trying for a better look at a pretty girl's ankles
> as she rustles past – but you can't see a thing
> except scraps of fog. No wind; only stillness.
> Indirection. Around a bend
> streetlamps trail off like white ellipses,
> followed by nothing but a smell of seaweed
> and the outline of a pier. No wind.
> And stillness like the whinny of Victor
> Emmanuel's never-faltering cast-iron mare.
>
> ('San Pietro')

Hallucination, connection – echo as an acoustic version of fog – transmutation and denial: these are perhaps more truly the properties of a Brodsky poem. It occurs to me it is like experiencing the nineteenth-century material world subject to the vagaries of late twentieth-century doubt.

Brodsky isn't a highly specific writer. His poems are occasional ('December in Florence', 'Mexican Divertimento' and so on), but had the occasion or the circumstances been different, the poems wouldn't have differed by very much. True, his England isn't the same as his Russia or his Italy, and I am sure he would have passed Flaubert's coachman test to Flaubert's satisfaction, but it wasn't what he was interested in. His poems – light verse aside – resemble one another much more than they differ, and what they most resemble is one single long poem. 'One life, one writing', as Robert Lowell put it – though Brodsky would have put at least a semicolon and more likely a whole new paragraph between them. The poetry – and the prose too, and the prose with the poetry – is rare in our time for being the elaboration of an expansive and coherent body of thought and experience and reflection composed of, or dealing with, among other things, time and space, mortality, personal virtue, geopolitics, silliness, rhyme, water, evolution, art in a mass society, things, mathematics, provocations, places. To get involved with him – to get involved with these last two books of his, say – is to get involved with all that, and to have it come at you with the author's inimitable and irreplaceable urgency, eccentricity, wit and intellect. He foresaw it all such a long time ago, when, still in his mid-thirties, he wrote, lapidarily: 'What gets left of a man amounts/ to a part. To his spoken part. To a part of speech.'

Increasingly, after his exile, this speech was English. In his essay, 'To Please a Shadow' in *Less Than One*, Brodsky describes buying a small portable typewriter in the summer of 1977, to write at first prose, then translations, of himself and others, and in the end original poems in English. I was told a story of how, some time before that, probably shortly after his arrival in the States, Brodsky holed up in an apartment block in uptown New York with a television set, and for a month took what Baudelaire, along the lines of his 'bain de foule', might have called a 'bain américain'. Once, in a moment of characteristic expansiveness, he rang a friend across the Atlantic to order me some volumes of a no doubt enormous and ongoing American dictionary of slang. They never came, but no matter. He put them to better use than I think I could have done. I think American English was part of the making of Brodsky in English; the British version would have been grotesquely stiff, cramping and naysaying, incompatible with his democratic breeziness, his illusionlessness, his rapid skimming of surfaces, his colour and knockabout.

Some of this is in the vocabulary of the poems, 'boy' as an exclamation, 'salad days', 'scumbag', 'beaver' for pudenda, 'hairdo', 'zipper', 'dude', 'breaking new hearts and balls' or the joky portmanteau 'Tampax Americana'. (Pleasingly, British translators like Alan Myers put him back in the melting-pot with Britishisms like 'comfy' and 'wanker'; in essence, it isn't that Brodsky orientated himself towards American in particular, as much as towards whichever nourishing and appetitive linguistic environment beckoned – mostly American). At the same time, Brodsky's Americanism is not so much a matter of the vocabulary – and a lot of the terms I quoted are very eye-catching, off-the-boat Americanisms, and are also used as such – as of such things as rhythm, grammar, pitch and tone; and, less in the poetry than in the prose, in can't-be-bothered put-downs like 'the four-seasons routine', in the studied use of slang like 'goes big with', in nuggets of cracker-barrel wisdom like 'Well, it wouldn't be evolution if it didn't swing back and forth', in the prevailingly frisky and *salopp* tone and manner. All this, it seems to me, is American, or it's where American and Russian fortuitously connect, in massively rich slang, in mixed registers, in the rhetorical power of the demotic. One of the great delights of the prose, to my mind even the greatest – and I'm sure this isn't confined to people who actually heard him – is the way you can hear Brodsky speaking in it, with all his fussy and fizzing connectives and hedgings and hawings, 'to say the least', and 'what's more' and 'well' and 'now' and 'in short'. He made himself an anarchic gift to his adopted language.

To go back to poetry, Brodsky's adoption of an American timbre makes sense of his claim – which otherwise I can't agree with at all – that, 'because of a greater cultural heritage, a greater set of references, it usually takes much longer for a Briton to set a poem in motion [than an American]'. Well, but even if urgency, economy and drive are a lost art in contemporary American poetry, Brodsky still had it. His beginnings – address, aphorism, statement of (grammatical) subject, cinematic shot or noun phrase – were always among his strong points. As an example of Brodsky's writing in English verse, here is the first half of a poem called 'Exeter Revisited':

Playing chess on the oil tablecloth at Sparky's
Cafe, with half & half for whites,
against your specter at noon, two flights
down from that mattress, and seven years later. Scarcely
a gambit, by any standard. The fan's dust-plagued
shamrock still hums in your window – seven
years later and pints of semen
under the bridge – apparently not unplugged.

These aftermath-poems are often quite starkly done by Brodsky, and this one is no exception, but almost more than the starkness ('that mattress', 'seven years later' and the shocking 'pints of semen') it is the linguistic delicacy of the thing that strikes you: the first sentence's persistent refusal of a main verb through its choking series of adverbial – or adjectival? – phrases; the pithy second sentence, also verbless; the unobtrusive 'hums' in the third. Consonantal – half and half – rhymes pull the thing together. Below the tacky and talky surface are plays on electricity ('Sparky's' and 'unplugged'), on colour ('whites' and 'specter'), on milk ('half & half' and 'pints') and on sperm ('hum', apparently, is US slang for it – remember Frank O'Hara's 'hum-colored cabs'). The oddly substantial – though of course proverbial – bridge balances the real but spectral 'two flights', the fan's dust seems to settle on the oil tablecloth, the oil seems to gloss the 'matt' of 'mattress', 'gambit' to shade into 'shamrock', and 'unplugged' into 'pledge' in the line following – 'pledge', perhaps, to see off the dust. In its second eight lines, the poem, I have to say, loses me in a blizzard of five rhetorical questions, but the opening shows the kind of verbal density and trickery that Brodsky could achieve when writing in English.

The reluctance to accept Brodsky in English – in particular, in his own English – always seemed rather churlish to me: the successive books, *A Part of Speech* (1980), *To Urania* (1988) and *So Forth* (1996), each have their distinct quality as language, moving from quite smooth to pretty rough, but I couldn't ever see Brodsky's own involvement in the translation as a major factor. His own versions of 'A Part of Speech' are as good as anything produced by the roster of American poets working with him on the rest of the book; he always had the final say himself anyway; and while, I would say, it is obvious that 'Exeter Revisited' had to be written in English by the poet, I think one would continually make mistakes elsewhere in any 'blind tasting' of translations.

Finally, I think Brodsky was good enough to play by two sets of rules. Even in English, his poems have irresistible verbal authority, even when he writes such things as 'And in the sky there are scattered, like a bachelor's/ clothes, clouds, turned inside out/ or pressed' ('A Footnote to Weather Forecasts'), because I think he wrote in such a way as to draw on American and Russian at the same time. There is something binaural or bipolar about the writing, an uncomplicated and perfectly natural contract with the reader, whereby on the one hand Brodsky can write something like the above, the most arrant and wilfully provocative translationese, and yet the reader continues to endow it with the status of an original, fully intended and supervised in every detail – and I think because he accepts that it is only by some miracle that this writing exists in English at all. We read it, as it were, both with the English and the Russian parts of our English minds. How else to explain something like 'Ode to Concrete':

> You'll outlast me, good old concrete,
> as I've outlasted, it seems, some men,
> who had taken me, too, for a kind of street,
> citing color of eyes, or mien.

Undoubtedly, Brodsky's tolerance for eccentric English grew with time, as his desire to conform, perhaps, grew less, but even that I think has less to do with translation than authorship. *So Forth*, for all that the poet died at fifty-five, is *Spätwerk*. You see in it the garishness, murk, habits and shorthand of a late painter – say Munch or Monet. You hear the crack in the voice in 'A Song' ('I wish you were here, dear,/ I wish you were here'), the unfettered silliness of 'Centaurs II' (with Cary and Sophie, a racing-car and a sofa) or 'To My Daughter', which begins:

> Give me another life, and I'll be singing
> in Caffe Rafaella. Or simply sitting
> there. Or standing there, as furniture in the corner,
> in case that life is a bit less generous than the former.

and ends – in English *en route* to an afterlife – with its adorably elementary quip:

> Hence, these somewhat wooden lines in our common language.

His progress clarifies the apparently contradictory remarks in his essay on exile, that, on the one hand, exile 'slows down one's stylistic evolution, that it makes a writer more conservative' and, on the other, that 'Exile brings you overnight where it would normally take a lifetime to go'.

Brodsky's feeling towards America was first and foremost a passionate gratitude. It is expressed in the language of his prose and his poetry, in his teaching, in his uniquely and unexpectedly diligent tenure of the Laureateship in 1991, when he suggested putting poetry books in hotel rooms. Two of the best and sharpest essays in *On Grief and Reason*, 'In Praise of Boredom' and 'Speech at the Stadium', were originally delivered as commencement addresses at American colleges, and are good enough to make one wish one could have attended the establishments in question. Elsewhere, he describes American poetry as 'this country's greatest patrimony', going on, rather shakily: 'The quantity of verse that has been penned on these shores in the last century and a half dwarfs the similar enterprise of any literature and, for that matter, both our jazz and our cinema rightly adored throughout the world. The same goes, I daresay, for its quality. . . .' His reading-list in English poetry in 'How to Read a Book' comprises: Frost, Hardy, Yeats, Eliot, Auden, Moore and Bishop. But the only American poet he has dignified with an essay is Robert Frost. Perhaps his unspoken reservations about American contemporary poetry produced a rather tepid and defensive response from that establishment. It does seem to me incredible and contemptible that, for example, the Norton anthology has no place for Brodsky; or that the American Academy, having inducted Brodsky as a member, then decided, in effect, to terminate his membership by inducting Yevtushenko shortly afterwards. Still, I don't want to end on that sort of sour note. So let me quote instead from his account in 'Spoils of War' of seeing a Citroen 2CV in Leningrad in around 1960; as an example of his Rilkean and religious tenderness towards things (reminding me of Berryman's elegy for Roethke, 'Weeds too he favoured, as most men don't favour men'), showing his transsubstantiating imagination and his occasionally delectable diction in that word 'unemphatic'.

It stood there, light and defenseless, totally lacking the menace normally associated with automobiles. It looked as if it could easily be hurt by one, rather than the other way around. I've never seen anything made of metal as unemphatic. It felt more human than some of the passersby, and somehow it resembled in its breathtaking simplicity those World War II beef cans that were still sitting on my windowsill. It had no secrets. I wanted to get into it and drive off – not because I wanted to emigrate, but because to get inside it must have felt like putting on a jacket – no, a raincoat – and going for a stroll. Its side-window flaps alone resembled a myopic, bespectacled man with a raised collar. If I remember things correctly, what I felt while staring at this car was happiness.

MAX BECKMANN AND
JOSEPH BRODSKY

This year, I enjoyed two autobiographical accounts by two formidable types with a lot else in common: both moved from Europe to the States in adventurous circumstances, first the Midwest, then New York, Old World retro-moderns, possessed of huge personal authority, smokers, bullish presences. Max Beckmann's *Tagebücher 1940–1950* (Munich: Piper) are exactly that: a line or two *per diem*, the barest notations of the rudiments of his existence – what he was working on, what he drank, whom he saw, what he read. One begins perhaps by shrugging, then is slowly fascinated and latterly overwhelmed by the completely unexpected expressiveness of his sardonic teutonic melancholic macaronics. A note like '*tja, dieses Boulder*' ['Boulder, eh?'] is like the Odyssey in a sigh. Beckmann shades into Benn, as I think did Joseph Brodsky. Solomon Volkov's *Conversations with Joseph Brodsky* (New York: The Free Press) have been the subject of warnings from the poet's estate and there are obvious doubts about Volkov's method – each 'interview' is spliced together from remarks and answers made years apart – and also about the task that has fallen to the poor translator of getting Brodsky from Russian into English into Brodsky. Not, of course, that the poet comes out of it badly: the *Cantos* as 'a fictitious reality', the 'real library of a kitchen' in Auden's house in Kirchstetten, and much much more. For speed of thought, boldness of conception, range of reference and salt of wit, Brodsky is surely without peer in our time.

EUGENIO MONTALE

The first Montale poem to make any impression on me was 'Eastbourne' in the harsh translation by G. S. Fraser in the New Directions *Selected Poems*:

'God Save the King' the trumpets moan and groan
From a pavilion high on piles
That gape to let the sea through when it comes
To wash out wet
Horse-hoofmarks on the sand
Of this sea-shore.

Coldly the wind claws me
But a burning light snakes along the windows
And white mica of cliffs
Glitters in that glare.

Bank Holiday . . . It brings back the long wave
Of my own life,
Creeping and sliding, sluggish up the slope.
It's getting late. The brassy noise balloons
And sags to silence.

There come now on their wheel-chairs the cripples.
There accompany them dogs with long
Ears, silent children, and old folk. (Possibly
Tomorrow it will all seem a dream.)

And you come,
You, pure voice, long imprisoned, spirit now
Set free but with no bearings yet,
The blood's voice, lost and given back
To the evening of my days.

As a hotel's revolving door
Moves shiningly upon its four leaves –
One leaf answers another, flashing a message! –
So I am moved by a merry-go-round that sweeps
Everything up in its whirl; alertly listening
('My country!') I recognise your breathing,
And get up; it grows too stuffy, this day.

Review of Eugenio Montale, *The Coastguard's House*, trans. Jeremy Reed
(Newcastle-upon-Tyne: Bloodaxe, 1990)

Everything will seem pointless: even the strength
That in its gritty matrix aggregates
Living and dead, trees and rocks,
And from you, through you, unfolds. Holidays
Have no pity. The band expands
Its blare of sound, in the first dusk
An unarmed goodness spreads itself around.

Evil conquers . . . The wheel does not stop:

Also Thou knewest this, Lux-in-Tenebris!

In this burnt quarter of the sky, whence at the first
Clang of bells Thou departedst, only
The guttering torch remains that, already, *was*
And is not, *Bank Holiday*.

What first held me was this harshness, the criticism of the band's efforts, 'moan and groan', 'balloons and sags to silence', 'blare of sound', part of the sensuous pessimism of the poem's vocabulary. Public music is a wonderful subject (Rimbaud's 'A la Musique', Elizabeth Bishop's 'View of the Capitol from the Library of Congress', Joseph Roth's novel *The Radetzky March*), public music as a backdrop to private musings better still. Eastbourne, (August) Bank Holiday – 'the English *ferragosto*', Montale domesticates it in a letter – a country taking its ease, luxuriating in patriotism: but then it's the wrong country, neither Montale's Italy nor the USA of his addressee and of 'I vow to thee, my country'. Montale is in the wrong place, as everywhere since the beloved's departure is the wrong place, as indeed he has been in the wrong place from birth, feeling – a little histrionically for once, in an interview – 'total disharmony with the reality that surrounded me'. No doubt the band's harmonies don't help.

Like many of his poems, 'Eastbourne' has a way of communicating experience without depleting it. Finishing the poem, the reader doesn't say 'Oh dear!' or 'So that's what happened,' or 'Poor you!' The reader would be hard put to say what happened, and yet it's not because Montale has failed to be straight with him or talked about other things that don't matter. There is narrative, but of a uniquely interior kind, discontinuous scraps, observations that give rise to reflections. The poem exists on its own, it sticks to its own side of the net, it doesn't play pat-ball with the reader. There are things in it that have chronically troubled readers, and bamboozled translators: that wave, 'sluggish up the slope' (*troppo dolce sulla china*), the day, which is 'too stuffy' (*troppo folto*). One might note that it is impossible to locate the poet, the *tu*, or the reader in the poem; a series of external-internal camera positions is really the best one can do. It is another characteristic of Montale's poems that they are set in oceans of empty space. Nothing in the poem allows the thought that there is anything outside it – no brand-names or politicians – and the poem is characteristically situated at the very edge of land: as it were, at the limit of reference and experience and paraphrase. There is no such exclusion on time – there *is* in Montale's first poems, which often end on a frozen image: time passes ('It's getting late') and suddenly, at the end of the poem, we learn that a whole evening has gone up in smoke. A poem of Montale's is often less like the usual short story than like a novel. In its way, Eastbourne is as deadly and exotic as its 1930s contemporary, the Quauhnahuac of *Under the Volcano*, with which it shares the wheels, the holiday, the noise, the triumph of evil – as well as the basic situation of a man left by a woman, and thinking about his life.

A further reason why 'Eastbourne' made such an impact on me was that it wasn't among the ten Montale poems that appeared in Robert Lowell's 1961 book of translations, *Imitations*. I am saying, I suppose, that Lowell spoiled the ground in making it accessible. At this moment I would guess that *Imitations* is more influential than any other aspect of Lowell's poetic practice: the idea of a popular poet with a current style refashioning some body of foreign work in his own way, and in order to reflect his own concerns. 'I have tried to write live English and to do what my authors might have done if they were writing their poems now and in America.' It remains an attractive blueprint, and one that Jeremy Reed has followed in his own work on Montale: 'What I have tried to achieve in this book is a series of poems in which the poet's intentions are placed within a context of late 20th-century values.' Certainly, disdain for the poor conventional translator of poetry is always a strong card to play: 'Most poetic translations come to grief,' says Lowell simply. He calls translators 'taxidermists'; Reed

describes them as undertakers. And yet is *Imitations* anything
to be imitated? Should Lowell's *karaoke* procedures be encour-
aged? Which of his dirty dozen-and-a-half poets would one
actually choose in Lowell's version in preference to another's,
or to Lowell himself? Perhaps only the Rimbaud of the teenage
sonnets lumped together in a sequence called 'Eighteen Seventy':
'On the Road', 'At the Green Cabaret' and 'A Malicious Girl'.
These seem incorruptible in their freshness. Otherwise, I have a
hunch that anyone who knows one or other of the languages
of Lowell's originals will find his treatment of them especially
unforgivable, but will feel merciful towards the others; certainly
I find his Rilke, and even more his Heine ('Heine Dying in
Paris'), hard to take. *Imitations* doesn't even contain Lowell's
best work as a translator, which is buried without acknowledg-
ment in *Notebook* in a poem called 'Volveran': the original is
by G. A. Bécquer, who was one of Montale's favourite poets,
and from whom he took the epigraph for his Motets: *Sobre el
volcan la flor.*

Like most everyone rendered by Lowell, Montale appears in
versions so electrified and distorted by feedback their own
mothers wouldn't recognize them. 'A death cell?' is how his
version of 'The Coastguard House' begins. The originals have
no hope of asserting themselves against Lowell's *Gleichschal-
tung*, they are inaudible for all the crackle and pop and screech.
The result is that one thinks of them as weedy, characterless
and indeterminate – this is what I meant when I spoke of being
spoilt for certain poems by familiarity with Lowell's translations.
For years I kept a line of his in my head – actually it's from the
selfsame 'Coastguard House' – as evidence of Lowell's incredible
usurpation: 'For years the sirocco gunned the dead stucco with
sand.' The two Italianate words (neither exactly in the original),
the half-rhyming American verb 'gunned', the American fasci-
nation with European antiquity and decay – all extraneous and
false. Sometimes I think he used him as a pretext to evoke
ugliness and dirt:

> Come night,
> the ugly weather's fire-cracker simmer
> will deepen to the gruff buzz of beehives.

Termites tunnel the public room's rafters to sawdust,
an odour of bruised melons oozes from the floor.
A sick smoke lifts from the elf-huts and fungi of the valley –
like an eagle it climbs our mountain's bald cone,
and soils the windows.

The thoroughgoing concreteness of such a passage is matched
by its pervasive nausea. The poem as a whole may seem vague
and histrionic and shot to pieces, but individual words and lines
are of such force and brilliance that they make the efforts of
other translators appear puny.

The first three lines are unsurpassable, and the vigour of what
follows argues the case for 'imitations' as well as anything. And
then, even if the poem's last line, 'A porcupine sips a quill of
mercy,' is not to be found in the original, it is, first, extraordi-
narily beautiful, and secondly seems to have wandered in from
'Skunk Hour'. A poem kitted out with a top and tail like that
will quite reasonably seem unexciting in a more faithful or –
better word – normal version. A chaste approach like that of
William Arrowsmith, who all but forswears the use of diction,
is pretty unappealing: 'When the Italian text gives *ridere*, I have
translated it as 'laugh' rather than one of the more colourful
modalities of laughter: chuckle, guffaw, titter, and so on.'
Perhaps even the Italian original and other poems by Montale
will seem less worth persevering with to readers without much
Italian, like myself (while Italian speakers, in accordance with
my hunch about *Imitations*, should come down particularly
hard on Lowell's Montale, Ungaretti, Saba and Leopardi). This
explains my pleasure and relief at finding Fraser's 'Eastbourne'.

It may also help to explain why I am happiest reading Montale
in German, even apart from the fact that Henno Helbling's
versions are better and truer than anything I have seen in
English, and German, an inflected language with genders and
endings and a flexible word-order, is a better home for Montale
than English (*Montale: Gedichte 1920–1954*, 1987). It is only
since reading Helbling that I have been convinced of Montale's
greatness.

Lowell's example and achievement are as much a problem for
Jeremy Reed as Montale's original texts, which are printed *en
face*. At least Reed gives himself a chance – unlike Arrowsmith

– by allowing himself as much freedom as Lowell did. Also, he doesn't duck the challenge, including versions of all of Lowell's originals in his own careful and generous selection. There is a difference, though, in that while Lowell professes 'amazement' at Montale (perhaps not the best basis for imitation), Reed recognizes himself in the Italian: 'the imbalanced individual', the loner, the 'solitary upbringing on a seacoast'. These congruences are real and salutary, and they underwrite the hoped-for 'empathic collusion' between Reed and Montale. *The Coastguard's House* has had more poetic labour and feeling applied to it than any other English versions I have seen.

Reed's versions look reassuringly unlike the Italian opposite, more regular, often shorter, solid and compact – they are not translations in the geometrical sense, merely slid across the page. (In translations where the punctuation is scrupulously mimicked, I tend to fear that a similar attention has been paid to the words.) Reed has re-aligned and rephrased many of the originals, often breaking up sentences into shorter, punchier units. He has a superb sense of the music and tension of a line, and knows how to pace several lines in succession: this is perhaps the single crucial difference between a translation by a poet and the poetry of a translator. Take the beginning of Reed's 'Mesco Point':

> At dawn, unbending flights of partridges
> skimmed over the quarry's skyline,
> the smoke from explosives lazily puffed
> in eddies up the blind rockface. The ridge
> brightened. The trail of foam left by the pilot boat's
> beaked prow settled into illusory
> white flowers on the surface of the sea.

And that of Arrowsmith's 'Cape Mesco':

> In the sky over the quarry streaked
> at dawn by the partridges' undeviating flight,
> the smoke from the blasting thinned,
> climbing slowly up the sheer stone face.
> From the platform of the piledriver
> naiad ripples somersaulted, silent
> trumpeters, and sank, melting in the foam
> grazed by your step.

(The original stanza is eight lines long.) Two things are clear: that Reed has re-imagined the scene, and that he writes English verse to an incomparably higher standard. He even manages that daunting form, the short poem, which in less skilful hands can resemble a few bricks falling over one another:

> Insistently a cricket penetrates
> so many layers of vegetable silk.
> A scent of camphor rises, but can't rout the moths
> that fragment dustily in books,
> while a small bird creeps round and spirals up
> an elm tree's bulk, and stabs a sun that dives
> in its green whirl. Another transient gleam,
> and in the scarlet ivies, other fires.

'Poetry is less predictable than prose,' Montale said endearingly and – at least where his own work is concerned – accurately. 'A Window at Fiesole' is a beautifully made little poem, its corruption close at hand, then further away, at first colourless, then burning, small and then stellar, but all the time in whirling radii.

When Reed talks about placing Montale's intentions 'within a context of late 20th-century values', I don't really know what he means, but I'm sure that Montale, in the thirties or forties, did little to invite such treatment. (He seems to me neither marked nor deceitfully unmarked by what he called 'the mechanical culture of our time'.) That said, there are certain words like 'nerves', 'menace' and 'electric' to which Reed seems to be addicted, and which he brings in at the slightest opportunity; there are also smatterings of an almost Ballardish technoflash vocabulary: 'heliocentric', 'theriomorphic', 'the lever's/ hairline imprecision in locking the gears/ of the global spin'. On the whole, though, 'late 20th-century values' seem to mean the values of contemporary British and American poetry: a supple ten-syllable line (or eight or 12 or six, but seemingly always even numbers!), a quiet musicality and logical construction. He uses a predicate-subject inversion straight out of Joseph Brodsky: 'What startles is the screeching of the years/ on rusty hinges', 'What lives on here's the colour of the rat/ leaping through grasses, or the sudden dash/ of poisonous green metal.' Most of all, though, he has assimilated Lowell's style, less in the poems

Lowell translated in *Imitations* than in Montale's late work of
the sixties and seventies which I hadn't previously read and
which, in Reed's versions, is like Lowell *redivivus* or bootlegged:
words run together like 'chalkline' or 'deadmarch' or 'ripcur-
rent', final lines whammed down like aces, 'We hear you now
without a telephone,' 'Living, we're shadows blown out by a
breath,' 'Nothing's stable. The word dries on the change . . .', the
conjunction of humour and insanity in the astonishing sequence
'After a Flight':

> I lazed the day through reflecting that Lear
> and Cordelia suffered no such problems,
> and mooned around the tombs of Lucumos,
> the Piranesi streets of old Leghorn.
> The sky was gentian, no tragedians
> consoled the blinding self-truth of my age;
> I couldn't even claim to be your father.

The effect is so eerie it seems to me Montale must have a hand
in it as well as the translator. It would be interesting to know
whether Montale – who published late books called *Diario del
'71 a del '72* and *Quaderno di Quattro Anni* – read Lowell,
and, if so, whether he liked him (he was very severe on 'the vast
poetic reportage attempted by the new English poets from Auden
on'). Certainly, Reed seems to me to have done wonderfully well
to have enlisted Lowell on his side.

The only real criticism I would make of Reed is tautological:
that he is not Montale. There are passages, especially at the
beginning of poems, where decisiveness is muted into delicacy,
which his even iambic lines can't handle. The beginning of
'L'Estate':

> *L'ombra crociata del gheppio pare ignota*
> *ai giovinetti arbusti quando rade fugace.*
> *E la nube che vede? Ha tante facce*
> *la polla schiusa.*

> The kestrel's filtered shadow leaves no trace
> on dry bushes, but tricks a darkened cross
> on the heath's green awakening with spring.
> The earth reflects the blue mirror of space.

Or even more, of 'Barche sulla Marna':

Felicita del sughero abbandonato
alla corrente
che stempra attorno i ponti rovesciati
e il plenilunio pallido nel sole:
barche sul fiume, agili nell' estate
e un murmure stagnante di citta.

An orange cork-float drifts with the current
which eddies round overhanging bridges.
The chalk moon's a shadow of the sunlight,
and boats on the river seem half in flight.
The city builds behind as sluggish surf.

The English is far too commonsensical and humdrum: it is one
of the occasions where Reed fails to offer compensation for
what is lost. In this case, the deficit is enormous: the happiness
of the cork, a giddy world in which the bridges are upside-
down, and the sun and moon – brother and sister, maybe – are
together, an adumbration of the various perfect rounds and
arches, the whole thing touched with envy, and almost in the
form of a toast. For such things we have to use Lowell's word
for the feeling Montale induced in him: amazement.

IAN HAMILTON

When you get onto the big wheel of writing (or the little wheels within wheels of poetry), it seems clear to me that the people you look to and feel an affinity for are not – to begin with, anyway – the ones who get on immediately before and after you, still less the ones who've been on for ages – you want their seats – but the half-strangers you see through the struts half a cycle (half a generation) away, falling as you rise, rising as you fall. There were three poets I had my eye on – probably all appalled to be mentioned in each other's company, and by me: Joseph Brodsky, Tom Paulin and, most intimately though I knew him least, Ian Hamilton. When I sent him a copy of my first book, I realized I'd even purloined his initials for my title.

I wasn't of an age to have been reading, never mind submitting to, his magazines, *The Review* and *The New Review*, but when I started publishing around 1980, I had his book of poems *The Visit* (1970) on permanent loan from the English Faculty Library at Cambridge. It would fall due and I would renew it. I must have read it quite literally hundreds of times – and everyone else not at all! 'No one shaved, and only the turtle washed,' as Lowell said of the turtle in the bathtub. I discovered Hamilton, I suppose, and should explain, in the place of honour at the end of A. Alvarez's *The New Poetry*, second edition. When the time finally came for me to leave the rocky bosom of Cambridge, I was in a dilemma over the book. I couldn't live without it. Finally I said I'd lost it, paid the ten pound penalty, and thought I'd got away with murder: no doubt George Washington would have behaved differently. Now I'm the proud owner of four or five copies (whenever I come across one, I buy it), and moreover Faber had the grace to publish an enlarged version in 1988, *Fifty Poems*, so the library will be back in business too. Greetings, borrowers.

What I admire – not the word – about the poems is their intensity. John Berryman once said: write as short as you can, in order, of what matters. Surely no one – least of all Berryman

Review of Ian Hamilton, *Walking Possession: Essays and Reviews 1968–1993*
(London: Bloomsbury, 1994) and *Gazza Italia* (London: Granta, 1994)

himself – can have fulfilled the terms of that prescription as scrupulously as Hamilton. The majority of the poems are generated by one of two subjects: a wife's mental illness and a father's death from cancer. The few exceptions, just as sombre, are barely to be distinguished. There is something terrible and heroic in this narrow focus, in the way that these few poems, produced over many years, should have settled so close by one another, with their themes of break-up and breakdown, their shattered atmosphere, their identical reference points of hands and heads and hair and flowers and grass and snow and shadow. That 'silence on other subjects' that Brecht mentioned in a quite different context, is part of the effect. Nothing else, Hamilton implies, can have any being next to such losses. Each individual poem is pruned back to an austere and beautiful knot of pain. Poetry, by his practice of it, is not craftsmanship or profession, but catastrophe. I can't, in general terms, think of any better way for a poem to be. Most poems have a hard time answering the question: 'Is this really necessary?' Not his.

Fifty poems on 51 pages – there is one, 'Larkinesque', that goes 'over the page'. Exactly half of them ten lines or fewer. A verbal account of an image of an experience: a double distillation, a world away from the stuff that deserves the nasty label 'confessional'. A bit of 1910, a bit of 1960, and a bit of 1860 in the stately Matthew Arnold (Hamilton's current subject as a biographer) crumble of the lines. They are physical, without losing themselves in materialist drift; scenic without being pretty; verbally effective but not finical or clever for the sake of it. Thought wrestles with feeling, word with thing, and the poem balances. The 'I – you' stuff reminds me now of Montale; the beauty and compression and sorrow of Chinese poetry. The title poem 'The Visit':

> They've let me walk with you
> As far as this high wall. The placid smiles
> Of our new friends, the old incurables,
> Pursue us lovingly.
> Their boyish, suntanned heads,
> Their ancient arms
> Outstretched, belong to you.

> Although your head still burns
> Your hands remember me.

There is an echo of Yeats (impossible to hear 'ancient' without it), quite a bit of 'Waking in the Blue' in the humorous commingling of health and sickness, but the thing doesn't seem literary at all: the tenderness and delicacy and terror of the last two lines are original and primal.

One wishes, reflexively, there were more; but then again, why should there be, or what would there be? Hamilton talks about it in his pained and nobly frank Preface to *Fifty Poems*: 'Fifty poems in twenty-five years: not much to show for half a lifetime, you might think. And, in certain moods, I would agree. In certain moods, I used to crave expansiveness and bulk, and early on I had several shots at getting "more of the world" into my verse: more narrative, more satire, more intelligence, and so on.' More, in other words, would not, could not, be more of the same, and what then would be the point, beyond allowing the poet to think, as he puts it, 'like a poetry pro'? One realizes one has been thinking like a reading pro, and feels – not that Hamilton would have intended that – rebuked.

Stood alongside *Fifty Poems*, most things just look impossibly trite, leisurely and overstuffed. When Hamilton was judging the *New Statesman*'s Prudence Farmer Competition some time in the eighties, I remember he commented on how many of the poems had food in them. My own poems go like sequences of television quiz show prizes, undesirable prizes, prizes for losers, just one darn thing after another! Even with his example before me, how materialistic I have become, even in my own brand of negative materialism! How crass and compendious! *Fifty Poems* contains nothing in the way of comestibles: cigarettes, 'J and B' and 'a haze of cultivated blossom'. Pick your own! No, I'm wrong: the last poem on the last page, 'The Forties', ends:

> the neat plot
> For your (why not?) 'organic greens',
> The trellis that needs fixing, that I'll fix.

Well, it hardly reads like the Pauline conversion.

By grace of *anno domini* or whatever, Ian Hamilton is for me first and last a poet. If I'd been only slightly older, I would have been aware of the literary arbiter and infighter, the sixties *Wunderkind*, the builder and demolisher of reputations, the Ian Hammerhead of his friend Clive James's skit on literary London. And if any younger, he would be the author of the books he's published since, that nebulous thing, a jobbing biographer and writer, almost in the American sense of the word, a magazine feature writer, a non-fictionist, a prose pro. The poetry-centred view of Ian Hamilton does two things: it sees something, in Hamilton's own words on Aldous Huxley, 'sad and impressive' about the subsequent prose career; and it organizes the biographies and reviews, gives them a theme, a 'subtext' even, that otherwise they might not have. Still, always underlying everything is the callow, unexamined assumption that if a man has published a book of poems, he would prefer to publish more books of poems than anything else; and that if he could nominate fifty half-filled pages of his writing (all right then, 51) that would endure, it would be his poems. Poetry pro that I hardly am, I feel that, and I guess Ian Hamilton does too.

His biography of Robert Lowell came out in 1982 (at the time, I was half-seriously trying to write a PhD on him). Hamilton, as he writes in 'A Biographer's Misgivings', the first piece in *Walking Possession*, knew his subject fairly well: 'I had seen quite a lot of Lowell since his move from New York to London in 1970. I had published his poems, I had interviewed him, I had visited him now and then at home and in hospital. We weren't friends, exactly, but we were friendly enough allies, of a sort.' My feeling about the biography was that it was just slightly mechanical in its account of the rhythm of Lowell's life; and also that it was a pity that Hamilton had kept himself out of it. Thereafter, the role of biographer was imposed on him: subjects suggested were Pound, Plath, Berryman. 'The common factor in these propositions was, it seemed to me, insanity. I was in danger of being set up as an expert on mad poets.' But – invoking a characteristic separation or restraint – he turned down those ideas, and instead wrote his book on Salinger. There, ironically, as it seems to me, with a man he didn't know and would never meet, he proposed that 'the biographer would be a character in his own book.' Then came the book on writers in Hollywood – I realize that Hamilton is fascinated by variously enabling and disabling forms of compromise – and on literary estates, and their attendant difficulties for the biographer. *Gazza Italia* – whatever happened to the beautiful title *Gazza Agonistes*? – lets the Northeasterner and Spurs fan off the leash. Though not a deep or interesting or even particularly well-written book (by Hamilton's standards), it does fascinatingly combine aspects of all the others – like Salinger, Paul Gascoigne refuses to meet Hamilton; it's a book about difficulty of access, about a public figure withholding himself, about compromise (the white of Tottenham for the 'peculiar blue vest' of Lazio). Hamilton is even able to reveal that 'Gazza *is a poet*!'

The themes adumbrated above are all present in *Walking Possession*. It is an oddly but appropriately over-organized and compartmentalized collection, stratified into five sections on lives, poetry, fiction, Grub Street and leisure. The carapace is impressive but feels oddly unpersonal and *constructed*. A dance of five hats and no heart. Much of it is so-whatish – by contrast to the poems. The novel section, for instance, is either about the work of friends (Amis and Barnes) or American megalos: and Hamilton, interestingly, is an American specialist in these essays, never happier than when insolently ribbing the latest big-ticket imports. The poetry section is still weirder: Larkin one can understand, from Hamilton; also Alun Lewis, Roy Fuller, Frost and Graves. But Wilbur and Merrill, Heaney and Motion? I'm not surprised there's little evidence of attachment to their work, just oblique dismay. For any sort of poetic credo, you have to go back to the poems, or the essays in *A Poetry Chronicle* (1973), and even there it's scattered: 'no point-making or underscoring'; a kind of trust or trust in luck ('Already the most intelligent poet of his generation', John Fuller 'now seems excitingly prepared to place less than a total faith in pure intelligence'); a demand for intensity, for what Hamilton calls in W. D. Snodgrass 'a voice at once poised and inflamed'. Compared to that sort of engaged criticism, the writing on poetry in *Walking Possession* is either knockabout or demurral. One suspects the subjects have been chosen specially. They are refractions, distortions, opposites of Hamilton, rather than poets he might feel something for. There is Graves, 'encouraged to believe that he could finance poetry with prose'; the World War Two poet Alun Lewis: 'there are those who believe that Lewis's future as a writer would have been in prose'; Richard Wilbur, 'a poet of the "shallows"' who 'has under-extended his considerable talent'; 'What it all boils down to, or up to, is that Larkin the thrifty now has a *Collected Poems* of substantial bulk'; 'the parsimonious connoisseur had discovered the necessity of eloquence' (Stevens). All this is evidence of Hamilton's fascination at the road not taken; here is someone (inaudibly, to most readers), crying: 'Hold! Enough!'

Not only are Hamilton's pursuits scrupulously separated off, and kept away from his own poetry (and his kind of poetry), which might have given them a centre; his own critical persona is in pieces. It seems to me he hardly ever steps out and says what he thinks, in the first person, in his own voice. Instead, he pushes little columns of arguments to and fro. The book is stuffed with phrases like 'Some would say', 'the unkind view of Spender would continue thus', 'to our unkind observer, then'. He is impersonal and multitudinous. Even where he does come on in person, he breaks himself up by historicizing himself: 'so I thought', he writes, or 'as a bit of a mad poet myself, from time to time'. Even punctuation is called in aid. Hamilton has no equal with a pair of quotation marks. It's one of several techniques that has survived the move from poetry to prose. Here is the beginning of 'Critique':

> In Cornwall, from the shelter of your bungalow
> You found the sea 'compassionate'
> And then 'monotonous',
> Though never, in all fairness,
> '*Inconnue*' . . .

And here is the Graves ménage: 'The whole thing came under strain, though, with the appearance of one Geoffrey Phibbs, an Anglo-Irish poetaster of "unstable" yet (some thought) "demonic" character.' This is at once ironically circumspect, lethal and hilarious.

If the critic himself is largely absent as a set of explicit personal views and responses, he makes up for it through style. In the twenty years since *A Poetry Chronicle*, Hamilton has cut away much of his critical vocabulary and probably halved his sentence length. He now impresses less by argumentative rigour and marshalling of detail than by overall clarity, wit and mixed registers. His use of first names is straightforwardly wicked: Kingsley, Gore, 'the tiny Bron', 'the obliging Bron', 'Tambi', 'Junior himself'. He seems to reserve for American subjects that maddening British mixture of mateyness and snottiness. He is a master of phrasing, often, though not always, to debunk: Huxley's 'almost awed contempt for ordinary people', an 'obscure but powerful thwartedness' in Kingsley Amis, 'drowsily ecstatic' Frost critics, a 'sinister contentedness' in Wallace Stevens. When he writes 'stocky and efficient', can't you almost see little Isherwood on the left of the group portrait with Spender and Auden on Rügen? He cites the pair of Margaret Thatcher and D. H. Lawrence as Larkin's main men, refers to the 'crappy brainwaves' of Spurs chairman Irving Scholar and the 'uncolourful speech' of Andrew Motion, putting me immediately in mind of the 'brown teapot' in his Arvon Prize-winning poem of 1980, 'A Letter'. This lapidary gift is served, perversely and surprisingly, by wonderful timing. On the Hampsteadites and Islingtonians who went along to the Comic Strip: 'Most of them, it seemed, had never been called *cunts* before.' One wouldn't have thought it possible, but it's all in that 'it seemed'.

TOM PAULIN

Everybody knows – Paul Muldoon said it on the radio recently – that writing poetry can only get harder the more you keep at it. Against that is the belief, or perhaps the determination, that it shouldn't. That instead of the diminishing returns, spending twice the time saying half as much twice as cumbrously/flashily/winsomely, one should use craft and expertise to overthrow the stiflement and self-importance of craft and expertise – to be as uninhibited and fresh and airy as a beginner. Not continue to paint yourself into a corner with aching brush and paint gone hard, but take a line for a walk, as Tom Paulin says, taking a leaf from Paul Klee, whose daily wit, invention and application (not to mention his use of bastard materials) stand behind this, his fifth book of poems.

It is seven years since the appearance of Paulin's fourth, *Fivemiletown*. To say that was one of the best books of the eighties isn't enough: it is one of the best books I know, or for that matter, am capable of imagining: a corrosive and uproarious litany of bad sex, bad politics and bad religion:

> All I could try
> was turn a sly
> hurt look to soften her
> and that night in bed
> I stuck my winedark tongue
> inside her bum
> her blackhaired Irish bum
> repeating in my head
> his father's prayer
> to shite and onions.
> But my summum pulchrum
> said *I've had enough*
> *we rubbed each other up*
> *a brave long while*
> *that's never love.*
> 'Breez Marine'

Review of Tom Paulin, *Walking a Line* (London: Faber and Faber, 1994)

because you'd fallen for this young priest
he was a loiner Tim Ryan that's a lie
and driven with him July a heatwave
all through the West the East Riding
some harbour Hornsea Spurn Head it's pathetic
you were in cheesecloth he'd green shades I could scream still
the Society of Jesus White Fathers it's invisible
as that day the same day she and me
we made a heavy pretence of love
I mean we'd a drunken fuck in the afternoon
after a dockland lunch the Land of Green Ginger
its smell of sex herrings desire
                              'Sure I'm a Cheat Aren't We All?'

              for a geg one day
          I bought this tin
          of panties coloured
          like the Union Jack,
          but she slung it in the bin
          and never breathed
          the least bit sigh.
          'Va-t'en!' she spat,
          'I just can't stand you.
          No one can.
          Your breath stinks
          and your taste
          it's simply foul –
          like that accent.
          Please don't come slouching
          near my bed again.'
          So, real cool, I growled
          'Lady, no way you'll walk
          right over me.'
          Dead on. I chucked her then.
              'Waftage: An Irregular Ode'

The language flows as simply as blood from a wound, but
how multifarious it is, borrowed and pieced together, now like
a feather cloak, now like a lead painting, molten and jagged
and impressively crippled. Every poem varies its resources, while
keeping its outrageous 'spoken' feel: tags of Classical and
modern learning, literary debris ('winedark' and 'slouching'
from Yeats, or Homer and Yeats if you'd rather), the Shake-

spearean puns on place-names, the opposition of French chic and US cool; the anxious, dreary and deluded male protagonists; the way the whole literal scene seems forever on the point of dissolving into wicked metaphor. Some readers were alienated by its phallicism, perhaps bizarrely failing to grasp its misery: these are not phallocrats but losers, phallopaths if you like. What can one feel for the hero of a poem actually called 'Really Naff' but pity and contempt, the way his girl or boy does: 'but he's as bare as need, poor guy/ or the sole of that trainer'?

Linguistic richness on its own, or the tight thematic focus, would have made *Fivemiletown* a distinguished book: but with both, in harness, it was irresistible. It read like nothing else, even looked like nothing else: the columns of short irregular lines, broken by syntax, less and less truck with punctuation, occasional full rhymes and italicized scraps of learning, dashes or indentation to introduce dissent or chorus ('hear me sister!/ brother believe me!') – what other British or Irish poet was doing anything like this? Reading it, one couldn't even tell what Paulin had been reading. Only Zbigniew Herbert, with his construction and layout, his unpunctuated chorales, narratives and meditations seemed undeniably an influence: but where did Paulin's bizarre marriage of Ireland and America, of Paisley and Presley, come from? Was he reading William Carlos Williams, or were the influences all vernacular, as he, the vernacular anthologist, might have us believe? Whichever, it was an unforgettable performance.

Epochal books like that, invigorating and new, are a hard act to follow. A quick successor might only have betrayed Paulin's exhaustion. Instead, he has held off for a long time, and written most of his new poems towards the end of a seven-year lean spell. The new book is inevitably less focused, less fierce, it burns with a lower wattage. It demands to be read in a different way too, with latitude, amusement, appreciation for the features of Paulin's idiosyncratic style, tolerance if not approval of its new, almost unstrung mode. Both books deserve their jackets: *Fivemiletown* its thunderous black and grey, *Walking a Line* its little-boy blue and girl pink. It is somewhere between jaunty and kittenish. For someone who first made his name and his mark (in *A State of Justice*, 1977, and *The Strange Museum*,

1980) with austere and crunching formulations, it is an extra-ordinary pass to have come to. The style was one of the period styles, the Dunn-and-Motion style of the seventies (out of Auden and Larkin), the mighty encapsulation, a double-headed hammering abstraction, offering Truth and Compression and not much Pleasure, and Paulin was a natural at it: 'a buggered sun', 'a fierce privacy', 'a vegetable silence', 'a grey tenderness', 'an ignorant purity'. There are still, in *Walking a Line*, occasional echoes of this freeze-dried descriptiveness – 'the alum verities of dissent' – but this dominant feature of early Paulin has now almost disappeared. And on the other hand, the man of the senses ('the rickety fizz of starlings', 'the snarl of hair burning, its bony pong') and quirky word-spinner ('sweet, swea-ting explosive' – a play on glycerine; 'the bistre bistro'; and that patent-deserving Paulinism where he takes a man's occupation and cripples him with it, 'the boreal teacher', 'the hunched detective') who was such a grateful, relieving element in the earlier books, has now taken over the whole show. The things that make *Walking a Line* worth reading are either tiny or inconsequential: alphabetical sleights, puns, words run together as one, fantastically noisy descriptions of noise, a dash and a heckle, the gentle, almost pointless flips and flings with words. One of my favourite half-dozen poems in the book is 'Portnoo Pier', about a

> concrete quay
> built about 1905 by yes
> the Congested Districts Board.

'This disappointed bridge', Paulin writes, 'is home – home of a kind', because 'my namesake Tommy Pallin' goes swimming there:

> each morning in summer
> he goes running along the concrete
> then takes a header into the ocean
> – a contented man Tommy
> as he bashes the frameless mirror
> *come on on in and join us!*

I don't know that Paulin has ever sounded so happy in a poem; but, movingly, his happiness is either second-hand or empathic,

depending on things being twinned or doubled: 'Portnoo' and
'Portnua', Pallin/Paulin, the 'frameless mirror', even the two
'on's and the 'us' in the last line. All this adds up to the carefully-
sloppily qualified 'home of a kind'. The ease and grace of the
poem are of a kind that seem not worked for but almost inevit-
able – the reward for that craft and experience that I began by
invoking.

'Portnoo Pier' strikes me as an absolute departure for Paulin:
American and *parlando*, *plein air* and *bonheur*. A few more of
the most programmatic poems of *Walking a Line* take their
place with it: 'Kinship Ties', 'Almost There', 'Naïf', 'What's
Natural', 'Airplane' and 'Basta', which picks up the book's won-
derful epigraph from *Moby Dick*, describing whales swimming
through 'brit': 'As morning mowers, who side by side slowly
and seethingly advance their scythes through the long wet grass
of marshy meads; even so these monsters swam, making a
strange, grassy, cutting sound; and leaving behind them endless
swaths of blue upon the yellow sea.' 'Basta' is a *tabula rasa*, a
subject peculiarly congenial to Paulin's new mode and style:

> a reverse epic
> in our chosen mode
> – performance art
> so *krangg! brumpfff! shlump!*
> we took out the punishment block
> . . . the romper room
> – below the snapped electrodes
> what we found was simply
> a green field site
> its grass almost liquid
> like duckweed or cress
> – so we waded right into
> that watery plain
> that blue blue ocean
> and started diving and lepping
> like true whales in clover

'Reverse epic': where to stick craft and experience; the comic-
book violence of demolition; the touchingly, magically literal
adaptation of the dismal expression 'green field site'; the exul-
tation of jumping and swimming; the nod at Melville and,

punningly, ('clover') at Klee; all this in a rousingly surrealistic, more-than-realistic, finale – this is what Paulin is up to now. Think of a knotted string or tube: the knot, the dead end, the windsock (a favourite Paulin image) is the terminal volume *Fivemiletown*; coming out of the knot again, there is a new opening out, new positive feeling, new hope.

Walking a Line looks like a transitional book to me. While there are a number of examples of the new type of more 'open' Paulin poem, with almost unready, questioning endings – though maybe the opposite/ just happens to be the case?', 'no *ubi sumus*/ let's leave it there', ' – a tree that isn't a tree quite/ like the doubt in "literature"' – he is still a poet of quite a Manichean cast of mind, a poet of good and bad trees ('where the juniper/ talks to the oak,/ the thistle,/ the bandaged elm,/ and the jolly jolly chestnut' from *Liberty Tree* of 1983), more at home in black and white than colour, given to thinking in categories, forever working up alliances, parallels and lists of enemies. He actually criticizes this propensity here, when he speaks of 'so many fatuous binaries/ and all/ to too much purpose' – but he goes on doing it all the same. It remains difficult to imagine him surprised by motivelessness in himself! One could, for example, draw up a list of things endorsed in *Walking a Line* – Paul Klee, whales, the wind, the tongue – and find them all, perversely and paradoxically systematic: all amiable, dishevelling, square-fronted and blunt (or keen). Still, he seems to have entered more deeply into his metaphoric systems than ever before: they remain his cubist staging-posts, but what perhaps matters to him more is the deliberately sketchy, scribbled quality of the thinking-aloud and thinking-in-images with which he connects them. The poem 'A Taste of Blood' labours through a page and a half of imagery on a relationship, self-mocking and costive and excitable and trapped:

> – if she's a clamped oyster
> that may or may not have a liking for him
> then he can only be a claspknife
> that turns into Kinch
> the fearful Calvinist
> a hard penis

> a hand writing
> with someone else's pen

before shifting to the perspective of the woman:

> he lies on a lapsed futon
> always losing and chasing answers
> to his own question
> there's a dirty spatter of rain
> on the skylight window
> its skittery sprinkle
> falls on their amours
> and she knows this morning there'll be blood
> – blood and fuckyous
> between them

In the desperately reifying poem, the 'blood and fuckyous' have wickedly and ironically turned into words, giving the whole thing a wonderfully defeated shape. The notable thing about the poem is not any brilliance of analysis but its open-handedness and decompression. Its drama is much less lurid and electric than that of comparable poems in *Fivemiletown*, its despair more ordinary and endurable. Paulin seems to me to be embarked on a kind of *démontage* of his own writing – Yeats's 'more enterprise in going naked' comes to mind – which in the end may take him to some exhaustive pastoral or protocol, maybe a very long poem or perhaps a book of translations along the lines of Lowell's *Imitations*, for which his style, both distinctive and serviceable, would qualify him better than anyone now writing. In contemporary poetry, where voice is almost everything, he is using noise instead. One day he will compose a hymn to trash that will put everything in the shade.

PAUL MULDOON

Looked at in one way, *Madoc: A Mystery* is an extraordinary and unpredictable departure, a book of poems the size of most novels, with a title poem nigh on two hundred and fifty pages long, doubling Muldoon's output at a stroke. But in another way, it does remarkably little to change the sense one has of Paul Muldoon. It is a book for initiates, more of the same. Each of his previous five volumes has ended with something a little longer, a relaxing gallop after the dressage – even 'The Year of the Sloes, for Ishi' in *New Weather* (1973) was four pages long. Further, the structure of *Madoc* is actually identical with that of Muldoon's last book, *Meeting the British* (1987) – in fact, it seems like a monstrously curtailed and distended parody of it: the prose poem at the start, a section of short poems (no more than six), and then the *pièce de résistance*, which, for all its length, occupies just one line on the contents page, as though the poet were telling us it's no big deal.

  Madoc is a bigger canvas rather than a bigger splash. Perhaps it is Muldoon's fault, perhaps he has pre-empted himself. Already the most characterful and most imitated of contemporary poets, he offered more trademarks than perhaps was good for us: the pluperfect tense; the hoary Rip Van Winkle idioms stretching and disbelieving; the outrageously resourceful rhyming that came to preoccupy him more and more; the factual, ironical, provincial-newspaper beginnings; the little sea-horse emblems breaking up the poems and jointing them; the plain definite-article-plus-substantive titles; the erotic memoirs; the druggy meltdowns; the recurring totemic props that made each successive book more like a new religion than a book of poems. He has seemed for some time like a man in need of a challenge, the eponymous man in a previous long poem of his, 'The More a Man Has the More a Man Wants'. In 'Madoc', Bucephalus the talking horse lectures us

Review of Paul Muldoon, *Madoc: A Mystery* (London: Faber and Faber, 1990)

that Madoc himself is, above all, emblematic
of our desire to go beyond ourselves.

The impulse for 'Madoc' came from a selection of Byron that
Muldoon made for his American publishers. (One finds oneself
adopting this rather unlikely preterite and literary-historical
tone, partly because the poem is a conundrum and cries out for
a methodical approach; and partly for want of a strong or
reliable personal response to it.) There, Muldoon re-acquainted
himself with the literary politics of the Romantics, Byron's
poetics, his digs at Southey and Coleridge. He read up on 'the
Pantisocratic society of Aspheterists' (Coleridge), and even
perused Southey's poem *Madoc*, about 'the Welsh prince, long
believed by his countrymen to have discovered America in 1170'
(Chambers Biographical Dictionary). Muldoon's 'Madoc' is thus
a 'remake' – a notion that crops up in the opening prose poem in
the collection. The title is from Southey, the principal character is
Coleridge, and the prevailing spirit is not unlike that of Byron
in *Don Juan*:

> Prose-poets like blank-verse, I'm fond of rhyme,
> Good workmen never quarrel with their tools;
> I've got new mythological machinery,
> And very handsome supernatural scenery.

'Madoc' is predicated upon two non-events, 625 years apart:
the 'arrivals' in America of Madoc, and then of Southey and
Coleridge.

That is Muldoon's 'new mythological machinery', providing
him, on the one hand, with Welsh Indians, variously known as
Madocs, Modocs, Mandans and Minnetarees, and, on the other,
with a quarrelsome, unprepared, disreputable and idealistic
bunch of poet-philosophers and their hangers-on. Coleridge's
imaginary move is one that Muldoon himself really made, going
from Cambridge to America in 1987. 'Madoc' is also by way
of being a brief and selective history of the early years of the
United States, as Muldoon works in (I'm not always sure how)
some of the pioneers, the Lewis and Clark Expedition, the
(Celtic) Indian Wars, eventually returning home in the person
of the nineteenth-century (Irish?) artist and painter of 'native
Americans', George Catlin, whose *Rushes through the Middle*

graces the cover of *Madoc*. Oh, and one other thing. The narrative is sectioned-off into short, mostly self-contained poems, each given the name of a philosopher or quasi-philosopher (such as Frederick the Great or Schiller) to whose life or thought the poem makes some reference.

To sum up, then, 'Madoc' consists of two unequal chronological sequences: the philosophers in the titles go from Thales to Stephen Hawking, while the poems below cover the ground from 1795 to 1834, Pantisocracy, Madoc and the Welsh Indians, early pioneers, Lewis and Clark, stray Irishmen, the Satanic School of Byron and Moore. The two disciplines are pretty arbitrarily related – principally, I suppose, by the idea that Southey and Coleridge are poet-philosophers, and thereafter by some typical Muldoon punning and legerdemain, such things as the cryptogram 'C(oleridge) RO(bert Southey The S)ATAN(ic School)', and later 'Not "CROATAN", not "CROATOAN", but "CROTONA" ', this last a reference to Pythagoras's western place of exile. Occasionally, too, the philosophers have names similar or identical to the names of actors in the drama: Putnam, Lewis, Newman, Clarke and Hartley. The whole spooky procedure recalls the celebrated episode when Coleridge and Wordsworth were eavesdropped-on in the West Country, and were heard to speak of the sinister 'Spy Nozy' (the philosopher Spinoza): there is the same mad triangle of poetry, philosophy and subversiveness in Muldoon's poem as there was in that incident.

In his long poems, Muldoon has been drawn to and drawn from literary history and genre fiction, sometimes the one ('7, Middagh Street' is about the Auden-Britten ménage in Brooklyn), sometimes the other (the Chandleresque 'Immram'), but mostly a blend of both. This gives the poems their approachability and readability, a content, and a style both ripe for subversion. In 'Madoc', the genres are Science Fiction, Western, whodunit, and perhaps even children's writing – in nonsense words like 'signifump' or the delightful 'de dum' used for comic rhyming, dither, mock-epic, iambic filler or half-coconuts on the radio. The Science Fiction provides the frame, because the poem begins and ends in the future, where a character called South (descended from Southey), a 'wet-set', leads some kind of insur-

rection against the 'Geckoes', perhaps themselves descended
from Cayuga Indians. It seems as though the boot is on the
other foot, that the high have been made low, and that Kubla
Khan's 'pleasure-dome' has become some top-security hush-hush
installation. The narrative of 'Madoc' proceeds from the inter-
rogation of South, in best Sci-Fi manner: 'And, though one
of his eyes/ was totally written-off,/ he was harnessed to a
retinagraph', 'So that, though it may seem somewhat improb-
able,/ all that follows/ flickers and flows/ from the back of his
right eyeball.'

What takes the reader through the poem is pleasure and
puzzlement in roughly equal measure. Whatever Muldoon is, he
isn't the maths master type of poet, setting problems of the
correct level of difficulty: he seems rather unaware that there *is*
any problem. Essentially, he is taking his style for a walk, and
the style is mesmerizing. Muldoon is a star exhibit for Gottfried
Benn's view that a 'fascinating way with words' is an innate
quality, unteachable and unlearnable. One either has it or one
doesn't, and Muldoon has it. It is hard to imagine him using a
dull word or phrase – he certainly wouldn't use them in a dull
way. And yet this hard, glittering, *interesting* surface seems to
be at variance with the very idea of a long poem – of a middle
way, not high, not low, Wordsworth walking up and down a
gravel path. Muldoon's road is like one paved with cat's eyes.
It is an extraordinary idea, really, to have a narrative advanced
in this way, by Muldoon's slight little poems, very exact, very
fussy, never saying anything, but proceeding by ambiguity and
innuendo. And yet somehow they aren't overpowered by what
they have to convey: they pick up mass, but – against the laws
of physics – without decelerating, still at the speed of thought.
The reader is exasperated by his own dull-wittedness, but
struggles on.

One often feels tempted to throw the whole thing at a com-
puter and say: 'Here, you do it.' But that is the price one pays
for Muldoon's speed. Part of one's exasperation comes from
doubting whether the whole poem, the 'Mystery', resolves itself.
I am pretty sure it doesn't. If 'Madoc' were a novel, I wouldn't
persevere with it. But, as I have said, Muldoon doesn't set
problems. It is more that the poem is too full of solutions: no

body, no motive, but stacks of clues – what to do with all the recurring figures, the CRO-riddle, Bucephalus the (s)talking horse, the white (shaggy?) dog, the valise that survives into the SF future, the polygraph. Any one of them might lead to the heart of the matter. Take the last. It comes up three times, first in 'Pascal':

> Jefferson is so beside himself with glee
> that he finishes off a carafe
>
> of his best Médoc;
> his newly-modified polygraph
>
> will automatically
> follow hand-in-glove
>
> his copper-plate 'whippoorwill'
> or 'praise' or 'love':
>
> will run parallel to the parallel
> realm to which it is itself the only clue.

Why 'Pascal' I don't know. One notes the playful, not unexpected 'Médoc' and files it with an earlier rhyme, 'metic-/ulously across a mattock's/ blade-end'. Then one looks for the rhymes, in order of ease: carafe/ polygraph, hand-in-glove/ love, whippoorwill/-parallel, Médoc/ automatically and glee/clue. This last pairing summarizes the argument of my last paragraph. There are many references to codes and ciphers and 'sympathetic ink' in the poem – possibly self-references. The 'Médoc'/ automatically' rhyme is also an apposite one, when one takes 'Médoc' as 'Madoc'. The suggestion is of 'automatic' writing, reinforced by the 'polygraph': literally 'writing much', but also 'an apparatus for producing two or more identical drawings or writings simultaneously' and, figuratively, 'a person who imitates, or is a copy of, another; an imitator, or imitation' (Shorter OED).

The idea of a line or word parallel to an unseen word or line is highly suggestive: perhaps of the process of history first of all; of duplicity (tracking the Indians); of the idea of the 'remake' noted earlier; of something both forged and real; of an unlocatable original, since, famously, parallel lines never meet. A 'polygrapher' is the enigmatic, clue-dropping, rewriting Muldoon; is also 'multo-scribbling Southey', as Byron describes him. These meanings came into use around the turn of the eighteenth century; in its new, stupidly conferred meaning of 'lie detector', it has connotations of the White House and Nixon and Reagan, of the malpractice of 'hand-in-glove'.

The two further references to the polygraph, which occur in 'Kierkegaard' and 'Adorno', both continue the association with Jefferson (his retirement and his death); both suggest a kind of comic incompetence that may be Muldoon speaking about the production of his poem: 'In Monticello, the snaggle-toothed gopher/ tries his paw at the polygraph' and 'The polygraph at its usual rigmarole./ The gopher pining for a caramel'. (The gopher must be Jefferson; Washington himself had wooden teeth.) The rigmarole, the parallel lines and the idea of polygraphy all comment on Muldoon's writing of history in 'Madoc'.

'Madoc' may be enriched by reading it as or with a parallel text. Either a Dictionary of Philosophy (though not the Collins, which doesn't mention half his 'philosophers', not all of them philosophers) or something about Coleridge and Pantisocracy. (It seems the days are gone when one could read Muldoon simply unaided.) With *Madoc* I read Richard Holmes's *Coleridge: Early Visions*. Ironically, this wasn't used by Muldoon: *Madoc* would have been finished by the autumn of 1989, when it came out. Some astonishing correspondences between the two books are therefore coincidental, the meeting of two great minds. First and perhaps greatest is this: 'It is not impossible to imagine Coleridge, in some alternative life, flourishing among these original Susquehanna pioneers, and making his own distinctive contribution to the history of the Wild West.' The 'alternative life' is not remarkable, but the 'distinctive contribution to the history of the Wild West' is, because it is precisely what Muldoon does with him, enrolling him, for instance, with Lewis and Clark. Coleridge himself stipulated that a poet must have 'the *eye* of a North American Indian tracing the footsteps of an Enemy upon the Leaves that strew the forest'. Then there is a very personal judgment of Holmes's, tucked away in a note: 'Coleridge's version of the emigration scheme has, at times, almost a Science Fiction quality.'

There are further suggestive phrases and details: about 'Southey's enthusiastic dog Rover (also a Pantisocrat)', about pondering 'his emigrant's wardrobe – "what do common blue trousers cost?"' and his 'rapturous cartooning', not a million miles from Muldoon's approach (the gopher, say). But there are also things that Muldoon hasn't got and doesn't use, such as the fact that Southey's 'rooms were next to the college lavatories, by an alley that opened on to St Giles', or the fact that Southey 'left for Dublin to take up a post as Secretary to the Irish Chancellor, with a salary of £200 per annum, a characteristically efficient career move'. The point about these is not whether Muldoon knows them or not, but that his poem maintains the same intense and witty close focus upon its characters as Holmes's outstanding biography does, and that from reading the poem alone, one might not necessarily have known it.

Every reading – and still more, every new bit of information – makes *Madoc* a cleverer and more imposing piece of work. Perhaps one of the last details (I am not claiming to know or to have done one-tenth of what needs to be known and done) to be seen to is the securing of the seven short poems of Part One to 'Madoc' itself, for they are clearly appendices or codicils (a word which Muldoon might care to derive from *cauda*, a tail). And truly each one contains some chromosomes from 'Madoc': no other poet has Muldoon's expertise in forging such organic connections. In order, the poems contain: the idea of the 'remake'; 'Pythagoras in America' and 'some left-over/ squid cooked in its own ink'; a duel, like those between Burr and Hamilton, and Jeffrey and Moore; 'Asra'; an Irish immigrant to America; an amazing metastatic sestina patented by Muldoon; and this poem, 'The Briefcase':

> I held the briefcase at arm's length from me;
> the oxblood or liver
> eelskin with which it was covered
> had suddenly grown supple.
>
> I'd been waiting in line for the cross-town
> bus when an almighty cloudburst
> left the sidewalk a raging torrent.
>
> And though it contained only the first
> inkling of this poem, I knew I daren't
> set the briefcase down

to slap my pockets for an obol –

for fear it might slink into a culvert
and strike out along the East River
for the sea. By which I mean the 'open' sea.

The theme of this sonnet is the desperate – and comic – attempt
to hold on to something, to prevent it from metamorphosing
and accelerating away. In the context of *Madoc*, it is the wrestle
with his own new poem about the new continent, *in* the new
continent. Hence the force of the ' "open" sea': once escaped it
could go anywhere, most obviously 'East' to Ireland. (The poem
is dedicated to Seamus Heaney.) It is a kind of envoi, but one
with the opposite wish, namely 'stay, little book.' I was reminded
of John Berryman's epigraphs for his *Dream Songs*, from Sir
Francis Chichester and Gordon in Khartoum: 'For my part I am
always frightened, and very much so. I fear the future of all
engagements.' There is something oddly and deeply touching
about this fear in one of the most metamorphic poets alive, in
whom words and facts and things themselves are so comprehen-
sively and gracefully destabilized.

SEAMUS HEANEY

Seeing Things, Seamus Heaney's ninth volume of new poems, is aimed squarely at transcendence. The title has a humble and practical William Carlos Williams ring to it, but that is misleading. It is better understood as having been distilled from 'I must be seeing things', said seriously, and with a fair amount of stress on the 'I must'.

The greatest difficulty for the poet is how to go on being one. Randall Jarrell set it out like this at the end of his essay on Stevens: 'A man who is a good poet at 40 *may* turn out to be a good poet at 60; but he is more likely to have stopped writing poems, to be doing exercises in his own manner, or to have reverted to whatever commonplaces were popular when he was young. A good poet is someone who manages, in a lifetime of standing out in thunderstorms, to be struck by lightning five or six times; a dozen or two dozen times and he is great.' This is poetry as catastrophe, as Minnesotan roulette. Heaney in his *The Government of the Tongue* quotes the Polish poet Anna Swir to similar but subtly different effect: according to her, the poet is 'an antenna capturing the voices of the world'. Compared to the chilling folly of Jarrell, this is both pat and heroic. It is more statuesque, less adventitious, less calamitous. It allows less room both for the will and for good luck: what it expresses is not so much the poet's real agony and uncertainty as his function in hindsight – a poet struck by lightning will have become an antenna of sorts.

Neither quotation bothers to work out the effect on the poet of popularity and fame, but it seems easy enough: such a poet might not be inclined (in Jarrell) to go out in the wet so often, or (Swir) he might stop retuning his receiver, and stick to a familiar frequency. In the introduction to his 1988 selection of *The Essential Wordsworth*, Heaney seems uncomfortable, even compromised, as he discusses the starchy, establishment figure of the older Wordsworth, 'in his large, not uncomplacent house', seemingly 'more an institution than an individual', 'an

Review of Seamus Heaney, *Seeing Things* (London: Faber and Faber, 1991)

impression not inconsistent with the sonorous expatiations of his later poetry nor with the roll call of his offices and associations – friend of the aristocracy, Distributor of Stamps for Westmoreland, Poet Laureate'. In that padded, double-breasted construction, the double negative, Heaney would seek to offer criticism and mitigation at the same time, but in so doing he betrays his own anxiety.

I don't know whether Glanmore, the house where Heaney wrote much of *Field Work* (1979), is large and complacent or not (although I doubt it), but readers of *Seeing Things* learn that he has now returned to it as its owner-occupier, a condition which, with some more awkward double-speak, he celebrates in the seven sonnets of 'Glanmore Revisited' – in such lines as 'only pure words and deeds secure the house.' Of course, Heaney has also become the master of a 'roll call of offices and associations' of Wordsworthian distinction and dimensions, so it seems tempting to try on the 'institution' and the 'sonorous expatiations' for size as well. In the event, I don't think they fit. The new book is many things, among them Heaney's most plain-spoken and autobiographical work to date. It is a departure in style, tone and purpose. So nix institution and expatiations.

As much as any poet alive, Heaney has understood the need to move on, to remake himself from book to book. (In that same essay of his Jarrell quotes Cocteau's advice to poets: learn what you can do, and then don't do it.) Blake Morrison has drawn attention to the way Heaney likes to use the last poem of one book to suggest the nature of its successor, a pattern skilfully maintained over many books, beguiling his readers with a glimpse of the future. At the same time, though, in myself at any rate, each new Heaney book since *Field Work* has provoked an uncertain response. Either it was the poems that were slow to take, or I was slow to take to them – even such (now) obvious favourites as 'The Underground', 'The Railway Children' and 'Alphabets'. In retrospect, this must have been because Heaney was always doing something slightly different – here was a popular poet who was (mercifully) less conservative than his readers.

Each of Heaney's books since *Field Work*, at all events, has had a different concern and a different presiding genius. *Station*

Island (1984) had its Sweeney poems and its Dantesque sequence of colloquies with ghosts (suggested by 'Ugolino' at the end of *Field Work*). *The Haw Lantern* (1987) had its allegories and parables, drily enthused by Eastern European poetry somehow filtered through Harvard and America. *Seeing Things* is Heaney's most 'Irish' book since *North*. While seeming to hark back to the whole of his career and to resume it – the seaboard and rustic settings and subjects, the translations from Dante and Virgil that frame it, the elegies for dead friends, the poems about driving and fishing (it is also Heaney's most 'sporty' book) – it takes its note from the penultimate poem in *The Haw Lantern*, 'The Disappearing Island', and its last line: 'All I believe that happened there was vision.'

The 'unsayable light' of an earlier poem (one of the original 'Glanmore Sonnets') is here said. 'The rough, porous/ language of touch' that made Heaney famous is forsaken for what one might call the smooth slippery language of sight, the quickest and furthest, most abstract and disembodied, and most trusted and fallible of the senses. That sense of 'words entering almost the sense of touch', the deep historical familiarity for which Heaney strove earlier, has yielded to a kind of seeing that is half-dreaming. He takes up the cudgels against himself. He speaks quippingly of 'the thwarted sense of touch', and in 'Fosterling' writes:

> I can't remember never having known
> The immanent hydraulics of a land
> Of *glar* and *glit* and floods at *dailigone*.
> My silting hope. My lowlands of the mind.

The equivalent in painting of the 48 12-line poems called 'Squarings' that make up the second part of the book would surely be abstracts called Impressions, Improvisations or Compositions, numbered like the poems.

The Haw Lantern was pioneering in that it had at its heart a single physical or geometrical image or schema, the hollow round or sphere which appears in a variety of guises: as the haws of the title; the 'globe in the window' of another possible title; the letter O 'like a magnified and buoyant ovum' in the touching first poem 'Alphabets', about reading and literacy and

literature and read to the students of Harvard. There is the O
of 'Hailstones':

> I made a small hard ball
> of burning water running from my hand . . .

Then there are the many islands in the book, and there's the
sequence called 'Clearances' to the memory of his mother:

> I thought of walking round and round a space
> Utterly empty, utterly a source
> Where the decked chestnut had lost its place
> In our front hedge above the wallflowers.
> The white chips jumped and jumped and skited high.
> I heard the hatchet's differentiated
> Accurate cut, the crack, the sigh
> And collapse of what luxuriated
> Through the shocked tips and wreckage of it all.
> Deep planted and long gone, my coeval
> Chestnut from a jam jar in a hole,
> Its heft and hush become a bright nowhere,
> A soul ramifying and forever
> Silent, beyond silence, listened for.

The O is both something and nothing, origin and omega, mother
and rooted sense of self. Heaney consigns himself to living with
its equivocations, in the fullness of absence. The haw is not a
lantern, but he will live by its light, 'its pecked-at ripeness that
scans you, then moves on'. The round Os in the book evoke
maternity, self-sufficiency and the integrity of conscience: the
one image brings to coherence Heaney's personal loss in 'Clear-
ances' and the several meditations on the practice of his art.

Seeing Things has a similar geometrical leitmotiv or schema,
and that is the straight line, or pattern of straight lines, dazzling
as op art, and producing the sensation of depth. The lines are
not adduced from such obvious sources as waves, layers of rock
or clouds at sunset; they are rooted in experience and have more
to do with a way of seeing, or even a way of being.

Here is the transcendence of *Seeing Things*, the simple and
miraculous escalation from a sixth sense to a seventh heaven,
the lovely delusive optics of sawing and cycling and barred
gates. The miraculous is produced by patience, by attentiveness,

by repetition and work; there is no secret hinge the world swings on the way there is in Edwin Muir, a poet whose name has come up recently in Heaney's essays. The lines – for once not ploughlines, not lines of verse – have their meaning, just as the sphere or circle of *The Haw Lantern* did. The meaning is not as intricate, or as deeply argued, as it was there, but here again it has to do with mortality, and with the generations of men. In 1986, Heaney's father died, leaving the poet in the front line of the senior generation. The straight lines in *Seeing Things*, the visionary buzz, seem to me to be connected to Heaney's sense of the passing generations. The mower, the gate, the spinning-wheel, all have associations with death, as does the phenomenon of 'lightening', defined as 'A phenomenal instant when the spirit flares/ With pure exhilaration before death'. The book begins and ends with the descents to the underworld undertaken by Aeneas and Dante. At the same time, though, the dazzling, silvery lines are an epiphany, a standing vibration, and, for all their confusion, a stay against confusion and mortality. They are a paradox, the contemplation of something physical and at hand, giving rise to a long view of the human struggle, a meta-physics of light:

> Heaviness of being. And poetry
> Sluggish in the doldrums of what happens.
> Me waiting until I was nearly fifty
> To credit marvels. Like the tree clock of tin cans
> The tinkers made. So long for air to brighten,
> Time to be dazzled and the heart to lighten.

The straight line, the dazzle of abstract and op art, are the symbol and message – it seems an appropriate word – of the book, while its human content is drawn immediately from Heaney's life. Experiences from childhood, his courtship and wedding, the death of his father and memories of him, the birth of his children, the painting of his portrait (the one by Edward Maguire that appears on the back of *North*), the acquisition of a bed, a house, the lapidary events of a life – and not a public life, or even necessarily a writing life: all are recounted and alchemized, worked into dazzle, overbrimming, 'sheer pirouette', 'a dream of thaw', the marvellous, 'like some fabulous high-catcher/ coming down without the ball'.

In the second section of the book, Heaney displays his new form, the 12-line poems made up of four tercets and known as 'Squarings'. The 48 poems fall into four sections of 12, each one of 12 lines: squarings. He has perhaps found a compendious form for the work of his fifties, his version of Lowell's unrhymed sonnets and Berryman's *Dream Songs*. The poems are impressive for their freedom, their firmness of purpose, and their skilful arrangement – Berryman's and Lowell's forms retained, by contrast, the randomness of daily writing.

Naturally, not all of them are as good as the best ones – I would nominate v, xvii, xviii, xxviii, xxxiii and xlv – but there is nothing fuzzy about any of them, even the most mysterious. Their principle is the same transcendence as in the book as a whole: they are like homing devices, or Geiger counters, infallibly orientated towards the abiding surplus energy of the moments they describe. The aim is not to provide an adequate (and static) verbal icon, but to reflect in words some continuing effect, a vibration, a recurring figure, and this is how they end: 'Above the resonating amphorae', 'In a boat the ground still falls and falls from under', 'Another phrase dilating in new light', 'Sensitive to the millionth of a flicker', and lastly: 'That day I'll be in step with what escaped me.' These are more aftershocks than tied ribbons; they speak of the poems having located the source of the indestructible energy Heaney was after. Here, in full, is xxvii:

> The ice was like a bottle. We lined up
> Eager to re-enter the long slide
> We were bringing to perfection, time after time
>
> Running and readying and letting go
> Into a sheerness that was its own reward:
> A farewell to surefootedness, a pitch
>
> Beyond our usual hold upon ourselves.
> And what went on kept going, from grip to give,
> The narrow milky way in the black ice,
>
> The race up, the free passage and return –
> It followed on itself like a ring of light

> We knew we'd come through and kept sailing towards.

Here is the iterative motion, the abandon, the astrophysical in the playful, that characterizes these poems. The adjacency of being and non-being. CERN in Geneva ought to like them.

Stylistically, *Seeing Things* is plain as plain, sometimes 'awful plain' (Elizabeth Bishop, 'The Moose'). The gutturals of early Heaney are long gone, and now also the suave Latinity of what one can now call his mid-period. The poems have the most pedestrian beginnings, often stumbling over themselves, with humdrum idioms, and words repeated in the first lines, and rarely anything like a spark. An index of first lines would look dismaying. Occasional shafts of cleverness, against such a back-ground, are almost wounding to the reader: 'Like Gaul, the biretta was divided/ Into three parts' might look well on some poets, but one's jaw drops on seeing it here. There are still the puns – more and more like tics – which now seem characteristic of Heaney, but which he may have got from Muldoon or Lowell. They are puns without the spice of puns, where the second meaning is only an amplification, an organ-stop, of the first, like 'the free passage' in the lines I've just quoted. Because of its preoccupation with dazzlement and with energy, language in *Seeing Things* tends to be straightforward, unobstructive, building step by step towards its illuminations, without much in the way of decoration or distraction. One-word sentences and sentences without verbs abound, line-breaks can be so-so or worse, and, in going for clarity rather than elegance, he has even permitted himself several of those notably ugly adjective-preposition compounds that our parents and guardians always warned us against: 'un-get-roundable weight', 'stony up-against-ness', 'seeable-down-into water'. This wilful crudity and quiddity is evident in 'Field of Vision':

> She was steadfast as the big window itself.
> Her brow was clear as the chrome bits of the chair.
> She never lamented once and she never
> Carried a spare ounce of emotional weight.

In anyone but Heaney, and anywhere but here, this would be brutally demeaning, the person (twice) in terms of the thing, and then the vicious locution of the last line. I think it is the only passage in the book where pursuit of its dazzling philosophy has caused Heaney to be ruthless. As composed and constructed as his books always are – and as other people's hardly ever are – and with a surprisingly thoroughgoing devotion to the insubstantial for a book with that title, *Seeing Things* has taken Heaney to the edge of a new freedom, and to a set of poetic positions that are the very opposite of those with which he started out a generation ago.

OTTO DIX

... the English have long dreaded German art (literature, painting and music) as sure to be dreadfully ponderous, slow, involved and pedestrian.
Bertolt Brecht, to the members of the Berliner Ensemble,
5 August 1956

Unsparingness, *Schonungslosigkeit*, is a German virtue though not all Germans appreciate it – and an English vice. It is probably a matter of geography as much as taste: an island begs to be spared, by definition. The blue movies on the Kurfürstendamm sell themselves as unsparing. The art of Otto Dix is unsparing too, though not in a way the viewers of the blue movies would appreciate. Dix painted ugliness, and, being German, he did it unsparingly. When his retrospective comes to the Tate,* the English will have an opportunity to respond with their traditional discomfiture and dismay.

In the case of these big shows by great and distinctive artists – of which Dix, despite my initial doubts, is certainly one – not all the paintings are on the walls. The painter's vision is sufficiently strong and sufficiently clear to attach itself to your fellow exhibition-goers (this isn't an exhibition you should go to with anyone else), and even to leave the museum altogether. Dix had two of his best years, 1925 to 1927, in this same Berlin; he painted the same human types you see on the streets now or looking at the paintings, and in a similar atmosphere. For at the beginning of 1992 Berlin seems to be just coming out of a war. The city is full of miles and miles of wasteland, beginning just outside the museum with the Potsdamerplatz, once the busiest square in Europe, now a derelict lot. In the damaged East, reconstruction is beginning. Commerce squats in the form of product names on top of reprieved concrete blocks. From their new premises the banks proclaim, incorrectly, 'Investment is

*Tate Gallery, London, 11 March – 17 May 1992

an art', and, unoriginally, 'Money doesn't smell'. Hundreds of thousands of Russian troops are still in the process of being withdrawn.

You see their brown outsize caps and their coats and binoculars for sale. On the howling Stalinist expanse of the 'Alex', the Alexanderplatz, there is pavement gambling and a spot of black market. The most superficial wants are also the deepest, and are attended to first: coffee, newspapers (especially the *Bild Zeitung*), fruit, posters and pornography. The incredible scale of the Stasi's operations is becoming apparent; a quarter of the country tears itself up, the rest looks on, is concerned, gives advice. All this reflects on Dix, and he expresses it with his paintings of whores and cripples, his grey proles and louche portraits: social dislocation, impatience, submission, false glitter and the inadequate healing powers of capitalism. The person who penned the hymn to lost opportunity on a BMW hoarding that began *Gestern abend stand hier ne knackige Alte* (Last night there was this tasty old bird . . .) was Dix; and so was the Polish couple on the bus, mother and daughter, telling each other about the food, pulling out a tub of chocolate pudding as proof, a dark fake-fur coat with white highlights, and the kind of golden ringlets Germans (and no doubt Poles too) have painted, goldsmith-fashion, for hundreds of years, the latest and not the least of them 'Otto Hans Baldung Dix', as his friend Grosz called him.

The retrospective – and last year the centenary – exhibition of Otto Dix shows the work of an artist as protean as any this century, with the usual exception of Picasso; a man who got through the range of current isms very early in his career, and in his thirties found himself painting in Old Master style, like the pupil of Cranach, Dürer and Grünewald he occasionally claimed to be; an impressive, unsparing and unlovable artist in the German tradition of accuracy, the sublime and the unbeautiful. Dix was a member of no groupings of any significance for any length of time; he had no particular affiliation, no close associates (Grosz not very close); his name is not inevitably connected with that of any movement, unless it be that of Verism, a rather obscure offshoot of Neo-realism and *Neue*

Sachlichkeit, coined largely to accommodate and account for
Dix himself. His wilful and eccentric career was nevertheless
almost wholly contingent, at the mercy of every passing political
and economic change. German history shaped his output more
than that of any other German artist in the twentieth century:
the lovely, rather decorative pen-and-ink field postcards he drew
during the First World War; the watercolours that kept himself
and his family fed during the German Inflation, when nothing
more austere or expensive would have sold; his portraits in oils
in the late twenties, when he was the most sought-after and
alarming of portraitists; a handful of brave and ambitious large-
scale allegorical paintings (his triptych *The War, The Seven
Deadly Sins, The Triumph of Death*) done before and immedi-
ately after 1933 and Hitler's coming to power; the landscapes
he painted during the Nazi period as a form of emigration; and
the Christs and Christophers and Lukes he did in Dresden
after the war, in the Workers' and Peasants' State of East
Germany. Each phase is chronologically distinct, and refers you
to the political, social and economic circumstances in which it
was created.

And yet even this lightning summary of Dix's work raises
certain questions about his effectiveness, his intentions and his
methods. At each stage, he seems to be in a kind of tacit oppo-
sition to what is going on, but he never elaborates on this.
His contemporaries carried cards, sounded off and explained
themselves, but not Dix. There is the story of one of them trying
to persuade him to join the Party, and Dix finally saying, I've
had enough of this, let's go to the brothel. But the brothel,
according to many commentators, is a highly politicized
location: the painter, who sells his services for a living, identifies
with the prostitute. Could Dix not in fact be proving himself to
be *more* political than his would-be recruiting sergeant? And
so on. When Grosz draws and paints soldiers, industrialists,
politicians and priests, the intention is clear: to depict the enemy.
His pictures are *Feindbilder.* Dix's, though, are *Zerrbilder,* dis-
tortions, an exaggerated, not an embattled reality. What they
seem to say is not 'These are the oppressors' but (as Goya wrote
on some of his work) 'I have seen it' and 'This is how it was'.
Where Grosz uses caricature and metaphor, Dix refers you to

the reality of what he depicts. The prostitute is not a metaphor for capitalism but an actual prostitute. If the pictures are political, they are so in a less narrow and less purposeful way. In particular, their relation to change is very questionable.

There is a kind of unwisdom, ambiguity and perversity in many of Dix's attitudes and subjects. What made him settle on 'the dead and the naked' (the title of one of the studies on him) as his preferred subjects in the twenties? How could he become a religious painter – though not personally religious – in godless East Germany in the fifties? What accounts for the rigorously uncontemporary appearance of so much of his work, like the tiny sombre *Venus in Gloves* of 1932? The overwhelming tendency is for an over-literal interpretation of the subjects, to infer Dix's standpoint from them. Most famously, this is Carl Einstein's put-down of Dix as *malender Reaktionär am linken Motiv* (a reactionary painter of progressive subjects); but it is just as true of political and religious interpretations of Dix. Late in his life, when Germany was still divided, he lent himself, wittingly or not, to splendid political-aesthetic wrangles between East and West. Neither side really had much use for him, but he did make a bitter bone of contention. In fact, but for the re-unification, there would not have been not one, but two Dix exhibitions!

I believe the arguments about him are too intellectual and too theoretical. At the root of Dix's art is a desire to abash or confront or be unfashionable. With his working-class background, his severe provincial training and his four years in the war as a machine-gunner, he reached his thirtieth year in 1920, and no contemporary style or practice in art was able to impress him. The Expressionists painted the world in primary colours; to him it seemed grey and he painted it accordingly (*Working Class Boy, Woman and Child*). He never gave anything for the French or for abstraction. His experiments with Dada, Cubo-Futurism and a merely photographic realism were all gifted and promising, but of short duration. In the way he worked later, he was almost always alone, away from the moderating influence of others, on terrain that was his own, often eccentric, and sometimes incommunicable. The artists with whom he had any relationship were his students, or they were local Dresden painters, or they had been dead for centuries.

The painting from which Dix generally said he took his beginnings is his 1912 *Self-Portrait with Carnation*, painted when he was just twenty-one and a student. It seems at once a beautifully solid and achieved work on which to found a career, and a complete anachronism, perhaps 500 years out of date, with nothing in common with any living style of the moment. And yet it is a real self-portrait, not an exercise or pastiche. In its accuracy and painstakingness and style, it proclaims its identification with the traditions of the past and its agnosticism towards the present. It could be a Martyr or a Saint or an Unknown Young Man of 1500 or so, but a twentieth-century self-portrait – never! Dix is standing half-sideways on, like a duellist presenting a small target to his opponent (in 1915, he painted a *Self-Portrait as Target*). He looks serious, glowering, watchful, a Henry at Hal's age. The eyes are deepset, the brow frowns and the mouth is down-drawn: it is a picture of some sort of victory over a more generous and open self, an early maturity in the drab, armouring, magnificently painted corduroy. A helmet might go over the stringy fringe. You feel sympathy for the young man, putting on such a stern face to meet his portraitist – himself! The carnation (*Nelke,* also a clove, *un clou,* a nail), an emblem of pain, mortality, the Crucifixion (I don't know the exact iconography), has dropped into his hand from another century; he seems unaware of it even as he holds it, and is further characterized by it, as he is by the blue background – not a natural sky blue, but a heightened ethical blue, a rather sweet blue like a sugared almond.

This very early picture anticipates Dix's later practice: an unfashionable finish and perfection, both exaggerating and suggesting, the use of props and one-colour backgrounds (Dix says somewhere that everyone has a personal colour: Anita Berber's hot red; Sylvia von Harden's cool pink; the drapes, blue-green and German shepherd in *The Photographer Hugo Erfurth with Dog)*, objectivity tending towards caricature (this last perhaps signalled by another portrait of Erfurth, this time holding a photo-lens – the German word for lens is *Objektiv*). Dix stressed the importance of first impressions – which seems to me odd for a portrait-painter, especially one with such long drawn-out processes as Dix used – and said he preferred to paint strangers. Where many twentieth-century portraitists seem to paint just one type of face – think of Schiele or Beckmann, among Dix's contemporaries – Dix's are all different. The human face is a terrible place, someone once sang, and that is the impression one has from Dix: a keen, instinctual, almost doggish sense of alienation from other breeds, faces like smells, different, disturbing, unforgettable. Dix has obviously succeeded in capturing one's initial feelings of alarm, fascination and repulsion, a sense of the disproportion and strangeness of other people's features, before habitual looking makes them acceptable. But he manages in his portraits to combine the vehemence of first impressions with a studied and permanent form (his *Lasurtechnik,* many thin layers of paint and varnish, if I understand it correctly, generally applied on wood, and demanding the making of full-scale cartoons beforehand). This is the basic tug or contradiction in his work: quick reactions and 'low' caricatural subjects, executed in the most lavish, durable and historically dignified way; the colossal – ironic – discrepancy between technique and content, the twentieth century through the eyes of the fifteenth or sixteenth. Take the painting *Nelly with Toys* of 1925. Dix paints his two-year-old daughter like an Infanta by Goya or Velazquez. His characteristic pink and green palette, often used to repulsive effect, is here kept pure. Nelly's outrageous ribbon is a crown, her ball an orb, her jumbled and anarchic tower (her stare challenges the viewer to say it's wrong) a sceptre. Even her collar and cuffs might be ermine. Her fat fingers lie carelessly on the sumptuously grained table like Botero trotters. Her dark eyes blaze from their blue whites; her chubby mouth is an imperious curl; her own curls are lovingly chased by the painter in the Old Master technique that Grosz witnessed. The portrait radiates the wilfulness, poise, beauty and peremptoriness of the little girl. If she spoke, it would be to say, 'Off with his head!'

The 1920s were Dix's decade: with his portraits, his pictures of prostitutes, his big set pieces like *To Beauty* and *The Metropolis,* he supplied many of the enduring images of those years. At the same time, in the 50 etchings that make up *The War*

(1924), he produced possibly his best work, and, with Goya, the strongest visual response to the subject. Again, the delay is characteristic, necessary for the finding of a medium and form with which to communicate his quick impressions. What he sent back from the Front at the time, in the form of his decorative field-postcards and the watermelon-pretty spatter of his water-colours must have dismayed him by its serenity and merriment. The titles are veiled apologies for this: *Concrete Trench with Flowers* (1916), *Shell Crater like Blossom* (1916). The same quality in Dix that made his early *Self-Portrait with Carnation* so austere and memorable, his will to create strong effects, his unsparingness, his aversion to colour as consolation, drove him to rework his wartime experience later, in black and white, with absolute technical mastery and freedom. *The War* has an enormous range: from white to black, from fine, representational lines to an acid fuzz of pain and decomposition, from parodic sketching to papers that might have been stained by war itself. The 50 etchings seem to be in no particular order. Among the best in my opinion were I,4, a pattern of white receding craters, II,2, a gas attack by night, II,9, a lovely patterning of corpses on wire, and III,7, the dawn over a field of bodies. *The War* was quickly recruited for the anti-war movements of the twenties – and Dix's main trouble with the Nazis was that his work was *wehrzersetzend,* or liable to weaken the instinct to self-defence; but I have more sympathy with the view that finds these images neutral, horrific, yes, but not evaluative, not condemning, not propagandistic. The tone is once again one of 'I have seen it' and 'These things took place'.

Just as Dix's war art is not censorious, nor are his pictures of prostitutes; they are not prurient either. The fact that Dix was twice taken to court for obscenity is absurd; but just as absurd was his defence – which years later still made him burst out laughing – that these were deeply moral pictures, warning of the dangers of corruption and loose living. I simply cannot see Dix as such an infantile moralist. In his self-portraits and photographs, Dix always preserves a demeanour of the most tremendous earnestness. Even on the cover of a picture-book he made for his nephew 'Muggeli', he draws himself in profile, smoking, hair slicked back, brows furrowed, mouth down – and you wish he would relax, just for once. In fact, though, the po-faced, puritanical image is misleading. Dix didn't spend the twenties glowering on the sidelines. Other photographs show him wearing make-up and a monocle for Carnival; he danced so well he thought of doing it for a living with Martha his wife; he was a dandy, who sometimes took payment in the form of new shoes and a suit of clothes; he participated in the kind of scenes he depicted in *To Beauty* and *Metropolis*. When he painted his whores (many of whom were not), he didn't preach to them like Gladstone.

My point is that I don't think there is anything too considered, let alone too comprehensive, about Dix's subjects: his work doesn't add up to an anatomy of the society of the time, still less to an indictment of it. 'It's what I do!' he said. 'Say what you like. What it's good for I can't say myself. But I do it anyway. Because I know that's what it was like, and no different!' Dix was a provocative artist: he liked to paint what he knew people wouldn't like to look at. Even among his watercolours – to which he looked to make his living – there were many that were unsaleable because of their subjects: old people, ugly faces, suicides, murders, foul prostitutes. It's easy to pick out the ones that might have sold: slight and cynical skits on bourgeois happiness. What interested Dix was ugliness, which seems to him almost like a creed. When he said, later in his life, 'I'm not that obsessed with making representations of ugliness. Everything I've seen is beautiful . . .', he only succeeds in confirming its importance by suggesting a kind of *ésthetique du mal*, which I've argued is close to German art and writing anyway, in the poetry of Georg Trakl and Gottfried Benn. Many of Dix's paintings are truly horrible, vile, creepy: the first impression, under the many varnishing layers, like an insect trapped in amber. And yet they have a kind of beauty too, beyond the skill with which they were painted. The watercolours are surprisingly messy and sloppy and spirited: *Mieze, abends im Café* with an ocelot round her shoulders, a lapdog burrowed into her crotch, toying with a green beaker with flame-red fingernails; the luscious red-on-red *Sphinx; The Suicide*, with his red tongue and loosened red tie (Dix's joke?) hanging in his wan room.

In the oil-paintings, what is again and again arresting is the contradiction between a flawed or even disgusting face or scene and the perfection of its execution: *Still Life with Calf's Head* (like an illustration for some of Benn's *Morgue* poems), *Three Women, Elderly Couple, Three Prostitutes in the Street*, the disturbing *Nude Lying on Fur*. These and other paintings can't be reduced to coded or simple statements. The ugliness in them is a continual and willed, yes, finely controlled vibration: the curtailed, minced-pork-and-parsley palettes; the opulent backgrounds; the heroic, classicizing postures and arrangements; the array of physical types and physiognomies; an airless glow in the painting, pallor and garishness together. It seems that the more there is in each painting – the more Dix puts in – the worse it gets. There is a kind of incremental nausea provoked by draperies, carpets, velvet, veils, marble balustrade, carpentry, jewellery, ribbons, hair, flesh in the *Three Women* of 1926. It is as though Dix had found a way of depicting *ars longa, vita brevis* in a tiny, annihilating glimpse. The 'beautiful' – or at least the costly, the showy – is contaminated by the hideous human. It is as though one's nerves had become sated and couldn't bear to touch another gorgeous velvet or diaphanous silk, or see another piece of veined marble or porphyry. These props for cheap erotica become, in Dix's hands, the catalysts of disgust. Not the least disturbing part of this picture, and others (say the *Nude Lying on Fur*), is the absence of any reciprocal thought on the part of the model, or any mutual awareness if there are more than one. Each figure – and this is true of all of Dix – exists solipsistically. The models for his portraits seem not to be aware of themselves, not to know what is happening to them; and so, at its very worst, the nude is assimilated to her fur, her hair dribbles blondly into it, her foreshortened wishbone legs beg to be cracked open, she becomes a stupid cow or a piece of meat (is that the 'statement'?); and in the eerie 1937 portrait of Jean-Jacques Bernauer, the model becomes an aristocratic wax mannikin between the carpet and the tapestry. Everything is texture, and texture in the end is inert, as *Still Life in the Atelier* shows, where a mouldering stuffed doll mimics a live and pregnant model.

Dix's biggest, most ambitious paintings tend to be the ones I am least impressed by: they dilute his ability as a portraitist,

reality is diminished by allegory. *The Triumph of Death* is plati-
tudinous; *Metropolis* is much less than the sum of its parts, and
much less than something like Diego Rivera; *Flanders* and the
other war paintings are better in their black and white versions
in the *War* etchings. The religious paintings and landscapes of
later years are fey and uninteresting, except perhaps in the way
they extended Dix's range of creepiness. *St Luke Painting the
Madonna* seems to contain more hidden birds each time you
look at it; Dix himself as St Luke looks like a Florida dentist in
the pink steam of some Everglades – an appalling picture. The
landscapes are lurid, never-never landscapes under never-never
meteorological conditions in the Northern European manner
(out of Brueghel, etc.). Dix said that landscapes didn't interest
him, and these have only the mildest historical interest, as war
paintings by default.

If Dix's career had ended here, he would be seen as a brief,
inexplicable, almost accidental phenomenon who lit up one
decade, the 1920s, and did nothing else of note. Admittedly, the
later work is not very well represented in the exhibition, but
there is enough there to make a different case, in the form of
three heavy, bold and expressionistically painted portraits: the
Self Portrait as Prisoner of War of 1947, *Dr Fritz Perls* of 1966,
and *Self Portrait with Marcella* of 1969. The first of these is the
most moving – perhaps the only moving – painting I know of
Dix's: dark wintry colours, green, blue, ochre, turquoise, but
with black and grey breaking through everywhere, the paint
applied in little flecks as though it wouldn't spread; three heads
– or one in two mirrors – grizzled, numbered, in camouflage
gear, with a suggestion of camps and searchlights. It's a tragic
painting, more Christian than any of his professed Christian
work, perhaps with something of the *Odyssey* about it too. The
other two are lighter: Dr Perls with his curly Jewish face and
curly body posture, purple suit and mustard and cream back-
ground, a quick and wise piece of work – one survivor by
another; and himself with Marcella, a granddaughter, the
colours of youth and age, a light yellow and green to his own
dark blue and maroon, the possessiveness of age, the old fingers
holding this handful, a kind of crazy Bellovian joy in the eyes,
the whole thing under a child's fantasy of a tree. All three seem

to me great paintings, simple and sure, with a new and wonderful sense of colour, 'colour no longer space, line no longer explanatory', giving a likeness and even preserving the element of mockery – can this be true? – that accompanied Dix all his life.

ANSELM KIEFER

Exhibition openings in December and press dates in November meant that I wasn't able to look at Anselm Kiefer's new paintings in Dering Street or on the Peckham Road,* but instead saw a smaller and quite possibly different show just ending at the Galerie Yvon Lambert in Paris. Five enormous canvases, two workbooks and two rubbery photo-books in a room and a half. The physicality of the work, its enormous scale and the pressure of its details force me to write about what I've seen, rather than conjecture from transparencies.

But then contingency is the mother of coincidence: in Paris, I learned that Kiefer had left Germany and taken up residence in France. He has exchanged his brickyard at Buchen in the Oderwald, south of Frankfurt, for a former silkworks near Barjac in the Gard. As to when this happened, the catalogue is discreetly silent; and I suppose Kiefer must have 50 hermeneuts for one biographer. Still, we are to think of him, astoundingly, as remaking himself – perhaps – as a French artist, now scrawling French words on his paintings, addressing themes from French history, using French materials in his compositions. His new works, four pictures from 1996, one from 1995, include two – *Les Reines de France*, if you please, and *Maginot* – on explicitly French themes; even the cosmic paintings, like *Cette obscure clarté qui tombe des étoiles* (I don't know whose the line is, if indeed it is anyone's), seem more French- than German-cosmic, more Verlaine than Novalis. Certainly, the work seemed as though made to be looked at where I happened to be looking at it: it seemed rooted and local. The colours of the pictures, predominantly white and off-white, were everywhere in evidence outside: in the winter Paris sky, the stone hotels, the peeling façades and shutters of the Marais, the coarse sand of the boules pits. You can look at them and be reminded of – I don't know – Dufy. Or Braque. Or Tati.

* Anthony d'Offay Gallery and South London Gallery, February 1997

The last time Kiefer exhibited at the Galerie Lambert five years ago, his works were fashioned from lead, glass, brick and fire. A French critic, the late Jean-Noel Vuarnet – in the French manner more a rhapsode than a critic – anatomized his greys:

> iron-grey, grey-white, silver-grey, silver-white, the greys of clouds and sauerkraut ... an elemental, so to speak, *technological* colour ... evocative of film, of the cathode ray tube and of radar and VDU screens, of aeroplanes and rocketry.

Now, though, there is this mild and subtle and variegated off-white, not modern, not cutting-edge, not fearsome. One thinks, not of technology but of nature, of clays and shales. Or if of something man-made, then of buildings, and then not new buildings but things time has got its teeth into – a dirt road, crumbling plaster, cement dust on a workman's overalls. The French catalogue speaks of the 'violence' in Kiefer, but I feel this is no longer true. There is a kind of serenity or acquiescence in the new work. His endlessly resourceful and undesigning processes mimic time in the way they bring things to beauty or beauty to things. Something similar, I think, has happened to Kiefer's use of history and mythology: it seems less impersonal, less minatory, less imposing. France, historically equated with such values as lightness, grace and pleasure, offers these qualities to Kiefer, their unlikeliest recipient. On top of everything else, his recent work seems to be autobiographical.

The most explicit of the paintings – the one on its own in the half-room – is *Maginot*. The name of the French system of fortifications, built following the 1871 defeat by Prussia and simply bypassed in 1914 by the Schlieffen Plan, it is written across the whole width of a large canvas in Kiefer's spindly capitals. The whitish canvas, treated, distressed, slathered and gouged, built up and peeled off, aged and watchable, is pierced by scores of asparagus stems, which come out of the painting at the viewer. The initial effect is bewildering, a sense of feeble bristling – especially out of the letters of the word 'Maginot' – a suffusing of a dry yellow colour over the white, perhaps some illegible alternative script. Then, when one recognizes the withered, straw-coloured, agonized, practically *crucified* forms as asparagus, the effect is terribly moving. This is asparagus-

abuse: these twisted, inedible, unsucculent, unphallic forms have
become the antithesis of asparagus, a kind of anti-asparagus!
You stand in front of *Maginot*, and grapple with what you're
given. The thing itself – green, epicurean, spear-shaped, luxur-
ious, slick – but then countermanded, as it were, by its withered
condition, by the individuality and anguish – the personality –
of each dead stem, not least by its being levelled pathetically
against you, and then it sets up a sort of inconsolable vibration
with the word 'Maginot'. Is 'Maginot', with its historical fate –
an irrelevance, first and foremost, a sternly practical measure
turned uselessly quixotic, like the erecting of a row of windmills
– to be equated with those stalks; or did they pierce it; are we
to understand something of the Germans' motivation for
trying to conquer France (they wanted to eat it: Brecht, from
East Berlin, saw in a French cheese platter with 70 cheeses the
acme or definition of civilization; the German proverb for
the good life is *'wie Gott in Frankreich'*, like God in France)?
Or do we see in the painting, with the one-dimensional historical
resonance of its title, and the one-dimensional asparagus sticking
out of it, twisting in space, some oblique reference to the
painter's own move to France? A curving arrow like the German
infantry in World War One, like the asparagus? What does it
do when a German painter paints 'Maginot'? What if instead
he'd called it 'Spargel'? Or *'ceci n'est pas une asperge'*? I suppose
the painting is a voicing of historical guilt. Like his teacher
Beuys, Kiefer uses inanimate things to register trauma. His tragi-
comic asparagus is a notable addition to his expressive
repertoire.

Les Reines de France is in a far more straightforward relation
to its also less fraught title. It too can be read as an announce-
ment of or a commentary on Kiefer's change of address and
allegiance, and this time in a frankly romantic way. At the foot
of the painting a man lies on his back, in white trousers, stripped
to the waist. He looks a little like Lenin, a little like Gary
Numan, but is perhaps Kiefer himself – I have no idea what he
looks like, and of course the catalogue doesn't offer anything
so vulgar as a photograph of the artist. He is resting or dead or
dreaming or tanning. The ambiguity is not troubling, a reliable
tranquillity goes out from the painting. Above him, in a cloud

of history, is the entire distaff side of the French monarchy. Along the top of the painting, which is made up of nineteen hinted concave vertical panels, goes the march of time: '*4ième, 5ième siècle, 6ième*' through to '*21ième, 22ième*', for which there is predictably as yet no demand. In between the supine male figure and the chronometric scale are the names of the queens, scribbled on businesslike buff cards and stapled to the painting, one hundred and twelve of them in all, from Clotilde and Basile to Marie-Amélie de Bourbon-Sicile, in Kiefer's slapdash hand. The fantastic schoolboyish cataloguing zeal of the thing and its inescapable scruffiness are better conveyed by the work-book version: here the names are more legible for a start, the cards are numbered, the dates of the queens are included and even, in some cases, the names of their kings. In addition, the work-book has vertical ledger-like columns for each decade, and this shows you, as again the huge painting doesn't, the eccentric accuracy of the enterprise: each little card trimmed to the length of the queen's life, stuck down in precisely the correct position, and – a crowning weirdness – where there is doubt about the date of birth or death, the left or right edge of the card is trimmed in a pennant-like zigzag. Seen from a distance, the picture reminds me of the naming of mountain peaks in a panorama, but the strongest impression is that of schoolboy ardour and out-of-hours pedantry. It reminds me of our real and fictional teamsheets, of the defunct cricket game 'Howzat', of our perfectionist but ultimately unimpressive semi-practical 'projects', and, most specifically, of a piece of wrinkly pseudo-parchment I was bought in America at eight or nine, with the names and dates and pictures of all the presidents on it, and also, before long, in biro and in my awful Kieferish handwriting, my computation of their time in office. This, then, is *Les Reines de France*: a declaration of love to France – the book has a dried lily on its frontispiece and another at the end; Marie-Antoinette gets a yellow rose – and to French history and French womanhood. The names – and Kiefer has always found his prime inspiration in words and names; 'a name', he says, 'contains in itself a presumption, a feeling that conceals and reveals something' – are names to conjure with: Maria Stuart, Catherine de Medici, Anne d'Autriche, and so on and so forth. From the early names in particular, a historical pity or piety flows: Wisiogarde, Thédechilde, Suavegothe, Radegonde, Brunehaut, Meroflède – to our ears archaic, sexless, barbarous, beautiful names in which the French and the German-Gothic are still entwined (Charlemagne, after all, was also Karl der Grosse, and lies buried in Aachen or Aix). Febrile pencil lines connect the figure on the floor to the names in space, and three clots of an indefinable plant, trailing roots like a hair-piece, are a representation of feeling or longing. Even without the somewhat banal, balding male figure – the recipient of all that's above – one would read the picture as expressive of heart, vulnerability and affect. The caking, cracking ochre mortar and the bent, almost corrugated panels – as though taken from old 2CVs – make this an almost overly French picture.

However, the most arresting piece in the exhibition, for me, is *Sol Invictus*. 'Undefeated Sun', another huge and lofty painting, with the same recumbent man, this time lying head to the fore, feet diminished by perspective, naked this time, and under a gigantic and – thrillingly – real sunflower. The man is irredeemably banal – another painting, in the catalogue though not in the show, which has the sunflower sprouting in lieu of a penis, a thoroughly ill-judged idea, does nothing to change this – but the sunflower is absolutely splendid. This one reminded me of Blake – not his poem 'Ah Sun-Flower', but the final image of 'A Poison Tree': 'my foe outstretched beneath the tree'. One of the photo-books has a sequence of photographs of sunflowers, first a whole field of them, then moving closer and closer to their 'heart of darkness' till it ends with cosmic spatter, debris, very tiny or very distant matter: a rather hackneyed idea, I have to say, though it looks better in the two remaining paintings, *Cette obscure clarté* and *Homme sous une pyramide*. But the sunflower itself is wonderfully potent: left to stand in square fields until September or October when everything else has long been harvested, its yellow and green a memory, a ragged spine supporting a stricken face, massed, statuesque, anthropomorphic, a form and a face, a triffid. There seems to me something religious about it, in the way it is basically left to die in order to be reborn in its seeds, in the shape of it, a bell on a tower or again perhaps a crucifix, in its extended suffering the opposite of the fig in Rilke's Sixth Elegy, which fruits before it leafs. (As indeed I think there is something religious about the scale and the height of Kiefer's paintings, of which you can only see a half or even a third at all closely: the workings and details and textures of the top part you have to take on trust.) Here, Kiefer has nailed or smashed or glued an actual sunflower to his painting, subtly working it in with paint and varnish and other materials. Above all, with a wonderful seething, swirling, brewing mass of sunflower seeds – you can practically hear them buzzing on the painting. They are sinisterly beautiful, death-in-life or life-in-death, disposed with wonderfully natural randomness singly or in clusters, little flying wedges, both singular and 'incorrigibly plural' (Louis MacNeice), their shiny insect black softening to brown close to, and bringing out surprising pink and blue tints in the underlying thin and rather glossy white of this painting, falling with delicious ambiguity, like bomblets, like hard rain, like life from the air, on the ambiguous man lying in a field in fair France.

EGON SCHIELE

The private collection of the eye-surgeon Rudolf Leopold is perhaps less impressive than the twentieth-century section on the top floor of the Österreichische Galerie in Vienna – but only just. The Royal Academy has on display some 150 works from the Leopold Collection, including fifty Schieles and many other outstanding items by Klimt, Kokoschka, Gerstl and Herbert Boeckl. Only the fifth of the exhibition's five rooms, containing work done after 1920, is sheerly mediocre; Anton Hanak's ink-blot drawings, the mud-vision of Albin Egger-Lienz's grandiose 'Finale' of 1918, Alpinism and *plein-air* painting by various other hands.

In a rather prickly interview published in the catalogue, Leopold gives some rare insights into the problems of the private collector in – or perhaps in competition with – a small, not especially enlightened socialist State at the end of the twentieth century. What art in Austria really needs, he says, is a Mitter-rand. He himself does not want to be called an 'obsessive' collector; he allows 'passionate'. Artists have paid tribute to his 'eye' – it isn't just money talking – he has had to submit to interviews, amounting to auditions, in which he had to win the confidence of other collectors, artists or their legatees. Leopold tells the astonishing story of his meeting with Alois Gerstl, who confessed that he had been persuaded by a reputable art his-torian to cut one of his brother's paintings in half, in order to make it into two, one of himself, the other of a chair. After all, there was the example of Van Gogh, painting Gauguin's chair without Gauguin in it. Sixty centimetres of 'a light, broken green' were simply thrown away.

This is a personal collection: Leopold has concentrated on Schiele and Klimt, but only on certain aspects of their art. He prefers Schiele's 'expressive' paintings from 1910 to 1915, dismissing the later works as 'rather mannered'. The evidence of a strong personal taste and the unbiddable machinery of the

Review of *Egon Schiele and His Contemporaries: From the Leopold Collection, Vienna*, Royal Academy, London, December 1990–February 1991

market-place make *Egon Schiele and His Contemporaries* rather
hard to assimilate. It is almost too singular, without much in
the way of weak or merely supportive pictures – certainly from
Schiele.

One thinks of Schiele as the great painter of nudes, of women's
bodies and his own. However, he has a surprising range of other
subjects too. Perhaps his most conventional are the paintings of
mothers and children, and of religious heroes, in the formal,
allegorical manner of his friend and mentor, Klimt. He paints
Klimt and himself as 'Hermits' (1912), two lurching, black-
garbed, rather stylish figures in a single, indissoluble black mass;
the bearded, head-banded Klimt has both eyes shut, and
resembles Anchises or a dead Christ. 'Self-Seer' of 1911 has
intimations of skulls: the crossed wrists of the central figure
make a crucifix, and the right-hand side of the picture looks as
though it might refer to Schoenberg's terrifying humanoid in his
'The Red Stare' (1910), a nascent face in scarlet and ochre.
Schiele paints trees with a similar, anthropomorphic intensity.
The famous painting in Vienna of four autumnal trees is like
a biography of four people. The Leopold Collection contains
'Autumn Tree in a Gust of Wind', a flat, cracked and scratched
surface, in which the tree's limbs run like fissures. It looks like
a tree broken on a wheel. A few yellow leaves, like coins, are
held on its frailest twigs. Very different – perhaps Schiele's
calmest work – are the drawings and pictures of the houses of
his mother's village of Krumau. The conventional wisdom is to
regard these too as expressionist, but to me it makes no sense
to set them beside the Gothic warping and cramping of the
interiors in the films of Lang and Pabst or Schmidt-Rotluff's
night pumpkins, or Grosz's tenements, a murder in every
window. Schiele's houses might be the models of some child
architect. They are cheerful, complete and without distortions.
They have doors and windows, chimneys and buttresses, shut-
ters and curtains. Jaunty washing hangs out to dry. They are
positively Dutch in their allurement. Admittedly, they are
without trees or people: an ideal community from which the
artist is excluded, the promised land which Schiele saw only
from above, but never entered, painting it from postcards. Some

of these pictures – 'The Small Town', 'Dead Town', 'Krumau on the Moldau' – are among Schiele's loveliest.

Pre-eminent, though, are his pictures of women, and of himself. It is his treatment of these immemorial subjects that makes him modern. The contrast with Klimt is revealing: Klimt had no interest whatever in himself as a subject, and his treatment of women turns them into his favourite ethereal flame-shapes. His reaching for the textures and patterns of fabrics almost ceases to be that of a fetishist; it is more a drowning man's. In his perceptive catalogue essay, 'Not Blind to the World', Klaus Albrecht Schröder writes:

> So effectively is sex tamed in Klimt's stylized versions of the female form that Karl Kraus even recommended *Nuda Veritas* as eminently well suited to the expulsion of 'carnal thoughts'.

By contrast, when Schiele leaves his women partly clothed, as he often does, they are wearing their own things, stockings and shoes, not the fleecy accessories one feels Klimt kept hanging by the door for the purpose. 'Black-Haired Girl with Skirt Turned Up' shows everything under the skirt: stockings, petticoat, knickers, pudenda like a red fringed eye. You can tell exactly the feel of the crushed velvet skirt – with its green, red, blue and brown tints – and of the combed-out frizzy hair, the mouth painted and open, the eyelids painted and shut, the little smudge of the nose. The effect is candid but not, as has been said, provocative or depraved; it is most certainly not evasive or decorative either.

Schiele said, 'I paint the light that comes out of all bodies.' On yellow-brown or yellow-grey paper, he draws strong, bumpy outlines. Early on, he daubs strong watercolour like war-paint over the bodies: red shin, blue groin, yellow belly, green brow on his 'Nude Self-Portrait, Kneeling' of 1910. Sometimes he blocks in the form with heavy white. Later on, he marks stresses and edges with flurries of biro-colour, green and red usually, but also violet and black; cheeks, elbows, knees, kidneys and knuckles. The poses seem to become more stable, though they still emphasize defensiveness or sexual vulnerability. Acid-green, rust and red is a favourite colour-combination, seen for instance in 'Act of Love' (1915). The draughtsmanship looks on occasion like that of an acupuncturist, spiny lines at cross-purposes, a kind of secret geography of pain.

None of his contemporaries could draw remotely like Schiele, but there were some good painters among them for a time; it is interesting to note that, while Austrian literature survived for another twenty years, Austrian art ceased to exist as an international phenomenon in 1918, when both Klimt and Schiele died. Even so, Professor Leopold has some fine Kokoschkas, sketches of anorexically thin young people – thinness seems to be a leitmotiv of the exhibition – and a puzzled-looking 'Self-Portrait, Hand Touching Face', his lumpy, unplaned face against a tempestuous blue background. Herbert Boeckl has contributed some fine landscapes, very much in the Kokoschka manner, 'Large Sicilian Landscape' and the arresting 'Berlin Factory', the left half of which is a brown building, the top right corner a dazzling blue sky, and the remaining third an arrangement of three squares in a vivid red.

For the rest, it is good to see some more pictures by Richard Gerstl (1883–1908), even though none of them can touch the extraordinary 'Self-Portrait, Laughing' in the Österreichische Galerie. In 1908 Gerstl killed himself, apparently in the wake of an affair he'd been having with Mathilde Schoenberg, the wife of the composer, whom he'd been teaching to paint. His large 'Nude Self-Portrait' of 1908 is here, painted just weeks before he died. It shows him from mid-shin to uncut hair – maybe Alois sold his feet – one hand on his hip, the other held out, possibly holding a brush. It has been seen as a picture of erotic confidence, which seems possible. He appears to dazzle, standing in a blue-white light, his body all kinds of tender colours, pink, purple, yellow, pale-green, innocent, almost pastel colours. Behind him is a couch or sofa, in front of him the way out, in the form of a brown door. He stares, and his gaze seems to complicate things, signing itself in blueish spirals that twirl down to the floor.

GEORGE GROSZ

Surely the facts about George Grosz speak for themselves? The prodigy in war-torn Berlin. The mirror of Weimar. The sleek, handsome caricaturist, who liked to be taken for a banker or lawyer. Fleetingly, in the (Golden?) Twenties, the party member – more than could be said of the more committed Brecht. The lover of all things American – he claims to have copied out by hand the whole of James Fenimore Cooper's *The Last of the Mohicans* – who then had the misfortune of having to seek refuge there in earnest, in 1933. The loss of purpose and focus in the work he did in America. His return to (West) Berlin in 1959, and, within a few weeks, his death – squalid or tragic or avoidable – in the stairwell of his house.

Any 'revisionist account', like M. Kay Flavell's in *George Grosz: A Biography*, is under threat where there exists round its subject a mythology as formally and emotionally compelling as there is around Grosz. Even if the revision is scrupulous and persuasive, it is still unlikely to catch on. Rather, the new account will be believed or cherished only where it approaches the old myth. Flavell may have succeeded in altering one or two decimal places in her revision, but the myth rounds up or rounds down, and carries on.

As it happens, I don't think *George Grosz: A Biography* succeeds anyway. It is a book with the scope and ambition of an article, more argumentative than a regular biography, straining to correct an imbalance rather than offer a full narrative. It might be an intellectual biography, but it doesn't contain many ideas, and neglects to say whether its subject should be considered to be an intellectual himself. In the paraphrase form characteristic of the book, we hear Grosz saying that 'Writing was enjoyable, but it was also problematic since the thinking always had to come first.' Elsewhere, he says, 'An artist's ability to think independently or not tells one nothing about the level of his artistic ability.' One's uncertainty as to where to class

Review of M. Kay Flavell, *George Grosz: A Biography*
(New Haven: Yale University Press, 1988)

Grosz on so basic an issue is not resolved by this book, though it was comprehensively researched and years in the making.

Occupying the bulk of the book are the twenty-five years Grosz spent in the United States. Most earlier studies have passed over these in silence, complains Flavell, and the few others dismissed them out of hand. She is struck by the arithmetical injustice of John Willett, whose study of Weimar put Grosz 'alongside Tucholsky, in spite of the fact that the latter's life ended with his suicide in 1935 while Grosz survived until 1959'. A rueful line comes to mind, written by one exile, used as an epigraph by another: 'And the heart doesn't die when one thinks it should'.* Certainly, Cervantes, Goya and Orwell, those figures to whom Flavell turns most often for comparison, are much less effective than Tucholsky, who was a contemporary (at least to begin with), came from the same part of the world, went through some of the same political evolutions, used four pseudonyms and wrote about and fervently admired Grosz. 'If I hadn't been Tucholsky, I should have liked to be a Malik bookjacket', he once said (Malik was the publisher of Grosz and the photomontage artist John Heartfield).

Flavell's attitude towards her subject is essentially one of suspicion. Irritated and provoked by the simplicity of those earlier versions of his life that saw in his quarter-century in America only irrelevance and defeat, she interrogates Grosz's every statement and position for shadings of irony, provocation and dissembling. Often in such passages a kind of linguistic or analytical fatigue sets in. One begins to wonder whether Grosz was actually such a protean figure as all that – and if he was, then to wish for a somewhat more protean language in which to have the fact expressed. Grosz's own image for a plural (Flavell says 'shifting') personality – 'How many people live inside each of us? One on the top floor, one in the middle, and one in the cellar?' – is, one might note, couched in the interrogative; there is scorn in it, that a plain statement would not convey. Grosz *was* complicated, his views – like those of most of his contemporaries – changed, and above all he was addicted to telling people what he guessed they would most hate to hear. By the

* (Czesław Miłosz; Joseph Brodsky)

end, one feels word-blind and numb, but unshakeably convinced
in a Tucholsky-ish sort of way that in America Grosz remained
Grosz, and went on drawing and painting Groszes.

How much this matters depends largely on the quality of the
latter, and here Flavell again offers no opinion. A little flippantly
one might say that the word 'allegory' seems to mean a picture
that is neither good nor effective; Flavell at any rate uses it a
good deal. Something about being *dépaysé* – strictly speaking,
Grosz wasn't an exile – seems to have driven Grosz towards
the alternative country of art: tradition, continuity, salvage, the
search for a coded, all-encompassing expression to relate the old
to the new; even as an alibi, an occupation, the delusion of
ambition. When Grosz arrived in America, he advertised for
students by calling himself 'the finest living water-colourist' (not
a claim furthered by the samples reproduced in the book). It
was actually this 'art' side of Grosz, I think, that declined into
murky painting and cloudy drawing of subjects like mud and
fire, that moved towards the apocalyptic final image in his auto-
biography, 'the sponge soaked in blood' that will finally 'wipe
the slate clean'. Certainly, it is extraordinary to read – in one of
all too few technical notes in Flavell – about Grosz, of all people,
beginning a picture without knowing where it was going to
go, with a line on canvas: the Grosz who earlier had seen his
(purposive) black line as 'a sign of his control over death'.

'In those days "art" had a clear purpose', he wrote to a
friend in 1933 of those works of his that were now featured in
'degenerate' exhibitions or burned. He depended on having an
audience and knowing them. 'His personal life story seemed
intertwined at every point with the collective life story of
Germany as a whole.' As America yawed about among Commu-
nism, Surrealism, abstraction, McCarthyism, how obscure,
conformist and marginal a figure Grosz must have seemed! 'By
trying to say too much at the same time, Grosz runs the risk of
incoherence.' His paintings sprouted funny titles, commentaries
and correspondences with buyers and dealers, 'longer and longer
attempts, often in inadequate English, to spell out some of the
multiple levels of meaning he hoped the work might convey'.
What Flavell sets out in conscientious detail is not a counter-
argument for despair, but surely just its process, the mechanism

by which it overcame its object, Grosz. The comparison with the robust, temporary exile and optimist Brecht is stark: 'I am sending you here a poem that might be useful for Germany. It would be wonderful if you could make a couple of illustrations for it.' This was in 1947, and it is as though the preceding fifteen years had done nothing, could have done nothing, to shake Brecht in his educational project for German humanity. Grosz, probably, would not have believed in any of the concepts evoked: poem, illustration, usefulness, Germany, education or humanity! Flavell began her book by protesting at the image of Grosz as a nihilist, but she has brought us to that same point only by a long route. Grosz looks like an argument against evolution. 'Mild Monster Arrives' was how the *New York Times* announced him.

EDVARD MUNCH

Edvard Munch had the long, hinged, two-volume life of an apostle or a saint: 1863–1944. (By way of comparison, Knut Hamsun, with whom, bafflingly, he seemed to have so much in common and so little to do – Hamsun's biographer Robert Ferguson says that Munch simply quarrelled with everyone – lived from 1859 to 1952.) The hinge was a nervous breakdown in 1908–9, after which he spent much more time in Norway, won official recognition and yet lived as a virtual recluse, a monk, as his name suggests and signifies. The pictures in this exhibition are taken, bar one self-portrait of 1909, from the first half of his life, when he was a somewhat scandalous figure in Paris and Berlin.

There is a class of artist who, though startlingly handsome in appearance, tall and dark, solidly built, were nevertheless frail, haunted, imperilled creatures. In photographs, Munch looks imperturbable, rock-solid, a great-grandfather in the making – but he never married and was neurotic and unstable. In some of his pictures, his figures that are allegedly representative of himself are distorted out of recognition. One that shows him clearly is the lithograph, 'Self Portrait with Skeleton Arm', done when he was just thirty-one. The neck is rather ambiguous – clerical, military, severed? – so that the head alone looms white out of a special blackness he compounded from different inks. The handsome face is finely done, tender, almost veiled, the eyes deep and somewhere else, the large ears tapering down to the square chin, little ink on it, left almost white – in contrast to the crude, almost scribbled arm-bone resting along the bottom of the picture like a premature frame. The face and the fineness of it, the picture seems to say, are just one option; the violent arm is the other, and that will prevail. It is a challenge to himself and the viewer to see the skull beneath the skin.

Edvard Munch was the son of a deeply religious army surgeon and his much younger wife, a woman of peasant stock who died of tuberculosis when the boy was six. A sister died of TB

Review of *The Frieze of Life*, National Gallery, London,
12 November 1992 – 7 February 1993

also, and another ended up in a mental institution. In the some-
what lurid and hysterical prose that characterized him – Munch
wrote one autobiography, and painted another – he puts it like this:

> My mother came from strong-willed peasant stock, but tubercles had
> already attacked the roots. As you know, on my father's side my
> forefathers were poets, men of genius, but they too already showed
> signs of degeneration. When I was born, I was hurriedly christened,
> because no one supposed I would live. My mother already had the
> seeds of death in her. Six years later tuberculosis robbed five small
> children of their mother. Disease, madness and death were the black
> angels standing over my cradle. They accompanied me all my life.

The passage is pure nineties: mixed parentage, the doomed
scion, 99 per cent in love with easeful death. It could be early
Thomas Mann, stripped of irony and guile; it has the intensity
of parody. The way Munch began painting receives a similarly
literarized treatment: a quarrel with his father about the length
of time the damned were tormented in Hell, a visit to his father's
room to make things up with him, the sight of his father, seem-
ingly oblivious to his knocking, deep in prayer, and then: 'I shut
the door and went back to my room. I took out my sketchbook
and began to draw, I drew my father kneeling at his bedside.
The light from the bedside lamp cast a golden shimmer over his
nightshirt. I got out my box of paints and added colour. At last
I felt pleased with my drawing. I felt calm, and fell asleep right
away.' By 1880, in his eighteenth year, Munch had decided to
be a painter. He quickly became known on the Christiania scene,
dividing people into admirers and scornful opponents. In 1885,
he painted his first important pictures, 'The Day After', 'Puberty'
and 'The Sick Child'. Subsequent versions of the latter two – he
claims to have made twenty versions of 'The Sick Child' – are
included in *The Frieze of Life*.

In the next two decades, he lived mostly abroad. In 1889 and
1890, he went to Paris on Norwegian state scholarships; in
1892, he was offered a prestigious exhibition in Berlin, but when
his work was seen by the stuffy panel, he was controversially
disinvited. Public scandals and obscurely dramatic incidents are
a recurring feature of Munch's early years: if anything, though,
he used them to his advantage, as publicity, scenes and com-

ments in newspapers didn't seem to have much effect on him.
Germany was important to Munch, although he took much
from visits to France as well (Van Gogh, Gauguin, Toulouse-
Lautrec, print-making). There was a strand of French opinion
that was offended by him, that described him as 'literary' and
'Germanic', a 'barbarian'. Munch for his part would make dis-
paraging remarks on 'paintings of apples and crocked pots', and
in the catalogue his teacher, the Norwegian painter Christian
Krohg, is quoted hailing him as 'the father of Matissism' – a
rather too sibilant and somewhat nonsensical judgment.
Germans, not taking offence at Munch's 'Germanic' (nor
perhaps, for that matter, his 'barbarian') qualities, were his
buyers and patrons; he exhibited there regularly (a version of
The Frieze of Life was first shown in 1902 in Berlin); and
Germans from Macke and Beckmann to Goebbels (who sent
the – yes – 'Germanic' painter a birthday telegram in 1933)
took him to their hearts. Perhaps most interestingly of all, the
celebrated theatre director Max Reinhardt got him to design a
set for Ibsen's *Ghosts* on Ibsen's death in 1906. Though Munch
may have been technically unprepared for theatre work, it does
seem a wonderful idea. Reinhardt raved at the results: 'The
armchair says it all. That shade of black is the mood of the play.
And then the colour of the walls! Like diseased gums. We must
try to find wallpaper with that colour. It will put the actors in
the right frame of mind.'

Munch was bewilderingly – contradictorily – gifted as an
artist. A theatrical sense (stageyness, when it doesn't work) was
one of his prime qualities: the significant, rhythmic arrangement
of figures in a particular space, a sense of moment, of different
characters responding separately to a single drama. It is the-
atrical organization, blocking, use of the stage, not painterly
arrangement that you see in the picture 'Death in the Sickroom',
now with added colour – copper, drab green and blue – in an
oil version, with fleeing floorboards and carved faces in the
lithograph. Most artists with that ability to deploy figures would
make it their speciality: not Munch. He has, for a start, a
related but separate 'filmic' gift: a face or figure close-up, and a
background warping behind it (in 'The Voice' or 'Red Virginia
Creeper'). But many of his pictures are 'nowhere', they deny

space altogether; instead, the figure emanates vibrations or waves of feeling, of itself, like his 'Madonna'. Elsewhere, Munch shows a wonderful, classic appreciation of light: his 'Sick Child' is hungry for light and almost dissolves into it as it enters the painting from the right. The outcry provoked by that painting in Christiania in 1886, when it was first shown, appears quite inexplicable: it seems like other paintings of its time, only vastly better than most. In the 1890s, Munch developed an interest in etching, and many of his paintings were translated into the new medium; perhaps because of that, he can be associated with a simple, robust and sensational image, the kind of thing that thrives in reproduction, and survives (I would bet) shrinking down to the size of a postage stamp: 'The Heart', 'Separation II', 'Young Girl on the Shore', perhaps even the infamous 'Scream'. Munch can do other things, such as the claustrophobic and caricatural 'Green Room' sequence – not an authentic part of *The Frieze of Life* but added on to it by the present exhibition organizers – paintings that are called 'theatrical', but that actually seem to be enacted in a lift, and snapped by a fish-eye lens. His great skill, though, lies in the handling of paint and in the etchings of line and texture. Here he was a supreme master. Again, it appears there was nothing he couldn't do, from leaving the surface untouched to marks of every conceivable weight, delicacy and brutality. Such is his mastery of paint, and so fascinating and autotelic in its detail, it seems surprising that he didn't abandon figuration altogether; looked at purely as paint, in the right half of 'The Voice', say, the copper and indigo verticals of pines, or the brilliant boats, scarlet, gold and white in the top left against the blue water, are sensationally lovely.

Munch was occasionally criticized for his range, and it may be that he felt he had to work against it and offer some other coherence or consistency. In 1889, the idea of a thematic arrangement of his work came to him, the idea for *The Frieze of Life*. This was – or became – a movable feast. Some paintings would be sold and had to be replaced by others, new work had to be fitted in; it was, though, basically his work of the 1890s, made into cycles on 'Love', 'Anxiety' (a weak and implausible word in English, a smug sign over a drop) and 'Death'. It is this arrangement and selection that I find unsatisfactory.

It seems to be, for a start, the idea of a young man, someone with a keen sense of his own gifts but seduced into a premature packaging of them. Munch said 'my paintings are my diary', a humble and intimate function; and yet his 1893 exhibition (only his second in Berlin, he was thirty) was entitled 'Eighteen Motifs from the Modern Life of the Soul' – pure period jargon and cant. Munch the diarist is plausible, but not Munch the dissector of souls, the preceptor, the thinker who followed Nietzsche in warning us about women, the guilty hellfire merchant whose pictures are painted as sermons. His experience was too narrow and too intense to be the basis for a series of lectures, and if that presumption was the movement of its time, the 1890s, why should we, a hundred years later, still have to endure them? They made Sin into a long drink, and sat over it until they fell off their bar-stools.

Second, there is the 'literary' quality of the work. In an interview of 1897, Munch was asked: 'Have you ever thought of writing instead of painting?' To which he replied: 'I have. And perhaps that's what I should have done. Almost everything you see started off as a manuscript.' Munch, it seems, commentated on almost all his paintings, and this incapacitates the exhibition. He is a first-class painter but a poor writer, who, in a literary decade and among a literary circle, put the former in service to the latter. The pictures are dependent on the prose – who can walk past a painting without reading what is written alongside it? – and the prose is basically *de trop*. The result is to show a commanding and innovative painter as the helpless victim of his own emotional storms. The characteristic 'delay' of most of Munch's paintings contributes to this: he may have called them his 'diary', but elsewhere he writes: 'I do not paint what I see – but what I saw.' His rounded, organic forms and corroded colours are hauled dripping from his memory – and from old literary accounts. His first love-affair with Millie Thaulow is reflected in his paintings of the 1890s; a shooting incident of 1902 when he lost the tip of his left middle finger is ludicrously melodramatized in paintings of 'The Murderess' and 'Death of Marat', five years later. 'An extraordinary life . . . almost like a novel', he claims, and the strenuous prose of it pushes the paintings around. O for an apple, or a jug, or the view from a window.

The Frieze of Life seems both small and maximalist: eighty-five works are exhibited (but only two or three dozen separate images – the rest are reworkings and variations), and to see Munch as a sage on the basis of these is to take him too seriously, and to take the worst of him at that: columns of moonlight as phallic symbols, men wrapped up, destroyed by the long hair of women, it is dreadfully obvious and unpersuasive. An exhibition drawing from the whole of Munch's life, one that would have freed itself from prose and biography and the Nervous Nineties, and brought out the modern painter, would have been preferable.

Munch always lived with his paintings. Just like Rodin as Rilke describes him, he liked to be surrounded by his work. When he sold pictures, he made copies of them for himself, and when he could afford to, he stopped selling. He repainted most of his motifs many times, sometimes conservatively, often in an evolutionary way. He kept copies of his portraits in a row, and called them his 'Life Guards'. His paintings generally were referred to as 'his children' – though, disconcertingly, he was an appalling curator to them, leaving them exposed to wind and weather. 'They're used to that', he would say, and 'When they get a few things wrong with them, then they'll be really good. Rather a good painting with ten holes in it than ten bad paintings with no holes.'

The Frieze of Life – never completed, never definitive – seems no more than an early manifestation, fortuitous and magniloquent, of Munch's habit of keeping his paintings together. Ironically, the most coherent group, 'The Green Room', was never even a part of it. There is, however, a handful of masterpieces in this exhibition: the second 'Voice', the first 'Kiss' (the almost entirely blue picture with the decentred couple behind the curtain), 'Evening on Karl Johan' (like an illustration for *Hunger*, as Robert Ferguson has said), 'Sick Child' and 'Self Portrait with Bottle of Wine'. However, what mostly stays with me is a composite memory of the others; a scene by a curved Northern strand, Darwinian rockpools, a livid sky, dead water more like the underground lakes in Jules Verne than the open sea (grim the soul it symbolizes, if it does), a man and a woman, or two men and a woman, heathery, licheny, parasitic colours, an ancient dissatisfaction.

ARTURO DI STEFANO

As I see it, Arturo Di Stefano's previous work (which I know from the catalogues of '91, '93 and '95, and a few stray pieces in studio and gallery) was broadly of two types: there were the enigmatic, even tormenting facades of buildings, public spaces, bits of architecture that commanded his attention and his extraordinary expertise; and then there were the human figures, many of them, gratifyingly enough, literary, as well as painters and mythological figures (often from the *Odyssey*), and portraits of family and friends. The two types of subject were kept rigidly apart, so far as I know. The separation invited you to see the architecture as the present (or maybe absent), and the human figures as the past and the future, they were Di Stefano paying his dues or aligning himself with A or B. Put them together – as he never did – and you get an oddly disjunctive, hesitant and fugitive autobiographical painter. An autobiographical painter – one thinks of Munch or Beckmann – is already something of a rarity, given that you are free not to be representational at all, and even if you are, a model or the view from a window or a bowl of fruit is all the subject you need; but an autobiographical painter in whom the self is bracketed out and invisible is even rarer! Here, I'm convinced, is the source of power and mystery in Di Stefano's work. The silent connection – the reason governing the choice of this building or that person – is palpably *there* in Di Stefano's pictures, but with impressive delicacy, he doesn't offer it to us. The places are his *haunts* and the people are his *familiars*, and the ghostly overtones of both words are absolutely appropriate. There is a kind of immanent narrative quality in many of the pictures that is never remotely made explicit (and that I, though I know Arturo a little, and have asked him about this and that, don't propose to make explicit now either!). The urgency of his repeated, almost obsessive approaches to places, sitters and subjects underscores – if that were needed – their necessity as images, and their part in an oeuvre that none of us can probably yet understand. To take just one example, what about Di Stefano's most characteristic

Catalogue copy for *Strands* by Arturo Di Stefano, Purdy Hicks Gallery, London, 22 October – 28 November 1998

subject, his arcades – represented in the new exhibition by
Arcades, Paris and *Camera Lucida*. Now, I suppose they have
their own almost étude-like value to the painter, in the geometry
of their recessional perspectives and their hardening colour; but
beyond that, what about the possible connection with Arcadia
('the ideal region of rural contentment' in my Oxford dictionary,
and thus identified wistfully or ironically or both with the Italy
of Di Stefano's forefathers); then, doesn't the narrowing shape
call to mind the passage taken by the arrow of Odysseus (arc =
bow), the way he ultimately proved his identity to wife and son
on his return, an image or emblem of the whole idea of return;
and I suppose too there is an allusion to the work of Walter
Benjamin in his Parisian exile, *Passagenarbeit*, he called it,
Arcades. And so something one might suppose merely to be
classicizing décor ends up being freighted, even fraught, with
meanings of exile and home, or both at once (see Di Stefano's
1992 painting *Sicilian Avenue, London*). In fact, the way the
titles are so often thickened by puns (*Penelope, Rove* I remember,
or *Strands* from the present show, or, I suspect, *Pier*), or by
allusions or misdirections, is utterly literary. They are the kind
of titles or plays I wouldn't be surprised to find a poem turning
on; but I hardly expected their ambiguous light to illuminate a
painting or a series of paintings. But there they are, probably
the most overt signalling of complexity in Di Stefano's work,
and you ignore or underestimate them at your peril.

There is the implicit suggestion that one might go to Di
Stefano's *vita* – born in 1955 in Huddersfield, the son of Italian
immigrants, school followed by art school in Liverpool, then
Goldsmiths and the Royal College of Art, based in London since
1974, visits to Italy, notably to Turin in 1986, married with a
young son, Piero, nothing too indiscreet there, I hope – for
a predictably disappointing 'explanation'. A fuller and more
helpful way of bringing people and places together might be
sought in the area of technique: the extraordinary array of
impairments, scratchings, removings, jumblings, patternings,
scribblings, mirrorings (in the etchings) and re-mirrorings to
which Di Stefano subjects his painstakingly accurate images,
giving rise to the grave and frail 'Sudaria' sequence of 1986, the
somehow 'speaking' series of artists' portraits of 1989–90, or

the blurring and smudging that makes the sky seem to bleed in the fantastic 1994 painting, *Royal College Street* NW1 (aptly, as it's where Rimbaud and Verlaine housed together for a time in 1873 – a further instance of buried content in the work lurking behind the anodyne, even misleading title – it's nothing to do with the college where Di Stefano was a student!). These defacements, which Di Stefano has found ways of producing in the many different media he uses (notably, here, in the absolutely charming series of aquatints called *Strands*), seem somehow to lend solidity to the world in his paintings, the sky, the pavements, the concrete and stone facings, and to make his human shapes even more imperilled and ghostly in their eloquence.

I'm sure people have written more authoritatively – are even now writing more authoritatively – about Di Stefano's technique, but I have a little to say about it too. It is, firstly – modestly, destructively, hair-raisingly – a way of unmaking. I remember reading how Caspar David Friedrich's wife let it be known that her husband should not be approached on days when he was painting sky; I imagine Di Stefano's overpainting, varnishing, and then papering and part-stripping his canvases, first, disposably, with newspaper, lately with good Japanese paper on which the results were preserved as 'counterproofs', would be his equivalent. Certainly, it would be a wonderful and alarming thing to witness. But even without being in a position to 'report from the front', as it were, I see it as a terribly evocative type of procedure. It is to reinstate chance after the exercise of his own skill as draughtsman and painter. To unmake, having made – like Penelope at her loom. To split colours, as, curiously, the paintings and counterproofs have completely different sets of tonalities from one another, as well as movements and rhythms. To peel off a bandage from a fresh wound. To lend an impression of speed to something static – for instance, in the wonderfully brooding *Crucifix Lane* SE1. To strengthen the sense of absence by the 'wiped' effect – we seem to be seeing the dying echo of a human aura, to be witnessing the immediate aftermath of something. To give the paintings almost a non-visual dimension, in the way that in an imperfect electrical circuit, some of the power goes on heat and noise; look at *Crucifix Lane* SE1 for long enough, and it will rustle at you like the soundtrack of an Antonioni shot. To show not the surface, but in each case, the middle, the epicentre of paint; this bringing the depth to the surface is what you might say Di Stefano endeavours to do in all his work. And perhaps last but not least to keep the possibility of the process in the mind of the looker, so that in instances in which Di Stefano has not used it – ironically, for example, in *Demolition Site, Mill Street* SE1 – we are aware of it, and feel it, that thin, integral blue of the sky, that scorched red of wall. There almost seems to be a kind of inversion, whereby the stripping and blurring of paint – or, in *The Smoke*, the barely controlled adding of patches of colour – seems to be an indication of human agency and possibility, something at any rate, that relieves the barely tolerable 'photographic' precision.

These 'findings' are variously put in question or muddled or carried forward by Arturo Di Stefano's new work. In some of the big paintings, especially *Camera Lucida* and *Pier*, there is almost a struggle for ascendancy between the human figures and a typically monumental and unyielding background. Does the presence of the people make the place more liveable? I find them difficult to read. Instead of inferring the human from the un-human, as I'm used to doing with Di Stefano, I almost find myself being asked to choose between them. In *Camera Lucida*, everything is so gridded and mapped, it's like graph-paper. The strange, hurtful collision between the Classical pillars and the 'Elizabethan' beams, the shutter behind the boy like an exercise book, and of course all the shadows just as intransigent. The colours are unwontedly harsh too, the stripe of lime at the edge, the burnt orange floor, the lavender wall. The little boy, all in white with his blue hoop for hope, seems to be standing at the starting line. Surprisingly, the painting seems to be still harsher and bleaker – I suppose because more vulnerable – than the obviously daunting and unpopulated *Crucifix Lane* SE1, with its massy Victorian commercial building, its steel railway arch (no train on it, this isn't Impressionism!), its marked tarmac that looks as though it's been washed with puddle-water, its unrelenting single-yellow lines, the black bollards and triangular road-sign, seen from behind, *stahlgrau*, all of it saying what a hard place this is, and how hard it is to have been put here but

somehow beautiful too, and inspiriting. The dark underpass is
where Sally Bowles goes to scream. By contrast, it seems to me
there is something nervous and mute in the paintings with people
in them. Perhaps it's to do with ownership: who holds the stage,
who prevails, why are the penguins such small sharp, marginal
figures in the house built and named for them? In Di Stefano's
unpopulated or unpeopled paintings, there is no question but
that we are, in the words of the American poet Robert Lowell,
'poor passing facts'. Their hero is the city of London, almost
imperceptibly lived in, bulky and massive and surviving as we
who in our lifetimes will only add or take away a few crumbs
of grime from its epidermis, will not survive. Di Stefano's diffi-
culty – or more likely mine – comes from the attempt to switch
his attention and his faith away from the unreflecting and imper-
sonal city to a chosen personal group. *Pier*, equivocating between
the pier and Piero, is in a kind of tense suspension. The Germans
have a proverb, all beginnings are difficult, and it looks to me
as though Di Stefano has got himself a new myth; after years
of thinking about the *Odyssey*, this new group is closer to the
little band with which Aeneas came to Rome.

In the three 'Dutch interiors', we are back on more familiar
terrain, though with a difference. They are like an indoor version
of Di Stefano's outdoor nooks and corners of buildings, sec-
tions of parks and streets and public space. Just as with the
outdoor pictures, we see how marked and un-pristine everything
is. Just as with them, we are left not knowing why this motif
or that view, but the raptness, even the unlikeliness of it, assures
us that there is a reason. What is so brave about these paintings,
and sets them apart from even such wonderful early works like
Royal College Street NW1 or *Orange Street* WC2, is the utter
lack of character of their subjects. In earlier paintings, Di Stefano
was able to discover a lurking character or a hidden story in
scenes that most of us would have passed by, all unawares. The
revelation of *85 Rokin, Amsterdam Stedelijk Museum,
Amsterdam* and *Stairs, Stedelijk Museum* is the revelation of
anonymity. The weary perspective, the parquet desert, the *pas
perdus* of the modern museum; the two-tone passageway
(redolent of hospital or municipal building), the door-bell and
(conjecturally) name-plate, the doormat with the alien and

inturned *Welkom* on it, and all the little security details on the door – doorknob, two mortice locks, and Yale; and then the grey concrete stairway, plastic-coated banisters set in the wall. Surely all this is the unspoken becoming the unspeakable? What else do all these subjects say, other than 'we are unworthy. We should be better than what we are. We should have had red and blue and yellow (beyond the yellow of the letter box in the passage). We should have had light and life.' These are the inert things – the door no one comes through, the stairs that don't lead up or down, the gallery walls with no art on them, only power-points – through which a life passes, the coffee-spoons of Prufrock, or the water-glass that is handed to the king in Rilke's wonderful sonnet called *Ein Frauen-Schicksal*. Only *these* things, once touched, are not thrown away, because unlike us, they are permanent. They are relics of no religion and of no intrinsic aesthetic worth (only un-worth!), but still they somehow contain us and are valuable to us, because they were once – presumably – brushed by a certain hand, and a certain eye. They experienced, unlikely though it may appear, a miracle. A great soul once gave them something of himself. And that is what Di Stefano shows us in his painting, and what he gives us too, when he looks at our streets, our buildings, our city.

PERICLES

Families nowadays might be heroic, but that doesn't make it any easier to relish them as heroes, which is what *Pericles* proposes. Imagine the *Odyssey* with Odysseus replaced by a collective (all right, the Trinity of Husband, Wife and Holy Daughter), and you have *Pericles*. Restrict to a mere half-dozen locations scattered over the Eastern Mediterranean, put in nine sea-voyages to connect them up again, add an emcee called Gower with a wicked tetrameter ('To sing a song that old was sung, / From ashes ancient Gower is come') and you have what in *Fanny Hill* was called *le tout*.

For the director of what might be called an 'interestingly bad' play (it is uncertain how much of it is Shakespeare and when), there are broadly two alternatives: a po-faced and rather embarrassing doctrinal approach, playing it for the – only very intermittent – poetry, stressing Diana and chastity and family values and hanging everything on the emotion at the reunion, or a show based on music, spectacle, Mark Thompson's design and Jonathan Lunn's choreography. Phyllida Lloyd, obviously, and to the delight of the audience, has gone for the latter. The 'message' and even the general drift of the action are as nothing to the pleasure and diversity and surprise of the individual episodes. The motto for the production might have been 'Top that!' as the funny hats come on, the ones that look like cheese-makers' and then the beekeepers', the padded bottoms and the farthingales, the aquamarine Tyrians and white Pentapolitans, knitted Assyrian beards and marcelled astrakhan hair, the stick-fighting and bull-fighting and tumbling, the hoisting into the flies or lowering into the drum, the revolve spinning, tilting, once almost upside down but rarely still. One thinks of Candide or Gulliver or Alice in the rapid, sometimes gormless and (for all the visuals) still talky toing-and-froing of Pericles (played by Douglas Hodge); of Fellini's *Satyricon*; or, perhaps most of all, of the dippy music films of the 1960s (similarly, the group as hero, and the same plot idea: Band Member Goes Missing) with

Review of Shakespeare's *Pericles*, Royal National Theatre, London, 1994

the Beatles or the Monkees or Amen Corner for all I know. A
potentially rather prissy play is thus gloriously subverted to (or
is it: by?) a tolerant and swinging vision of ancient coastal
civilizations, be they African or Eskimo, *qu'importe*, anthro-
pology, ethnography, the most comprehensive and purposeful
cross-casting I have ever seen, and the family at the end, a frail,
almost random assortment who have never lived together, and
solicitously surrounded by white-clad figures that look sus-
piciously like doctors or analysts, but are actually nothing worse
than the acolytes of Diana.

The text is quite regularly undercut – and is probably the
better for it. Hodge, as it might be, or Henry Goodman playing
Gower, look around oddly and apprehensively after delivering
themselves of their lines (as though thinking, 'Who wrote this
guff?'). 'A crew of pirates came and rescued me', Marina (played
by the Irish actress Susan Lynch) tells Pericles, with much rolling
of eyes. As Gower gives the good tidings to the Pentapolitans,
'Our heir-apparent is a king!/ Who dreamed, who thought of
such a thing?' Hodge stands there modestly with an aw-shucks
expression. 'When peers thus knit, a kingdom ever stands', the
stuff of the Histories, is delivered with contemptuous ponderous-
ness by Helicanus (engagingly played by Selina Cadell).
Occasional wordplay is ignored (better than trying to make
something of it). But then, in the midst of all this, words fly out
and catch in the audience: in II i, Pericles' comparison of the
sea to a tennis-court; his 'a man throng'd up with cold'; the
'puddings and flapjacks' of a fisherman in a classic Shake-
spearean prose-scene, the language typically compressed and
fascinating. The brothel scenes in IV are similar: Boult's (Toby
Jones) 'Performance shall follow', his beautiful, wheedling 'Oh
sir, I can be modest', and many of the words of the Bawd (one
of three parts played and animated to their fingertips by the
incredible Kathryn Hunter), Jagger-ishly drawled and purred
and chewed: 'creatures', 'continual', 'action', 'qualities'. For the
audience, the experience is the gradual incarnation of Shake-
speare (it is claimed he wrote most of the last three acts).

With Lloyd and Thompson, the choreography of Jonathan
Lunn and the percussion-driven music of Gary Yershon (often
close to the Eastern fringes of the Beatles), *Pericles* is presented

as a ravishingly superficial spectacle (but, of course, there *is* no depth of character), Douglas Hodge in his *Sgt Pepper's* drummer-boy jacket, a playing-card king. In his sorrow he grows first his hair, then a Rasputin (or, more likely, Roy Wood) beard. For the happy family ending, he is shaved and trimmed. The people of Tarsus are poor and starving; he tosses them mimed food, they twist off their dust-coloured wrappers and flower in red-and-yellow. The Ephesians are cargo-culters, with old bathtubs and an elephant's-foot umbrella holder. For the reconciliation scene, the revolve is tipped right over, a hole in the middle is open, the steel struts and unconcentric circles look like Mount Palomar or something, the stars come on, and Pericles babbles about the music of the spheres. I think this is as good a production as three hours can get you; it would take about seven to produce mythic depth and to dissipate the words sufficiently.

EUGENE O'NEILL

Two qualities characterize Peter Stein as a director: a fanatical attention to detail, and a seemingly limitless technical ambition. His production of *The Hairy Ape,* in his own admirably slangy German translation, is as intensive and extensive as anything I have ever seen: it is a staggering accomplishment, a cathedral display of theatrical vision and expertise.

When the curtain first rises, it reveals the proscenium arch entirely taken up with a riveted, grinding, uneasy surface of steel plates. When these eventually part, it is at a point some twenty or thirty feet above the stage, and it is at this unfamiliar and exhilarating height that we see the first scene unfold of Eugene O'Neill's anti-capitalist tragedy of the stoker Yank. There are sixteen stokers, stooped and grimy and stripped to the waist, bawling and drinking and playing music in their iron-furnished cage in the steerage. They drift loosely and dangerously from one point of interest and authority to another, from Long, the socialist agitator – who pathetically stands up on a soap box, which, in that confined space, means that he has to stand bent double – to Paddy, the old Irishman who has seen clipper ships, to Yank, their backbone and spirit and spokesman who declares himself alive by virtue of the twenty-five miles an hour his labour produces – without asking himself whom it benefits. O'Neill's strenuous stage-directions are carried out to the letter: the uproar 'swelling into a sort of unity', the 'Neanderthal' appearance of the men, and perhaps most crucially and powerfully, 'except for slight differentiation ... all these men are alike'. Their matted hair hangs into faces dominated by high foreheads and prognathous jaws, their limbs resemble grey, oiled tubular steel, they do the ironic choruses (at the concepts of love, justice or God) 'of hard, barking laughter' with a will, and even – a clever touch of Stein's – fall in with the conclusions of speeches, showing their utter familiarity with arguments that are as issueless as the cycle of labour in which they are trapped.

For the next scene, one has to crane one's neck even more: it

Review of Eugene O'Neill's *The Hairy Ape*, Royal National Theatre, London, 1987 is up on deck, and so, accordingly, at the very summit of the towering steel hull. Against a passerelle, with the ironic presence of a couple of foghorns next to them, are Mildred, sociologist, slum-voyeur and millionaire daughter of the owner of 'Nazareth Steel', and her aunt and chaperone, viciously slagging each other off. Stein's interpretation of the text has them every bit as limited and entrapped as the stokers – their passerelle is only a more agreeable kind of cage – and they too are played as apes: always swaying and changing position, the vermilion aunt with her fist pressed to her hip; even the wax-white, cloche-hatted, pneumatic Mildred belongs only to some particularly exquisite subspecies.

The pointing of these underlying affinities is a feature of the production. In O'Neill's text, it is only Yank and the stokers who are apes, and caged in steel; in Stein's brilliant interpretation, it is everyone: the capitalists and their feathered wives, screeching and squawking in the Fifth Avenue scene, the policemen falling over each other to club Yank, the prisoners in the 'Zoo', the trade-unionists in their male nest, and the apes themselves. When Stein has the reactionary Senator Queen speak from a lofty balcony, we see with horror and disgust that his knee curls over the parapet in an uncontrollable simianism.

Lucio Fanti's astonishing designs, for all their breathtaking variety, always have steel bars as a kind of vestigial presence, while their savage inclines suggest the unfairness of society. Even the flat upper-deck of the calm voyage (the only scene, I think, played on a horizontal plane) allows the two women as little headroom as the stokers in their hold. Stein has made O'Neill's play deeper and darker; the class stereotypes are all poisoned, so that even revolution could change nothing of man's essential nature, of chattering in groups behind bars: the Industrial Workers of the World are played, scathingly, as a harmless act. The most human sounds are those produced by the apes in their cages, whimpering as Yank is killed; and the favourite pose of the gorilla is Rodin's 'Thinker'. Everyone associated with this production deserves to have their reputation enhanced: be they the Schaubühne Company, the West German Embassy, or Mercedes Benz.

ÖDÖN VON HORVÁTH

Glaube, Liebe, Hoffnung was in production in Berlin in 1933 when it was abandoned as the Nazis came to power; it was eventually premièred in 1936 in Vienna. Now, in Christopher Hampton's translation, it is presented in Britain for the first time. The play is about a young woman, Elizabeth (played by Julia Ormond), who is gradually destroyed by the consequences of a trivial infraction of the law. It is set in the world of 'die kleinen Paragraphen' (the little laws); and is based on a true story told to Horváth by Lukas Kristl, a court reporter who is credited as co-author. The play carries the subtitle *A Little Dance of Death*; it would have a strong claim to Hardy's epigraph for *Jude the Obscure*: 'The letter killeth'.

Horváth is one of the great idiosyncratic writers of the century. Hampton, who has already translated two of his plays, and installed his ghost as narrator in his own play *Tales from Hollywood*, has been smitten with him for years. Heribert Sasse has been brought over from Berlin to direct. *Faith, Hope and Charity* is a handsome, munificent production, with at one point a dole queue of thirty or forty people stretched right across the stage; with a stucco arcade in just the right Austro-Bavarian shade of mustard yellow; with a saxophone player sitting on the revolve in a dead-eye spotlight. No half-measures or cutting corners. And yet it is such a desperately disappointing evening that one is hard put to account for it.

Part of the problem is the picturesqueness. There is no hint of sordor or stray parts about the Anatomical Institute, the handsome mustard building. The lighting, by Sasse and Leonard Tucker, is positively Mediterranean. The 'minimal front garden' of the Social Security Office might be an Italian piazza; some negligent patron has kindly left bentwood chairs and marble-topped tables lying around. The set breathes culture, leisure and human scale; the small Bavarian shopping street might have seen a millennium of peace and pigs' trotters. Surely, nothing will happen to you, so long as you remember to greet the

Review of Ödön von Horváth's *Faith, Hope and Charity*, trans.
Christopher Hampton, Lyric Theatre, Hammersmith, London, 1989

neighbours and sweep outside the front door. But – 'There'll be civil war soon, it's just insanity.' A couple of shots ring out, raffish bobbies rush on to the stage, their whistles thrill in your ears like hummingbirds. It might be a Monty Python sketch.

Just as disabling is the language. Much of Horváth's fascination comes from his ear for the corruption and clichés of speech. There is macabre humour in the way that his unemployed speak like bureaucrats, and his little people come on like 'little paragraphs'. The suggestion is that there is a horrible collusion between victim and oppressor: the human grist volunteers for service in the State's mills. Horváth's diagnosis was made for the 1930s, but it is instructive for any society that promotes cravenness, conformism and fear of officialdom in its citizens. This doesn't come through in Christopher Hampton's translation, though it may not be entirely his fault. The genius of the English language is wrong for it. There is no English equivalent of *Amtsdeutsch* – 'legalese' is just another form of 'gobbledygook'. English is naturally unfussy, demotic, debunking. It has little tolerance for pompousness, mystification, specialization. Inarticulateness is respected as a sanctuary. Speech does not confer power. All this makes Horváth impossible. How can you have a bureaucratic tragedy, where 'kleine Paragraphen' – practically the murder weapon here – is translated as 'pissy rules'? How can the plain-clothes policeman who turns up in Elizabeth's (exquisite) garret be seen as one of the Furies? He appears more like a mild pervert who has happened along. The linguistic and psychological springs of the play have been broken. The production is quite extraordinarily lacking in menace; normalcy stands in for caricature (the dissectors are decent enough chaps really); apart from a few Alan Bennett-like lines such as 'I shouldn't climb steps with my glands', the humour is gone. It is lumpy, slow and abruptly, over.

THOMAS BERNHARD

I was curious to see how Thomas Bernhard, the monologist in prose, would arrange himself with drama: the answer is that he doesn't. For all that *Elisabeth II* (why the 's'? She's not Austrian) sounds like a history play, and, unbelievably, has a cast of thirty-two to match – a nervous ripple goes through the *klein aber fein* audience when one of the characters asks, 'Is there actually room for forty people here?' – the play is basically a monologue. The other thirty-one pile on to the scales against him, but Herrenstein (literally 'Masterstone', commandingly played by Julian Curry) remains unmoved.

As perhaps happens in the theatre more readily than in real life, the wheelchair is a seat of tyrannical and eccentric power. The crippled magnate Herrenstein is like a cold sun. His two old retainers, manservant/companion/lover(?) Richard, with twenty-five years of service, and Fräulein Zallinger, with forty-two, are his closest satellites; beyond them are Victor, his nephew, and Holzinger, his business associate; and beyond them the space-dust and asteroid belt of Viennese society as it raucously, greedily and hypocritically spills into his flat on the Ringstrasse to wave at Her Britannic Majesty on the occasion of a royal visit. The tiny Gate stage pluckily plays the enormous flat, there is a greenish simulacrum of daylight outside the curving French windows giving on to the balcony at the back, and the whole thing happens practically in real time. An average but none the less historic day in Herrenstein's life: breakfast with Richard; a business visit from Holzinger at eleven; at twelve, a buffet for forty people (the Top 40) who want to catch the Queen before going on to the funeral of a jeweller at three, for which everyone is already blacked up. If there seems to be a kind of sarcastic sneer at such a diary, well, there is. Bernhard never expressed much relish for human society.

As a real, as it were drawing-room, character, Herrenstein of course doesn't stand up. One knows of no industrialist (weapons, I believe) so widely read in literature and philosophy,

Review of Thomas Bernhard's *Elisabeth II*, trans. Meredith Oakes,
Gate Theatre, London

musical, misanthropic, virulently anti-Nazi, so scathing about Austrian society, the piano, the Burgtheater. These are all Bernhard's own positions, and Herrenstein is merely a stone set rolling by his master, Bernhard: a wielder of theatrical power, a speaker of crushing, zanily poetic judgments, a man who has suffered all the pain and outrage of life and voices it.

If a Greek dramatist had ever written a play in which the protagonist, a man of undoubted scale, had abused and humiliated all the other characters, entertaining a special hatred for the Chorus, whom he had finally sent to their deaths in an offstage catastrophe – such a play, one would say, would be an antecedent for *Elisabeth II*. As none exists, I am reduced to describing Herrenstein and his creator as Promethean.

The play is wall-to-wall spleen. But then, one goes to Bernhard for Bernhard, not for variety. Words like 'curmudgeonly' and 'crotchety' and 'crusty' suggest themselves, but they are all short-run and Bernhard is marathon and epic, and never draws breath. He stays crusty to the bottom of the glass. There are plenty of laughs, but aren't there always? Bernhard isn't funny, though, he is so frighteningly sour that people laugh out of fear: 'I don't think I'm going to that nest of Nazis any more. The most beautiful parts of Austria have always attracted the most Nazis.' (The translation by Meredith Oakes is admirable.) In his will, Bernhard banned all productions of any of his plays in Austria, and, watching *Elisabeth II*, I imagine it was something related to this laughter: he didn't want Austrians to go to his plays and amuse themselves, question the legitimacy of his birth and the naturalness of his death in the intervals, amuse themselves some more, and go home feeling reformed, shriven and progressive.

David Fielding has directed and designed with the attention to detail and professionalism one always expects at the Gate. Julian Critchley would have approved Herrenstein's aristocratic suit with its four-button cuffs and sheer socks, with Richard in a shinier two-button servitor's version (Ian Gelder is quite superb: repressed, wary and emollient, a politician-class performance). The black and white formality of it all reminds me of Beckmann's paintings: a modern evening carapace, but the same sense that at midnight everyone will be in tigerskins, swinging clubs.

FRIEDRICH DÜRRENMATT

Max Frisch called *The Visit* 'the greatest play in the German language since Brecht', and he may be right, but the comparison, if pursued, would be severely to Friedrich Dürrenmatt's disadvantage; Brecht has it all over him in wit, dramatic richness, depth of characterization and purpose.

The Visit is a theatrical fable for the classroom. Even in Maurice Valency's up-to-date adaptation, and no doubt kicked around by the company, the story of a monstrous and monstrously wealthy old lady, Clara Zachanassian, visiting her hard-up small-town birthplace of Güllen and offering 'one beellion' for the life of her rascally former lover Alfred Schill, remains resolutely un-thought-provoking: it never leaves the theatre. One N. Tolschenova once said *The Visit* was 'a play about the secrets of fascism' – but only if one is determined to think it so. In fact, I strained to think of it in relation to the assimilation of East Germany, or the privatization of Poland, but its jokes and hints were never anything more: the audience tittered at the refrain 'But this is Europe!' and references to the IMF and newscasters called Jeremy, but we were never made to feel uncomfortable. Perhaps the play cuts off too soon, just where things get interesting: what happens to the good people of Güllen once they have committed their collective murder and been recapitalized: do they get into guilt or gilts? The play seems what it is, a tinny contraption not much better than a mousetrap. That said, it does get an enjoyable outing in Théâtre de Complicité's vigorous production, in which Kathryn Hunter as the old lady is quite outstanding.

If she is one star of the production, the two others are Rae Smith's design, and the interplay of the company, who have lived with *The Visit* for three years now, with everyone doubling and tripling up. It is astonishing to check the programme afterwards and see it has been mounted with a cast of only eleven. The production by Annabel Arden, with Simon McBurney, is rich and busy, with a lot to look at and listen to. Individual

Review of Friedrich Dürrenmatt's *The Visit*, trans. Maurice Valency,
Royal National Theatre, London, 1991

moments have been brought out quite brilliantly; magic tricks, spoof ballet and choruses of Rod Stewart's 'Sailing' and 'There's only one Clara Wascher' (Zachanassian's maiden name) are both wildly eccentric and perfectly apt. The internationalism of the cast is also used to good effect, with a babel of reporters and Lilo Baur chattering away in her native Swiss. It is sometimes a bit madcap, and it does lack all menace. What most hurts the production is Simon McBurney's performance as the sacrificial victim Schill, a role in which the guying and laddish actor seems strenuously ill at ease.

Covering the back of the stage and both sides are what look like enormous abstract expressionist canvases, bright orange at the bottom shading into battle grey at the top. They are roughened or texturized by having old clothes, shirts, trousers and dresses stuck to them. They are the human equivalent of coral. Their detail and relief means they take Luke Sapsed's lights wonderfully and are extremely adaptable and responsive. There is a similar effect in Clara's balcony which is stuck with corsets. The use of cloth suggests, variously, entrapment, compromise and mastery: the hauling of immense sheets over tables for Clara's civic reception and for the judgment scene at the end, the scattering of confetti, and above all Clara's wedding dress, which trails for a sensational twenty yards behind Hunter's tiny dogged gimping frame, glad rags of brocade and bunny fur. No doubt she adds to it with every husband, more corsets appear on her balcony, and the backdrop of Güllen will grow and grey.

Hunter's outfits give her a wonderful start: little tsarina fur bonnets, cruel 1950s shades, bejewelled 'Louis XV' crutches like gold-plated twiglets (though mourning is worn in the last scene, such is the attention to detail of the production and the design), and an array of boots and miniskirts: the look is fantastic senile ice-dancer, equal parts sex, wealth and infirmity. She speaks in low tones, enunciating brutally with out-turned lips in an accent somewhere east and south of Vienna – perhaps she caught it from her husband's Armenian oil-wells. Her movements are clockwork and pain. In perhaps the best scene in the play, she zigzags across the stage like the business end of a centipede, dragging her train behind her, and mounts of all things a ladder to smoke a cigar; whereupon the town doctor and schoolmistress scale an eight-foot wall and crawl and hurdle their way through a variety of obstacles to put their case for the regeneration of the town to her: a totally physical account of the difficulty of coming to money, and the inaccessibility that money confers.

VOYAGER

The story, simply, is this: Faber (Sam Shepard) likes to travel. He likes to travel alone. But as he is so irresistibly attractive, women are forever wanting to accompany him wherever he goes. Stewardesses leave their planes carrying his suitcases. The woman he writes a 'Dear John' to – she is called 'Ivy' because she clings, but all women cling – has the gall to be waiting back in his apartment with a lobster dinner and floral wrap. Clingwrap. The woman at the beginning, which is also the end, an archaeologist in Athens (Barbara Sukova), wants to fly away with him. But unfortunately the one person he could stand to travel with, he can't: first, because she died, and second, because he's learned that she is his daughter.

Astonishingly, this shoddy, self-regarding and sentimental plot (taken from the novel *Homo Faber* by the late Max Frisch) presents itself as tragedy. From the stupefying and irrelevant distance of June 1957, Faber tells us, in the way he tells us most things in this most undramatic and unfilmic of films – in Shepard's affectless voice-over – that his life is ruined. 'What I wished was that I'd never existed at all', he says, his words taking up a refrain of Classical tragedy. Like Oedipus, he fears for his eyesight. The final scene shows him in Athens airport, waiting for the Furies to arrive (or is it just that he doesn't want to board?). Really, you need Oscar Wilde's heart of stone not to laugh at this snobbish and portentous piece of film-making by Volker Schlöndorff, after Frisch's worthless and dated original.

Voyager is – possibly unconsciously – a catalogue of failed attitudes and aspirations from the 1950s. There is the coquetry with taboos and with Classical mythology. There is the hunt for a new type of hero, a man from the New World, a technocrat, a man of facts; Faber builds dams. His answers to three successive questions are: 'I'm an engineer', 'No thanks. I don't read fiction', and 'I don't dream either'. (Frisch, himself an architect, wasn't joking then, and I don't suppose Schlöndorff is now.) There is Existentialism, or preferably just an Existentialist who hasn't

Review of *Voyager*, dir. Volker Schlöndorff, 1991

been told, who knows of Sartre only that he's 'that Existentialist guy who wears black and drinks espressos'. (Don't worry, that's good enough.) He can then be let loose agnostically in front of Europe's cultural sites, a passionless traveller. Finally, there's the looking for new arrangements for men and women to live together – though the results look to me like the usual male chauvinist pipe dream. All these things are finished, passé, discredited. No one takes them seriously any more. These are the 1990s: a hurrah goes up each time a dam *isn't* built. How Schlöndorff can set himself (s)lavishly to make a film of them is baffling.

What's left is costume drama. Fair-haired, round-faced Elizabeth Piper (Julie Delpy) in a series of nice frocks and stripy T-shirts, lean, taciturn Sam Shepard, in hat and horn rims, in stunning Armani suits that have lines like the very best skyscrapers, wearing his hat and vest (undershirt, that is) in bed like Crocodile Dundee, freckles on his palpable Nebraska farmer's shoulders; old cars offering you money on the screen, old boats, old buildings, best of all an old aeroplane.

As a director, Schlöndorff's forte lies in making things look nice. *Voyager* has no drama, a dead agenda, a foolish breathless rhythm (there can't be many films that make a Mexican funeral disappear as though it had never been), strikingly ineffective intimate scenes, indeterminate relationships (I have no real sense of how they are together, Shepard and Delpy), over-explicit casting – but it does look good. It does. It is very well framed and lit, and the colours are about as deep and pleasing and well composed as in any film I have seen. However, it is a little static – it is more like looking at a sequence of beautiful photographs than a film – a little packed and a little obvious. In a scene in Paris where the two leads are having lunch, not only does a fight break out in the background, but a drunkard in the foreground looks straight out of Cézanne. The lunch itself? She was hungry. He paid. He looked at her through the window afterwards. The dialogue? Something about an extra cup of coffee. Schlöndorff can't seem to get words and pictures to work together, a fair old disadvantage if your business is making films.

WINGS OF DESIRE

The sky over Berlin – the original and more apposite title for
Wings of Desire – is populated by a heavenly host. All-seeing,
all-hearing and invisible (except to children and the camera),
they pad about, pick up the babble of people's worries, follow
the destiny of a particular individual, swap titbits of news with
their colleagues. I take them to be recording angels, they have
little power to intervene in people's lives. They are suave crea-
tures, a little reminiscent of otters, and their get-up – which
promises to be as influential as any since Werther's 200 years
ago – consists of long tweed coats, woollen scarves, slick hair
and thin ponytails. On both occasions when I saw the film,
there were already angels plainly visible in the audience.

Damiel (Bruno Ganz) and Cassiel (Otto Sander) would appear
to work in some angelic leisure division: they hang out at monu-
ments, a public library, an up-market car showroom, a film-set,
a circus. Thus, they suffer more keenly than most the discontent
of the divine bystander; at one point, they trade lists of human
sensations and experiences: what it must be like to feed the cat,
to blacken one's fingers reading the newspaper, to eat roast
lamb. What finally leads Damiel to take the plunge is the sight
of the trapeze artiste Marion (Solveig Dommartin). But, with
the human story only just beginning – it is, I think, the first
man–woman couple at the centre of a film by Wim Wenders –
and cries of 'Nous sommes embarqués!' ringing out, the film
ends. The promise 'To be continued' rolls up before the credits,
but that may be perfidious English. *Wings of Desire* is only
prehistory.

Wenders has set himself a formidable range of tasks for this
film: to say something about love, to say something about Berlin
and its history, to make a film-essay on the singularity and
intensity of life on earth. (Imagine, for this last, Rilke's *Duino
Elegies* on celluloid, and you will have some idea of the rather
hallowed atmosphere of great stretches of *Wings of Desire*.) He
has used a daunting array of means: the film begins in black and

Review of *Wings of Desire*, dir. Wim Wenders, 1988

white and ends in colour; encompasses accelerated sequences, historical footage of bombed Berlin, and the gorgeous camerawork of the veteran French cinematographer Henri Alekan, full of long, curving, inquisitive shots. It is also remarkably full of words, many of·them in lengthy poetic catalogues spoken in voice-over. And it finds room for a great deal of music (by Jürgen Knieper). Its climactic scene at a Nick Cave gig is easily the best concert footage I have ever seen.

In the end, intentions, messages and techniques crush the life out of the film. It is cosmic, static and romantic, where Wenders's best early work has been none of these. *Wings of Desire* is perfect kitsch: Kundera's 'the dictatorship of the heart', inducing feelings 'of a kind the multitudes can share'. Wenders, the brilliant improviser, has actually made a film groaning with unfreedom, with numerous false starts and false endings hedging it about, and swaddled in clouds at either end. He has come on like a godless, religionless prophet. He has made a glittering, stainless film in praise of – Yeats's word – mire. He has elicited from one of the most feeling and expressive actors in Europe, Bruno Ganz, a waxy and withheld performance as an angel, allowing him no interaction and only a dimpled readiness-to-smile. (Admittedly, once the wings are off, Ganz is tremendous in his half-hour as a human being; his walk past a row of shopfronts – wild and clownish and private – is worth the price of admission.) There is a debilitating solemnity, as though Wenders has kept one eye on craft and another on significance, and lost sight of his film.

UNTIL THE END OF THE WORLD

The dedications proliferate, the credits roll on seemingly forever now, with vast crews working in nine countries (the technical, financial and logistical management for the project is awesome to contemplate), a five-hour cut awaits release, international star actors – Max von Sydow, Jeanne Moreau, William Hurt – appear where there were once friends, chancers and whims, but the result is still – just – a distinctive Wim Wenders product, more confident, more sophisticated and more grandiosely chaotic than its predecessors, but with the same strengths as for twenty years now. The combination of Robby Müller's camera-work and a loud rock soundtrack communicates a physical thrill that only Nicolas Roeg and Jim Jarmusch in contemporary cinema can match. The other features and preoccupations that have come to overlay these it is less easy to be positive about.

To begin with, *Until the End of the World* is a caper movie, a two-dimensional and metaphysical quest-with-twists of the kind you get in strip cartoons and opera. It is set in 1999, with an Indian nuclear satellite out of control, and the world facing extinction. Into this situation – which is disappointingly rapidly lost sight of – steps Claire Tourneur (Solveig Dommartin), followed in short order by a couple of French bank-robbers, a hitch-hiker (William Hurt), an Australian bounty-hunter, Claire's novelist boyfriend, Gene (Sam Neill), and a German detective, the lugubrious Mr Winter (Rüdiger Vogler). This unstable ensemble goes careering round the world very enjoyably for an hour and a half or so – you expect them all to turn into *ghee* as they pursue each other round and round the corridor of one of those Tokyo hotels where there are no rooms, only wall-safes to sleep in – and finally goes to ground in the middle of Australia.

There, what is effectively a separate film begins. This one is a domestic sci-fi film about the William Hurt character, his parents, a whizz scientist and his blind wife (von Sydow and Moreau), and Claire. The project is to restore Moreau's sight

Review of *Until the End of the World*, dir. Wim Wenders, 1992

by a computerized camera, whose images are fed directly into the cerebral cortex, bypassing the eye and the retina altogether. When this succeeds and Moreau dies happily, almost a third film is broached when the invention is reversed and becomes a way of screening one's dreams – the vision of the angels in *Wings of Desire* – to which the two men and Claire become helplessly addicted. Claire is finally cured of 'the disease of images' by 'the healing power of words and stories' – she reads Gene's new novel – and returns to the real (sci-fi) world, which has miraculously survived: she has herself shot up into space, to work as a pollution-spotter for 'Greenspace' – no doubt in the space equivalent of a rubber dinghy. A fair swap for the rogue nuke.

Even by Wenders's standards, the film has been a long time coming – fifteen years since its first glimmerings, when his first sight of the Australian landscape 'seemed to cry out for a science-fiction story' – and is not necessarily the better for it. His tendency is to graft and overload initially simple-seeming ideas. Perhaps the five-hour version is the one to see; on the other hand, there is the German proverb 'less is more'. What is difficult about *Until the End of the World* is the number of ultimates that it proposes, one after the other: first the end of the world, then money, then love, then the restoration of vision, the watching of one's dreams, stories, and perhaps finally doing good in the world.

The problem is that Wenders gives the viewer too much to think about, and in too unfocused a way. Stylistically, there is no problem – and that's a tribute to the skill which he and his army of helpers are now able to bring to making films. The future is a *noir*-ish world – actually, it's more *brun*-ish – the 1940s with a little leather and metal; a few gadgets like video payphones, and pocket computers for the private dicks; brownish light, overcrowding, total mixture of races. The static final hour in Australia is largely indoors in a Prospero's cave that looks rather cheap and cheerful – tinfoil-and-binliner – less James Bond, even, than *Doctor Who*. The video images that so much is made of – both as positive and negative – are crudely reminiscent of Impressionist and Fauve paintings.

It is now obvious that – almost as much as with music –

Wenders was always smitten with technology: the Polaroid camera – one of the very first – in *Alice in the Cities* and later in *The American Friend*, the video camera in *Nick's Film*, the innumerable radios and tape- and record-players. Technological progress in his films has been at the expense of veracity, dignity and human interest. The belief in showing, in capturing something, implicit from his earliest films, has split and turned into a concern for medium on the one hand and message on the other. There is a technical fix. When one of the characters in *Kings of the Road* goes home to his father, the editor of a local paper, he sets up a message to him in the form of a page of newsprint, runs off one copy and leaves it with him. We don't see what he's written, or not much of it. But Sam (Hurt) goes around shooting the most cloying messages for his mother, so that the magic camera seems like merely a way of transmitting awful video greetings. The more improved the medium, the more impoverished the message.

Until the End of the World probably has more actors in it than all Wenders's previous films put together. He directs them beautifully – the ones you don't expect to be good (Neill, Dommartin) just as much as the ones you do (Moreau, von Sydow). Sometimes there are multitudes up on screen, it's like the theatre with spear-carriers. But it's not a film about people; it's a film about too many other things, and hence about nothing. Dommartin skips bare-legged through it all like Superwoman. The men biff each other once in jealousy, but the scene is a comic one. William Hurt speaks Peter Carey's crass lines (some change from the fey Peter Handke who wrote the screenplay for *Wings of Desire*), as though they weren't for real. The overall atmosphere is of a charmed harmlessness, serenity, absence of menace. It's a feelgood film. Nothing much is at stake. Hence its best moments are those where you forget about story and dialogue and the *auteur*'s preoccupations: Hurt and Dommartin trudging through the desert, chained for some reason to the door of a light aeroplane, with some raucous band on the soundtrack. It's magnificent. It's what Wenders can do, what he has always been able to do, and no one can touch him for it.

THE SACRIFICE

Despite its long running-time and essayistic freight, *The Sacrifice* may be reduced to a short parable: the man who sets his own house on fire has a son whom he has taught to water a dead tree, and who will go on doing so when his father is gone. The film begins and ends with the tree, a tall and spindly pine. It is dedicated, 'with hope and confidence', to Andrei Tarkovsky's son Andryosha.

The fruit that falls away from this hard, poetic core is strangely soft, mealy and half-hearted. At times, it seems as though Tarkovsky has pitched his film as far as possible from where he means it to go, and set himself the most arduous and circuitous journey. *The Sacrifice* is a plea to man to unhouse himself, and yet its stars are the two houses where most of it is shot, among old glass and old wood, wrought iron bedsteads and the liquid, waxy run of floorboards. It is about personal duty and personal salvation (the house and the tree), and yet in form it is a chamber piece and has taken on board half a dozen clamorous and ill-differentiated characters. It is against words, and yet it has a chattering screenplay of fifth-rate Chekhov, full of gripes and complaints, containing long passages of boned 'philosophizing' as Chekhov deprecatingly called it. It is anti-materialistic, and yet the best part of it is in the solid, sombre photography of Sven Nykvist with a noisy and physical sound-track. It is clearly Eastern in orientation – one thinks of the Hindu pattern of old age, giving away one's possessions, leaving one's house and becoming a beggar – and yet there are only two hints at this: Alexander's black yin-and-yang kimono, and someone's *mot* about Gandhi having one day a week on which he would not speak. Instead, it is shot on Gotland in the Baltic Sea, along the nuclear corridor of flatlands that runs down from Scandinavia through East Anglia and the Low Countries to Bavaria. It bothers with things like the doctor's decision to emigrate to Australia, and Adelaide's statement that she has loved one man and married another, conventional 'story-elements' that

Review of *The Sacrifice*, dir. Andrei Tarkovsky, 1987

can hardly have exercised Tarkovsky, and do not now exercise the viewer.

However, what we cannot help being exercised by is the hypothesis of destruction that Tarkovsky makes. At one time in the script the agency was illness, now it is nuclear war. (It makes little difference, it is something always available, and, though each occasion of its use may seem wanton to the spectator, that makes it no easier to resist.) It is this that leads Alexander (Erland Josephson) to pray and to offer to destroy or forsake his entire previous life. The television makes its announcement and falters, the electricity fails, the whole place turns the dead grey with ghosts of colour that befits this blend of catastrophe, the Dark Night and the Scandinavian night. As ever, human behaviour is not the strong point here; the characters are a huddle of variously expressive gargoyles, which is all they have to be. The conjunction of eros and terror is brought out in Susan Fleetwood's kicking hysterics on the floor, and in Alexander's half-fuddled, half-mystical decision to seek out Maria, one of the servants, in her house. 'Save me,' he says, 'save us all.' In the end, when the threat has been taken away again, as suddenly as it arose, it is only Alexander who has been changed by it, and who decides: 'Du musst dein Leben ändern.' The tree is more important than the house.

Tarkovsky's care and intensity in visual and tonal compositions are always more impressive than the organization and writing of the film. Perhaps his point is to load us with things we only want to ignore, to let us hear endless, meaningless chatter, to show us the soft pulp of modern life and show it collapsing. It is only by having to endure all that, that we are privileged to see his blue grass, to hear distant foghorns (the most articulate things in the film) and the singing of glasses shaken on a tray, and to watch the lovely effect whereby light and wind come in together through sheeted windows and doors.

JAMES BUCHAN

I don't believe this country has a better writer to offer than James Buchan. I can't think of anyone who concedes so much of his own intelligence to his protagonists – doesn't mock or belittle them – and gives them so much world to do battle with. I see no particular limitation to his scope or style: his stunningly curt dialogues and ravishing recitatives are equally persuasive. No one writes better short sentences; he has a strong grasp of form; an Occam-ish economy (this is his first book over two hundred pages); and is utterly without the factitiousness – the I'll-pretend-to-write-a-novel-and-you-pretend-to-read-it – that seems so current in England. In the end – though this is bizarre – he is probably a religious novelist, whose theme is salvation, though I'd be surprised if he's actually used the word anywhere. Most tantalizingly, he is still better than any of his books.

Two things set Buchan apart: first, his understanding of the factual world – I remember his magisterial reportages for the *Sunday Indy* on Thorp and on high-street banks – such things as politics, money and abroad; not forgetting how little such understanding counts for with others:

> Adam was often drunk at this time. He had been abroad a year but nobody much wanted to hear about it, least of all Mary, who did not like abroad and could manage only a smile of puzzled sympathy. (A *Parish of Rich Women*)

Buchan studied Persian and Arabic; he has worked in the Middle East, Europe and America; the German in the new book is demanding and faultless. Novelists tend to be amateurs of information, believing a little to go a long way; Buchan is a pro. Nor is this just another way of saying that he was for ten years a foreign correspondent of the *FT*; his authority (like Joseph Roth's, say) is altogether deeper, more committed, more structural, than that of journalism. He reminds me of Washington DC in Lowell's distich: 'The stiff spokes of this wheel/ touch the

Review of James Buchan, *Heart's Journey in Winter* (London: Harvill, 1995)

sore spots of the earth.' It is a complex, macro-historical, moral-aesthetic authority:

> The Osteria Ischiana is an Italian restaurant in the Remigiusstrasse in Bonn. Its wonder years were the late Forties, when Christian Democrat politicians, de-Nazified and with certificates in their waist-coat-pockets to prove it, spun webs of intrigue between the padded booths; when the Bundestag still convened among the stuffed animals at the Museum König a hundred yards away; and the political city had not yet marched south into the villa gardens, fields and allotments between the railway lines and the river; before the journalist-hutches and diplomat-silos had sprouted at the Tulpenfeld.
>
> By 1983, the restaurant had fattened in the yeasty Rhineland air. Women in hats and fur collars worked their way through extended midday meals. Flour and cream glutted the sauces. The pasta burst with egg yolk. But you could still sense, under the Rhenish phlegm, the warmth and genius of Italy. (*Heart's Journey in Winter*)

How animated history is here, by costume and cuisine and clientèle: the calorific content of democracy; peace and self-confidence translated into avoirdupois; a Caesar-like contempt as vision; an audible sigh for risk! Energy turns to mass, 'webs' to 'padded' to 'stuffed', minceur to Bonn femme. At the same time, though, there is a sinister military rumble under the contentment – the book is about the bringing of Cruise and Pershing missiles to Europe to counter the Soviet SS 20s – in 'marched' and 'silos' and 'burst'. The second thing, incidentally, about James Buchan is how extraordinarily well he writes: compared to his, how unthinking, unsupple and uninteresting most prose is.

Buchan's protagonists like to know things – they treat with the world on the plane of knowledge, co-terminous, almost indistinguishable (as above) from the plane of the senses. They are experts, connoisseurs. He uses the word 'good' in his novels in a very specific way, auctioneer's shorthand, cool but with an undertow of almost frantic valedictory feeling: 'good furniture', 'good paintings', 'such a good part of London', 'The black risotto is outstanding, if you like good things.' His protagonists are people of the utmost discrimination, and yet they are able to take correspondingly little comfort from it. If anything, it seems to be a further source of danger to them: Adam, in *A Parish of Rich Women*, intensely knowledgeable about Middle

Eastern politics, unable to save his Chelsea friends from heroin addiction and himself from taking his chances in West Beirut; John Chadwick, who leaves the City to pay for the running-costs of his wife's damp and dilapidated house in Italy with dodgy investments and asset sales, in *Davy Chadwick*; Richard Verey in *Slide*, after spells in the Foreign Service and on Wall Street, effectively on the run from himself, finally forced back to what he knows best of all after running out of world:

> I might not be here, in this ridiculous landscape, hurrying down with my wife and child towards the tower of Wareham church, but I would still be I, Richard Verey, 35 years old, an Englishman of the upper middle class.

Or, now, Richard Fisher, historian, writer and observer by temperament, drawn into the dirty world of action at the crisis of the Cold War, in divided Germany in 1983.

If knowledge is one way of testing the limits of existence, action is another, and in a sense all Buchan's protagonists find themselves overtaken by action. The life they end up with is the one for which they are least suited; they are Hamlets forced into being Fortinbras. 'I thought: I was born for this stuff,' it occurs to Richard Fisher in a moment of dangerous elation. This sort of cross-casting – of which, in a sense, Buchan is himself a victim, with the expectation of genre in his pedigree and surname, the gold lettering on his first book and his fourth touted as a 'meticulously authentic thriller' – is a powerful device: putting a superfine piece of equipment in a mundane circuit, casting an insider (someone like Richard Verey) adrift, or perhaps installing someone with the nerves and awareness of an outsider as an insider. Characters with knowledge and sensitivity to burn, people who ordinarily, in fiction, would coin a few bon mots, give the encyclopaedias a run for their money, or stare fascinatingly out of the window, are made to be action heroes. It makes the books both harder and softer than you think they will be, or than other books. A brighter intelligence burns more unavailingly in greater darkness. In the end, though, they aren't really about their stories but about the embroiling of an individual, an innocent, in the affairs of the world, *die Weltmaschine*

as my father once wrote, and the way that life converts time
into memory.

All Buchan's books might be called *Heart of Darkness* or *In
Search of Lost Time*. Their text is 'What shall it profit a man if
he gains the whole world and loses his own soul,' although this
is given a further twist by Buchan's understanding that gaining
the world is an impossibility, that absolute possession is also
absolute loss because it only exists in the past, in the phantasmal
currency of memory, and finally comes down to a pawky
delirium of absence:

> My mind filled slowly with maddening touristic souvenirs: shrimps in
> Lübeck, cloudberry brandy in Helsinki, the heaving sea at Norderney,
> Leicester Forest East motorway services in rain, two quails in a cage
> in the Cahors Friday market, the warmth of paving stones on bare
> feet at Anacapri.

What remains of us is not love but memory, at best the memory
of love. Richard Fisher says, 'You have to love to be able to
enter history,' deliberately misquoting Marx. Buchan's books
are the histories of people who love, and who, as a result,
find themselves in the wrong lives: Adam Murray in his friend
Johnny's, John Chadwick in his rival William Nelson's, Richard
Verey in absolutely anyone's but his own, Richard Fisher in that
of the American spy Polina Mertz. The governing myth, I think,
is Grimm's. It is the story of the ferryman who presses the oars
into the hands of a passenger, who is then himself compelled to
ply the crossing until he in turn can find someone who will take
over from him. What Buchan has to offer is not primarily thrills
and spills but *Glanz und Elend*, splendour and misery, or, as
Lowell wrote: 'All life's grandeur/ is something with a girl in
summer . . .' His books are elegies to being alive. They are more
like Brodsky's definition of poetry, 'melancholy disciplined by
metre' – if you substitute 'story' or 'character' or 'prose' for
'metre' – than anything else.

At the end of *Notebook*, Lowell observes: 'Dates fade faster
than we do.' 1983 hasn't merely faded, it was practically obliter-
ated by the seismic shift in European politics. Now, it seems like
Rilke's unicorn, 'the beast that never was.' So it is oddly effortful
to retrieve Andropov, Reagan, Schmidt, the medium-range bal-

listic missile, the Twin Track approach, Geneva, Paul Nitze and Yuli (Yuri?) Kvitsinsky (Kvitinsky?) and the Walk in the Woods. These are the characters and developments that frame James Buchan's fourth novel. God knows they seemed vivid enough at the time, and Buchan brings them back with wonderful dash and economy. Political acuity is leavened by a fabulist's distancing lightness of phrase:

> Among the parricidal youth of 1968, whose heroes were not the founders of their prosperous republic but the peevish Marxists of the Frankfurt School such as Frank Lightner or the revolutionaries of remote and picturesque ex-colonies, the Soviets found a field ripe for subversion and recruitment.

(Who needs story, with exposition like this?) Between the big players, people like Genscher and Kohl and Petra Kelly and Margaret Thatcher – who, thrillingly, appear as themselves – and the fictional characters, Polina Mertz and Richard Fisher, is an intermediate layer of lightly fictionalized or disguised or à clef types, Polk and Kurtsovsky (i.e. Nitze and Kvitsinsky), Frank Lightner, co-founder of the Greens and Sebastian Ritter from the left of the SPD (Lafontaine? – but I really don't know). The function of Mertz and Fisher is to puncture the hermetic opposition of the two blocs: by their unexpected, human agitation to disrupt the colossal, grooved indifference of their political masters, and see that the timid hopes of Geneva ('the walk in the woods', which in the novel becomes 'the Golden Plough') get aired where it matters: 'In 1983, the two opposing systems were in such perfect equilibrium that the fall of a feather would tip the scale; and great events, for the only time in my life, came within the agency of individuals.' There is a wonderful interplay throughout the book between the personal-aesthetic and the political-functional, the spontaneous and the calculable, the ethical and the necessary, free will and determinism, love and espionage. Is there an aesthetics of history, Buchan asks; can you have ecstasy in politics? These questions are suggested again and again in the novel, whether it is in the youthful Ritter's Whitmanesque epiphany by the Thames, or the CDU's triumph in the '83 election ('the crowds round the TV sets, the wall-clock at 18.15, the arms going up, Kohl clambering, vastly, onto a table and, on Hannelore Kohl's face, a look of inconsolable misery'), or the Adam- or Cain-moment in Fisher's life after he's killed a man ('I was weeping because I'd passed out of the world I'd been born into, and lived in more or less at peace, and into outlawry, a windy and depopulated region where I'd scrape a hard living for the rest of an abbreviated life. I'd hoped to capture Polina for my world, or at least what remained of it; instead, she'd captured me for hers' – the ferryman story, as I was pleased to call it), or again, when Fisher, under interrogation from the Americans, is close to death: 'My body was dismantling. My chest and legs had broken off relations. My nerves passed out of central control. Grim little wars erupted, unreported, in my hands and feet. Muscles starved or hoarded. One by one, the great organs of my body shut down.'

The consciousness registering these dramatic public and private events is, as it often is in Buchan, partial, fragmented, even in ruins. (It is another way in which the anarchic, free and personal opposes the public and political: this isn't an impersonal narrative, though it touches on many things that are 'history'.) You can read the book as history; as dialectic; but also as a – mimicked – protocol of Fisher's memory as it is filtered by circumstances, by internal moods or external agencies like drink or drugs. There is a wonderful posture of inability or refusal that Buchan does (that 'excuse me, I can't go on with this' first seen in 'Felicia Hrabek' in *Slide*). Then, gradations of oblivion ('Of that evening at Gut Zons, I do not have continuous memory'), actual and predicted ('I suppose that, in time, Polina will attenuate into a female nude, bent at the waist to retrieve a bar of soap in a hotel shower in Marburg'), then colloquial vagueness ('that eel thing Manfred loves'), then on to many less easily describable degrees of precision, from the more generalised ('about to seal a masculine friendship in a welter of Leftist defeatism'), to the scrupulously swaggering ('the boats sliding under Holy Loch and the Vulcans of enamelled cast-iron and the Plateau d'Albion and the nuclear arquebusses in the Vosges'), to the constatation of impairment ('I was dazed with sunshine, Kirsch and sorrow'), to a raddled curve of thought ('she was looking at me and then the road: happy yet suspicious: what sort of civilian anyway, severe bruising, opioid intoxication, weight loss, dehydration, bed rest, 5 mg Vitamin B anticoagulant on the IV, fishy, leave it'), to the fabulous Lowellian catalogues ('everything about Jack Polk was faded, cracked, oiled, supple, expensive, fraudulent' or 'the world tasted and smelled of Patty Livingston: the hot spruces, the kraftpaper in the supermarket, the bloom on blueberries, the clamshell under the rake, the nylon of her white bathing dress drying on the deck, the flake of paint and creosote, the cool air on my legs as I jumped up in my shorts in the morning, the hot granite rip-rap and the icy sea, the yellow warblers flickering through the woods; tobacco, menthol, corn-bread, Budweiser, lobster claws, hot dogs, kerosene and, Hey, guys make great cooks, don't you believe that crap!') to tiny observations of hallucinatory clarity: a fly in a trout-stream spinning 'histrionically', or darkness 'cutting off' pieces of a bar at closing time. There is a wonderful half-page of crossword-type false leads about the Golden Plough: 'The Golden Plough is a place. The Golden Plough is an idea. A late and inordinately difficult novel by Henry James. A work of amateur nineteenth-century anthropology. An icily snobbish hotel in Salzburg, Austria. [. . .] Whore's slang for pissing. The strait forming the entrance to San Francisco Bay. A Hapsburg order of chivalry', and a lovely two-page apostrophe, Troggishly hymning Bonn ('Little city of dentists! I think I forgot to say I loved you.')

Last thing. The title. A Zukofsky-type pun on Goethe's wonderful poem 'Harzreise im Winter' about the unfairness and violence and unpredictability of the world. For all its historical circumstance and materiality, *Heart's Journey in Winter* is a meditation on just that: 'For the first time in my life, I thought: All this is going to end soon, in war or peace.'

MALCOLM LOWRY
Letters and Studies

Malcolm Lowry's response to fame, as expressed in his short, sharp, shocked poem 'After Publication of *Under the Volcano*', reads like a summation of his personal phobias, the hells of fire, alcohol and syphilis:

> Fame like a drunkard consumes the house of the soul
> Exposing that you have worked for only this –
> Ah, that I had never suffered this treacherous kiss.
> And had been left in darkness forever to flounder and fail.

By the time he died, in 1957, he may have felt he had recovered that 'darkness': neither *Under the Volcano* nor *Ultramarine* was in print in English; in the previous ten years, he had published just two short stories, a score of poems, an essay and a book review; and, although he was engaged on three or four new works of fiction, they had been in production for some time, and it must have seemed unlikely that he would manage to complete any of them, or, if he did, get them published. The diffident and sceptical wit that marked his dealings with publishers is one of the triumphs of the *Letters*: 'As to the Swedish, Norwegian and Danish translations, I understand they are out, but I have not seen them. Nor, I imagine, has any Swede, Norwegian or Dane.'

How Lowry would have reacted to posthumous fame and 'classic status' is anyone's guess. Not, presumably, with the easy irony of Pound's Sextus Propertius: 'I shall have, doubtless, a boom after my funeral,/ Seeing that long standing increases all things regardless of quality.' In fact, Lowry has had two such booms. The first, in the third lustrum after his death, saw the original publication of his *Selected Letters* (1967), his two unfinished novels *Dark as the Grave Wherein my Friend is Laid*

Review of Harvey Breit and Margerie Bonner, *Selected Letters of Malcolm Lowry* (London: Penguin, 1985); Gordon Bowker, ed., *Malcolm Lowry Remembered* (London: BBC Ariel Books, 1985), Ronald Binns, *Malcolm Lowry* (London: Methuen, 1984); and Chris Ackerley and Lawrence J. Clipper, *A Companion to 'Under the Volcano'* (Vancouver: University of British Columbia Press, 1984)

(1969) and *October Ferry to Gabriola* (1971), and a biography
by Douglas Day. Now ushered in by the film of *Under the
Volcano* (something that seems to have been mooted for almost
forty years, since the book was first published, in fact), there is
another boom, an after-boom, a secondary boom with new
material not *by* Lowry, but from him and about him: a paper-
back edition of the *Letters* (which have been long out of print);
a collection of reminiscences, a short critical account, and a
companion (*compañero!*) to *Under the Volcano*. Bibliographies
in some of these further attest to the interest in him, and there
is even a *Malcolm Lowry Newsletter* to keep up with new
developments.

In a passage in the *Selected Letters* Lowry talks about the
'purely romantic reasons' that drew him to Melville,

> but mostly because of his failure as a writer and his whole outlook
> generally. His failure for some reason absolutely fascinated me and
> it seems to me that from an early age I determined to emulate it, in
> every way possible – for which reason I have always been very fond
> of *Pierre* (even without having read it at all).

Lowry's continuing fascination, a generation after his death, is
prefigured by his attachment to Melville: it is personal and
romantic, and has to do with his 'failure', with the remoteness
of his life in Mexico and British Columbia, with his struggles
to write and to publish and then to get over publishing, 'and
his whole outlook generally'. Not only does Lowry create the
taste by which he is appreciated, he seems to have established
the mode of its transmission, pre-eminently (before the film) by
word of mouth, by osmosis, by adoption, as he adopted Conrad
Aiken as a father and David Markson as a son. Ronald Binns
remarks that *Ultramarine* reads as though Lowry had 'ransacked
his set books' at Cambridge, but John Davenport, reminiscing
in *Malcolm Lowry Remembered*, actually lists the works he
found in his rooms, 'Knut Hamsun and Hermann Bang, B.
Traven and Nordahl Grieg', and observes (with understatement)
that his reading 'was integrated in an unusual way'. David
Markson writes that 'a novel became a kind of introduction,
for Lowry, to the author personally', and another passage in the
Letters has Lowry quoting Aiken: ' "something about us doesn't

like to share our favorite authors with anyone", perhaps not even with the author himself!' Lowry's personal feelings for other authors, his adoption of them to the point of plagiarism, his possessiveness and possessedness, are attitudes for which his own books now provide the objects. In his letters, he tells (or makes up) the story of how his copy of *La Machine infernale*, together with his dark glasses, was stolen by a bearded Mixtec Indian. How should the books written by such a man reach their public by any ordinary route?

All Lowry's books are *Künstlerromane*, observed his American editor Albert Erskine, half-complainingly. Ronald Binns makes the point differently when he refers to him as a metafictionalist. Geoffrey Firmin, Sigbjørn Wilderness, Kennish Drumgold Cosnahan, Bill Plantagenet and the rest of them, all artists with words or jazz, are all Lowry surrogates. Lowry found it almost impossible to let a book go, and even years after publication – with *Ultramarine*, with *Under the Volcano* – he wanted to call them back for changes that were not mere details, but that would profoundly affect their autonomous status. *Under Under the Volcano* was how he referred, not altogether frivolously, to his second Mexican novel. He wanted to include all his books, written and unwritten, in a cycle consisting of three or five or seven books, called *The Voyage That Never Ends*. Impossibly beautiful titles for projected or never-published works ghost through the *Letters*, shuffled into various sequences: *In Ballast to the White Sea, La Mordida, Swinging the Maelstrom*. His reading of Ortega y Gasset helped him to remove his life and his work to the point where they meet as parallels, continually creating one another: 'Is man a sort of novelist of himself who conceives the fanciful figure of a personage with its unreal occupations and then, for the sake of converting it into reality, does all the things he does – and becomes an engineer?' The result is a kind of involution of art, biography and personal myth, a weird, inextricably connected limbo which in the end affects the reader.

This is what Stephen Spender feels when, in his introduction to *Volcano*, he writes, 'It would be altogether pardonable to confuse many facts about Lowry's own life with the fiction of Geoffrey Firmin's.' It so happens that the 'fact' from Lowry's life that was omitted from Firmin's – his eye-trouble that left him nearly blind in his childhood – may not have been one at all, but one of Lowry's gloomy mythical embellishments. His brother Russell discounts it in *Malcolm Lowry Remembered*. It makes no difference, though. The reader with that bit of information may – Spender almost says he ought to – incorporate it into his reading. And the myths are so compelling anyway, so refractory, that despite biographical questioning they assert themselves in the reader's mind.

All these factors – personality and myth, possessive reading, autobiographical protagonists, moves to reclaim and subordinate published texts (*Under the Volcano* was to appear as a novel 'written' by Sigbjørn Wilderness in Lowry's finished cycle) – make Lowry a kind of complex revenant in twentieth-century literature, neither myth nor fact nor fiction, neither life nor text, never completed or authenticated or dismissed or quite fathomed. As Lowry wrote of *Under the Volcano* in his celebrated 'Cape letter': 'It can even be regarded as a sort of machine: it works too, believe me, as I have found out.' The first chapter ends, 'backwards revolved the luminous wheel'.

The tenacity of the Malcolm Lowry phenomenon is evidenced in all of these four books under review. In the *Letters*, one can note how Lowry sends not only his fictional characters but his own name on quixotic jaunts into the world: 'Lowry's and Penates', he coins, 'too-loose Lowry-trek', or best of all, 'delowryum tremens'. Gordon Bowker's witnesses are clearly and vividly enthralled by the man they knew: Kathleen Raine allows him (and only him) the ascription of 'genius' – before villainously going on to read *Under the Volcano* as a description of her marriage to Hugh Sykes Davies. Conrad Aiken, John Sommerfield and Charlotte Haldane included Lowry-characters in their novels. Arthur Calder-Marshall is robustly, even rudely disparaging. Lowry's first and second wives variously glow and enthuse (Gordon Bowker's unearthing of a 1975 film interview with Jan Gabrial is the one big discovery here, although there are also notably gracious pieces by Hugh Sykes Davies and David Markson, and an interesting, though unfortunately very short item from the Canadian poet Earle Birney on conditions in the Lowrys' shack in Dollarton). For the rest, it is interesting to note how many conflicting observations and opinions there are, and how, by extension, any clean, authorized version of Lowry's life must be an impossibility.

Ronald Binns, although he uses 'metafictionalist' as though Lowry might have had it on his passport, follows his subject's precept that 'writing should not stand still but perpetually evolve' and develops fresh ideas and formulations. He has a beautifully apposite quotation from Sartre, writes about textual de-familiarization in Lowry, about the collage-like appearance of the writing, and has interesting points to make about Trotsky, Joyce and Hardy in connection with *Under the Volcano*. Chris Ackerley and Lawrence Clipper quote Lowryesque misprints of their own making ('pub' for 'pun'), put Ackerley's own photograph of 'el Farolito', the Consul's 'terminal bar', on their cover, and use 'no se puede vivir sin amar' as their epigraph. At one time, Lowry had himself envisaged putting notes at the end of his novel, and their thorough, occasionally fanciful *Companion* is very much in the spirit of his extraordinarily patient and detailed letters to Clarisse Francillon and Clemens ten Holder, his French and German translators. Their work in analysing allusions and making cross-references is very much what the reader must set himself to do, and it may rob him of the fun and randomness of doing it for himself, but for the student and the impatient, it must be invaluable. Perhaps inevitably, there are further, unintended Lowryesque touches: in the index, a reference to Peter Rabbit ('everything is to be found in Peter Rabbit', it says in *Under the Volcano*) has a 'qv' to the cabbalist MacGregor Mathers.

Lowry's biographer Douglas Day writes: 'One must begin by realizing that Malcolm Lowry was not really a novelist, except by accident.' He says it in, of all places, his preface to the posthumous novel *Dark as the Grave Wherein my Friend is Laid*. It is a daunting observation, but not one that I would disagree with. He continues: 'It is difficult to know what to call him: diarist, compulsive notetaker, poet *manqué*, alcoholic philosophizing rambler – any of these would do for a start, but only for a start.' Lowry's gift, to my mind, is for the revelation of cosmic designs, inimical and later comic. Like Byron or Kafka, his name has sprouted a suffix and can be used to describe a whole class of experience: his territory is coincidence, the impingements and implications of signs and symbols, 'correspondence between the subnormal world and the abnormally suspicious'. It is the world of 'we shoota de espiders', of 'spectral chicken of the house', and of the red HELL lighting up the night opposite the Dollarton shack. Lowry is an adept at elaborating such signs, and, especially, though not exclusively, in *Under the Volcano*, at composing them into a vision of the world and of life. In the later works, the quest for meaning is allowed to suffocate the reality and the realism that are so powerfully there in *Under the Volcano*. (Ronald Binns rightly overrules Lowry himself on this point, and praises his characterization.) The first sentence of *Dark as the Grave* is like an elaborate, rhapsodic parody of that other first sentence, so coolly and chastely factual: 'Two mountain chains traverse the republic roughly from north to south, forming between them a number of valleys and plateaus':

> The sense of speed, of gigantic transition of going southward, downward, over three countries, the tremendous mountain ranges, the sense at once of descent, tremendous regression, and of moving, not moving, but in another way dropping straight down the world. . . .

The later books have the same world and the same way of looking at it, they go back to the same incidents and fears, but they distance and relativize, playing with Pirandellian mirrors. Where they score is perhaps in their very raggedness and exhaustion, leaving Lowry's skills as a writer almost nakedly on view: his comedy and grace and erudition, his cultivated vocabulary, the safety of pure play:

> It was the early afternoon of a brilliantly sunny day in Rome, a young blue midsummer moon tilted down over the Borghese Gardens, and under the awning on the sidewalk terrace of the Restaurant Rupe Tarpea, crowded by men and women talking, a lone man named Kennish Drumgold Cosnahan sat drinking a glass of milk with an expression of sombre panic. ('Elephant and Colosseum')

The young blue moon, the grimly named restaurant and the sombre panic are marvellous, but the reader might have preferred reading about anyone else but the man they have been given. There is no sting, no menace and only the familiar unfamiliarity: the final text for this might be a clause from *Dark as the Grave*, 'Sigbjørn watched the lost prose sliding past the window'.

The *Letters* are Lowry without this occasionally exasperating mirroring. He emerges from them as a man of outstanding patience, culture and goodness. The most harrowing stories of misfortune, accident and betrayal are told with almost incredible calm and grace: a long letter to an attorney about various chicaneries suffered in Mexico; dignified letters to publishers and agents, whose behaviour (to the Lowrys marooned near Vancouver) must have seemed appallingly fickle; letters listing afflictions and works-in-progress in roughly equal numbers. There are beautiful drunken sentences ('outside my window in the hospital was a leaning forest of small green nameless trees crowned by one very little sweet tree, blowing . . .'); a letter sending money to a friend even harder up, punning on 'trois étoiles', 'brand' and 'cognate' over several lines; letters accompanying a screenplay of *Tender is the Night*, a work of purest, most intricately patterned Lowry; endless hopeful sendings of stories or poems 'just right for' this or that magazine or journal. In the middle of one of many, many long and highly figurative constructions, is the short semaphore, ' – sentence impossible – '. But how many others there were that worked.

MALCOLM LOWRY
Life and Poetry

Quauhnahuac, his Cuernavaca, is overlooked by the two volcanoes, but Malcolm Lowry's life is ringed by non-events and no-shows that were even more spectacular, things that might have happened or threatened or promised to happen, but never did: such things as financial independence; a regular relationship with an editor, a publishing house, a landlord; a *modus vivendi* with alcohol; Jungian analysis in Zurich or lobotomy in Wimbledon. Above all, there is *The Voyage That Never Ends*, the cycle of novels that he mooted but never wrote, or wrote but never finished, with fantastic, phantom, harpooning titles like *In Ballast to the White Sea*, *La Mordida*, *Swinging the Maelstrom*. All these things – books, changed circumstances, surgery – are cures of one sort or another, for as Stephen Spender remarked in his introduction to *Under the Volcano*, 'with Lowry one is never far away from the thought that although there is an illness there may also be a cure.' They obtruded and impended like the gods in the life of a Greek, but when it came down to it, they remained offstage, sat on their hands, and he gave his life to their absence. He is the one whom the gods did not save. Despite the offer made to Faust in the third of *Under the Volcano*'s three epigraphs, 'wer immer strebend sich bemüht, den können wir erlösen' – 'whoever unceasingly strives upward . . . him can we save' – the gods did not come for him. And yet strive he did, indubitably. *Passim*. Even a graphologist would have to agree:

> At first glance it did not appear a letter. But there was no mistaking, even in the uncertain light, the hand, half crabbed, half generous, and wholly drunken, of the Consul himself, the Greek e's, flying buttresses of d's, the t's like lonely wayside crosses save where they crucified an entire word, the words themselves slanting steeply downhill, though the individual characters seemed as if resisting the descent, braced, climbing the other way.

Review of Gordon Bowker, *Pursued by Furies: A Life of Malcolm Lowry* (London: Harper Collins, 1993), and *The Collected Poetry of Malcolm Lowry*, ed. Kathleen Scherf (Vancouver: University of British Columbia Press, 1992)

There I think is Malcolm Lowry's Fable – to use Edwin Muir's word for the mythic shape of a man's life. He is the one whom the gods did not save. This is what gives his life its irredeemable sadness, its suspenseful struggle, its promise that was never cancelled and only once – with *Under the Volcano* – fulfilled, superbly for the reader, catastrophically for himself, as witness the poem 'After Publication of *Under the Volcano*' ('Success is like some horrible disaster') and the ten last lost years he had to live through after it. But Lowry's life is full of Muir-ish hinges, cruxes, palpably brighter alternatives, all ready to swing on its axis if only the right point were touched, the right word spoken. Even his death, choking on his own vomit, seems the most fickle and unnecessary way to go. A proud and terrible loneliness emerges from *Under the Volcano* – that of the Consul its hero, a man severed from every conceivable tie, and that of the book, all alone in what without it hardly deserves to be called an oeuvre. Lowry stands unexampled to me as 'a great author who happened to have written only one great book', in the words of Douglas Day, his first biographer. Faced with a three-book deal and the prospect of becoming his own assembly line, all he could think of was *Under Under the Volcano*. Robert Lowell writes:

> I memorised tricks to set the river on fire,
> somehow never wrote something to go back to.

Lowry was the absolute opposite, no tricks and a work he was unable to get away from. He described himself as 'a sometimes subtle if not good carpenter etc', the builder of a pier, projecting into the Vancouver inlet where he squatted, the *Volcano* by other means'. Alternatively, in *Lunar Caustic*, he was the 'SS *Lawhill*', 'a windjammer that survived more disasters than any ship afloat'. Granted, these things are all out of Lowry's myths about himself, but my point is that one has to use them; everything else would only diminish him. In terms other than those of myth, Prometheus can hardly be seen as a success, and Lowry was a Promethean figure. Appreciating *Under the Volcano* is easy, but one has to bring something like belief to the rest of his life and work, admire Lowry for the discipline of failure and suffering, and believe that *The Voyage That Never Ends* might

actually have come to something. The dead titles and the post-
humous publications – dreary, foot-slogging reads and ever-
diminishing rehashes of *Under the Volcano*, novelising the
novelist who wrote it, 'six authors in search of a character', he
said – are articles of faith.

Clarence Malcolm Lowry was born in 1909 to a Liverpool
cottonbroker, the youngest of four sons. His father was already
comfortably off and became more so over the years. (He was
also, in 1904, 'England's Best Developed Man', but no worries
there: his son inherited his physique, was a block off the old
block, except he had short arms, small hands and, apparently, a
tiny . . .) As a boy, he looked like I imagine Richmal Crompton's
William looking, tousled, grinning, pugnacious. He was sent off
to the Leys School, where one of his teachers was W. H. Bal-
garnie, the model for 'Mr Chips' (I don't know what that means
in practical terms, but both Day and Bowker tell you so). A
teacher remembers Lowry as 'a rather shaggy, laconic boy, "a
cat that walked by itself"'. His style was already emerging. To
thank his mother for some cushions, he wrote: 'The study now
resembles the bibliothèque of an Armenian professor of down.'
No biography can explain that, so much courtliness, imagination
and wit in a 17-year-old; it's the mystery of genius, attested to
by Conrad Aiken, who never knew a writer (Eliot included) 'so
visibly or happily alight with genius'.

Lowry finished at the Leys, spent the original 'gap' year on
ships to the Far East and back, giving him the material for
Ultramarine, the original 'gap' novel. With help from Aiken and
others, he scraped into St Catherine's, Cambridge, did English
in a desultory way – but all his life he had a wonderful and
well-exercised Latinate vocabulary: the word 'tabid' is already
something, but to use it of music, as Lowry does in *Under
the Volcano*, is something else. He impressed his Cambridge
contemporaries (with sea-songs and drinking), but as normal,
not the English staff, always more deadhand than deadeye. He
collected his Third in 1932, *Ultramarine* was published in 1933
(but not before the manuscript was stolen), and he stayed with
the Aikens, and in London and Paris, sometimes in temperance
hotels, more usually not. Neither Day nor Bowker can resist
mentioning one of his rooms, which you had to enter through

a missing door-panel. In 1934, in Paris, Lowry married Jan Gabrial, the first of two American wives, and followed her to New York, where he did a short stint at the Bellevue (see *Lunar Caustic*), which he later claimed was purely voluntary and fact-gathering. On 30 October 1936, the day before the Day of the Dead, the Lowrys arrived in Mexico. He began writing the first draft of *Under the Volcano*, a short story about a man and his daughter witnessing a murder on a bus. Jan – not for the first time – left Lowry, and Mexico too turned nasty on him: he spent Christmas in jail and was finally thrown out of the country. In LA he met his second wife, Margerie Bonner, a writer and onetime silent movie actress, and they moved up to Canada, initially so that Lowry could renew his visa, and then for keeps. They moved to a 'squatter's shack' outside Vancouver, in 1940 bought one of their own for $100, and worked and re-worked on *Under the Volcano*, and on Margerie's writing. In 1946, with Lowry and Margerie touring the old sites of the book in Mexico, they had news of its acceptance, and in 1947 they went to New York, via Haiti and Miami, for the publication. The Dollarton squatting life was hard to get back into, and Lowry lost his energy and focus among fears and fires, broken limbs, three books and a screenplay of *Tender is the Night*. In 1954, his publishers, Random House, pulled the plug on him, and the Lowrys went to Europe, finishing up in England, in a village by the South Coast.

As a writer's life of a certain kind – centrifugal, 'simple' in its attempted self-sufficiency – it is formidable, exemplary. For the biographer, it has a deal to offer: a subject with a cult following, but also with a certain amount of slack in his reputation ('almost certainly Lowry is the least-known British literary genius of the 20th century,' Bowker says, a little flatly); action (or its substitute, relocation); eloquence and wit in its subject's presentation of himself, a human noise at all times; medical detail (alcoholism); a flaw (ditto); a commanding presence in photographs; and the alternative conundrums of success or failure – how did Lowry ever manage *Under the Volcano*; why did the author of *Under the Volcano* fail to finish another book? On most of the things that matter, I prefer Douglas Day's 1973 biography to Bowker's, for all the latter's greater detail and

accuracy. Day's subject is Lowry: Bowker writes about Lowry's
life. Day organizes, presents and mediates the man, a little crash-
ingly at times, but what the heck; Bowker glories in recounting
sequences of events – drinks, legal proceedings, extradition,
Lowry's death – in such detail that they become hard to follow.
It was Day who said, 'one must begin by understanding that
Lowry was not really a novelist except by accident' – as helpful
a sentence as has been written on him; who presents his slapstick
charm; and who describes the extraordinary ripening of *Under
the Volcano* through its miserably unpromising drafts. Bowker,
whose misfortune it is of course to have a predecessor, offers
the Furies as a big idea. Lowry pursued by remorse over Paul
Fitte, the undergraduate he apparently egged on to suicide; over
Burton Rascoe, whose short story he plagiarized; over his
mother and his bad angel, Conrad Aiken. This material is new
and diligently researched, but it isn't itself the main story. And
too often Bowker turns out inadequate biography sentences
and biography paragraphs, ragbags of mood and events, faintly
risible shards of facts: 'It cannot have helped his self-confidence
as a writer to have received a letter from Evelyn [his mother]
just before Christmas warning him to remember what happened
to rolling stones, and saying: "How much I would rejoice to
hear of your success in life. Well! I shall just go on hoping."'
Or: 'Upset by the assassination of Gandhi at the end of January,
he disappeared for a day into Rouen.' Or: 'Margerie gave him
for Christmas a copy of Kafka's diaries, a writer he enjoyed
because he fed his heightened sense of persecution.' To all of
which as a reader I say ' – '. Why the suppositiousness, the
skating over one's essential ignorance of another being? Why
should Lowry not have giggled at his mother's letter, used
Gandhi as a pretext, or found Kafka an absolute hoot (which
he is, the funniest thing until, well, Lowry)?

Under the Volcano eats light like a black hole. It is a work
of such gravity and connectedness and spectroscopic richness
that it is more world than product. It is absolute mass, agglomer-
ation of consciousness and experience and terrific personal
grace. It has planetary swagger, it is a planet dancing: 'The
Thames, in the half-light, seemed not unlike the Yangtze-Kiang.'
(In the *Letters* there is Port au Prince 'like Tewkesbury, set

against the rolling, mysterious mountains of Oaxaca'.) How full of geography, vegetation, talk, drink, books, stars, birds. It is a novel that has swallowed an encyclopaedia. Everything is shuffled, intercut, larded, expanded. 'You have a line there I wrote in Africa 15 years ago,' a friend told him; others like John Davenport and Aiken merely kept score. And yet there is perhaps nothing in it as impressive as the first page and a half, a completely orderly progression of six paragraphs, massive and thrilling and utterly well-made, until the first line of dialogue takes up the story. When Lowry follows similar magpie/mosaic procedures later on, though, one merely fears for the results and imagines Albert Erskine, his New York editor, hearing how many hundred pages Lowry and Margerie had knocked out on whatever work was in progress, before some sheepish *bona fide* accident – a broken ankle going to the well, a broken back plunging into the sea. Lowry, of course, would rapturously incorporate the subsequent hospital experience into his work-in-progress. How could the voyage ever end? And yet this is how *Under the Volcano* was written.

So many things might have made a difference. Focusing on one particular work after *Under the Volcano*; an editor closer at hand, and more prepared than Erskine to put on gumboots and wield a pitchfork; a more complete or less distracting success than *Under the Volcano* enjoyed in New York – launch, parties, razzmatazz, author flown in specially (although he came by ship and bus, being Lowry), everything but talk-show appearances. Surely it was the earliest and most calamitous instance of modern book publication. I had to wonder if it might have helped Lowry not to be English, not to have to return to England, the one place where the reviews were curmudgeonly and sales were disappointing. It must be hard to be a 45-year-old prophet returning to your own country, especially if the country is England. From Bowker:

'The wild scarlet windflower of Greece is blooming in the garden and the cemetery is a riot of henbane. The stinking goosefoot is out, the mobile frying fish shop is advancing from the south-west, and there are two swallows nesting in the woodshed.' Soon they would have a cat and the landlady had lent him *The Psychic Life of Jesus*.

Or perhaps it's possible to write one masterpiece on packing cases, but not two. Perhaps we are just greedy.

The Collected Poetry of Malcolm Lowry isn't the missing masterpiece, but it does do something towards satisfying one's desire for more. It is certainly worth having, a completely different experience from the little City Lights *Selected*. Poems to Lowry were many things: he wrote tight-arsed sonnets, gloomy humoresques, travel impressions, sound-painting, jazz lyrics, twee love-notes to Margerie. They are all here, all five hundred of them, complete with variants, sober notes from Kathleen Scherf on compositional methods and paper dating, and 80 pages of annotation by the champion Lowry-ologist Chris Ackerley, the pretty-damn-nearly-omniscient co-compiler of the *Companion to 'Under the Volcano'*. The poems, as well as being of these various types, are also Lowry in the raw – the place-names, the rhetoric, the apocalyptics, the jokes, the vocabulary. It is the consciousness of *Under the Volcano,* but loose and purposeless:

> Where is Oaxaca, Vigil, you ask, what annex,
> Niche, pitch, is this? What age is it? What sex?
> Mexico? Is it not the place of the lost?
> Goal of all Americans who want to be divorced:
> Of all Norsemen who want to be unnorsed:
> Of all horsemen, already unhorsed:

If he had made it his major endeavour, and also let himself go, he might have made a poet like the Berryman of the *Dream Songs,* a cryptic spill, wild swings between thanatos and wit, the screeching and chattering of the brain. I think some of the smaller poems, like 'Kingfishers in British Columbia', 'Happiness' or 'Hostage' are purely good; in them he takes, as it were, Aiken's advice to 'put your complexity into reverse – and celebrate the sun':

> A day of sunlight and swallows . . .
> And saw the fireman by the fidley wave
> And laughed. And went on digging my own grave.

More important, though, everything has something to commend it, the *facetiae,* the Learish nonsense, the poems-on-poems-and-poets, the liquored-up improvisations with their echoes of Crane and Stevens and others, but distinguished always by the Lowryan note of joyful corruption:

> A dead lemon like a cowled old woman crouching in the cold.
> A white pylon of salt and the flies
> taxying on the orange table, rain, rain, a scraping peon.
> And a scraping pen writing bowed beggarly words.
> War. And the broken-necked street-cars outside
> And a sudden broken thought of a girl's face in Hoboken,
> A tilted turtle dying slowly on the stoop
>
> of the sea-food restaurant, blood
> lacing its mouth, and the white floor
> – ready for teredos to-morrow.

These poems – and it is a strange thing for poems to be – are Lowry at his most unfinished, and unless and until we are given facsimile versions of his prose manuscripts, that gives them their fascination.

PAUL BOWLES

There is something nicely adventitious in the way that the traveller and composer Paul Bowles came to be an author. In New York in 1947, he took some stories to the Dial Press, was told that – then as now – no publisher would look at stories without a novel, and that – then as now – a writer, to be taken seriously, needed a literary agent: then he waited while the publisher kindly rang up an agent for him, had lunch with her (one Helen Strauss), and heard, not much later, that Doubleday had offered him a contract for a novel, and an advance. So far, so mischievously industry-led. Then:

> I got the idea for *The Sheltering Sky* riding on a Fifth Avenue bus one day going uptown from Tenth Street. I decided just which point of view I would take. It would be a work in which the narrator was omniscient. I would write it consciously up to a certain point, and after that let it take its own course. You remember there's a little Kafka quote at the beginning of the third section: 'From a certain point onward, there is no turning back; that is the point that must be reached.' This seemed important to me.

The title – a variant on the words of a popular song – came to him on the same bus.

The book was written mainly in Tangier and completed in Fez in May 1948. Bowles described it to a composer friend, Peggy Glanville-Hicks – with not so much dead-pan as drop-dead irony – as 'a novel just like any other novel; a triangle laid in the Sahara'. He sent it to Helen Strauss, who delivered it to Doubleday, who 'unhesitatingly rejected it'. As they saw it, they had contracted for a novel, and he had produced something else. (So much for his 'novel just like any other novel'!) Subsequently, the book was accepted by New Directions, and just before them, by John Lehmann – which explains why it has British spellings. It was published in London in the summer of 1949, and in New York in November, and was enthusiastically received, becoming a selection of the Book of the Month Club,

Introduction to Paul Bowles, *The Sheltering Sky* (London: Penguin, 1999)

and spending several weeks on the *New York Times* bestseller list (up to number 9). It is easy to suppose, because *The Sheltering Sky* became a cult book and Bowles has largely been with small presses since – Black Sparrow, Ecco, City Lights, Peter Owen – that that is all it ever was, and Bowles himself merely a cult author, the sphinx of Tangier, waiting to be visited, as Nicholas Lezard nicely put it, by 'every white visitor not wearing shorts'. In fact, *The Sheltering Sky* has had both popular and critical success. Its first American paperback printing was 200,000 copies, and it has continued to find new and influential admirers, from Tennessee Williams (who reviewed it) and Gore Vidal to William Burroughs, Anthony Burgess and Patricia Highsmith. It was filmed in 1989 by Bernardo Bertolucci (I haven't seen it), and some time in the eighties there was an unforgettable *South Bank Show*, in which for a hilarious hour a wretchedly persistent Melvyn Bragg questioned a decorously disobliging Bowles. After its first fifty years, then, *The Sheltering Sky* needs little re-contextualization and no allowances. Whether you file it under Beat or Expatriate Literature, American Existentialism or African Gothic (according to a writer in *Life*) or – my own literary compound term – Travel Horror, it is there to be discovered.

One of the reasons for its continuing appeal is that *The Sheltering Sky* is not a 'literary' book in the bad sense of the word. It seems more like something found than made. It carries very little baggage, in the way of language or characterization or style or teaching, nothing to get in the way of naked experience. What one takes away from a reading of it is its split drama of death and survival; its relentless chronological and geographical progression; and a sense of the physical atmosphere of certain scenes – say, Port walking downhill to the edge of the town, at the beginning; the sickroom in Sbâ with its sheeted window; the tree under which Kit sleeps, wrapped in her coat, at the beginning of her new life; the complicated interiors of certain of the dwellings (Belqassim's, for example). So linear and direct is the novel that, if it had been a part of speech, it would surely be a preposition; it would be 'into' or 'through' or 'beyond'. Certainly, one wouldn't know Port, Kit or Tunner if one met them: they seem an anonymous, unstable, restless group of the sort that forms up to travel together, probably by the million – and much more common now than fifty years ago. *The Sheltering Sky* has the kind of self-taught appeal and freshness that Bowles's more established and craft-conscious composer friends, like Aaron Copland, always admired in his music; and it seems much less 'writerly' than the stories, say, 'A Distant Episode', which he wrote a little earlier, in 1945, and which in outline – Westerner gets lost – anticipates *The Sheltering Sky*, but is much more studied in its ironies and its effects, and is much more concerned with tone.

In fact, if one is seeking a literary point of reference for *The Sheltering Sky*, one of the places one goes to is Bowles's juvenilia – or not even his juvenilia, these are things he wrote as a boy of eight or ten. In his autobiography, Bowles remembers writing:

> two volumes about a woman named Bluey Laber Dozlen, who sails from an unidentified European country to Wen Kroy, where she immediately finds a huge sum of money and buys herself a self-steering automobile. During her first year she has many illnesses and recoveries, several marriages and divorces, and becomes a spy. During the second year she learns how to play bridge and smoke opium. Everyone else catches influenza and pneumonia and dies, but Bluey, blessed with excellent health, manages to survive and is last seen hiding out in Hong Kong from a vengeful housemaid she was once foolish enough to dismiss.

This type of straightahead narration, unafraid of lurid extremes, shocks and fatalities – in fact, irresistibly drawn to them – produces a story that, in the words of Bowles's biographer, Christopher Sawyer-Lauçanno, 'mixes, rather convincingly, the most fantastic adventures with commonplace reality.' It is, in fact, more or less the methodology of the mature novelist, as he relates it in his autobiography, *Without Stopping* (known in some quarters as *Without Telling*):

> The structure and character of the landscape would be supplied by imagination (that is, by memory). I would reinforce each such scene with details reported from life during the day of writing, regardless of whether the resulting juxtaposition was apposite or not. I never knew what I was going to write on the following day because I had not yet lived through the day.

Elsewhere, Bowles amiably remarks – shades of the Fifth Avenue bus – 'Sky I started in order to make the hotel room at the Belvedere in Fez more real than it was.' At the outer edge of his aleatory, improvisatory method was the moment – surely one of the strangest in the history of modern prose – when, having killed off his protagonist, Bowles realized he wasn't finished! 'The death of the main character does not make the book satisfactory. The book has to go on.' Drawing on early experiments with Surrealist 'automatic writing' – and on the local cannabis jam, *'majoun'* – Bowles 'shifted to automatic and went ahead full speed. It's the only way I can write a novel, not being a born novelist.' His unconventional methods brought Bowles into seeming proximity to the Beats. However, when William Burroughs, a long-time friend and admirer of Bowles's, showed him some 'cut-ups' he'd made of *The Sheltering Sky* to get him interested in the technique, Bowles had no use for it, and one can understand why: he had already cut together the 'fantastic' and the 'commonplace' in the way he'd written it.

Looked at in one way, *The Sheltering Sky* is one of the simplest and oldest kinds of story: the journey. It is the progress from Oran to Boussif to Aïn Krorfa to Bou Noura to El Ga'a to Sbâ, and then on to some – I think, unnamed – sub-Saharan coastal city. It is conducted on foot, by car and by train, by bicycle, bus, truck, camel caravan, plane, taxi and tram. It might be the chronicle of some expedition – with the curious difference that there is no destination or objective, and that even the next point on the itinerary, while inevitable (there are no other possible places to go!), still seems doubtful, obscure, little more than a rumour: 'Port spent the next two days trying assiduously to gather information about El Ga'a. It was astonishing how little the people of Bou Noura knew about the place.' This whole side of the book – linear, simple, strange, unpredictable – puts it with, say, Poe's *Narrative of Arthur Gordon Pym*, a deadly plunge South.

But *The Sheltering Sky* can also be thought of as the opposite: static, complex, real, deepening. It's a story of innocents abroad, not unlike a Henry James novel. With his highly self-aware characters (well, Port and Kit anyway!), Bowles even seems to be playing on, and with, the resulting expectations. The noisy film next door is called *Fiancée for Rent*; Tunner's presence provides 'a classical situation for Kit to exploit'; Lieutenant Armagnac finds the local Arab girls 'exasperatingly uncomplicated after the more evolved relationship to which he latterly had become accustomed'; an Arab bus driver, who is from the city, has no one to whom he can make any obscene remarks about Kit 'since there were no Europeans present, and the other Arabs were not from the city' and wouldn't have understood; when Kit finds herself being shared between Belqassim and his older relative, it says – alarmingly, scandalously! – 'she supposed that it was a gentleman's agreement, made for the duration of the voyage'. A really quite surprising strain of comedy of manners runs through *The Sheltering Sky*.

But then there are other elements one doesn't expect or register fully. Far from being a simple travelogue, *The Sheltering Sky* has quite a few cannily managed partings and re-meetings, usually involving Tunner and the Lyles. There is a certain amount of 'business' with the passports of Kit and Port, and with the money in Kit's valise. The state of the beds – made or unmade – and the comings and goings in the interconnected hotel rooms would not have disgraced a farce. (If he hadn't come by this in any other way, Bowles would certainly have learned the necessary timing and planning from his work as a – highly successful – composer for the theatre.) There is one further – erratic – element I wanted to mention too, though there's really nowhere to bring it in, and that is the presence in the book of several sentences that, in their concern with logic and gesture, and a kind of comic fullness that includes surprise, remind me irresistibly of Kafka. They wouldn't have stuck out if I'd read them in Kafka:

> The long main street was empty, cooking in the afternoon sun, whose strength seemed doubled by the fact that over the mountains ahead to the south still hung the massive dark clouds that had been there since the early morning.

> For some reason which he was unable to fathom, there were a good many small children running about the establishment. They were well-behaved and quiet as they played in the gloomy courtyard, exactly as if it had belonged to a school instead of a brothel. Some of them wandered inside the rooms, where the men took them on

their laps and treated them with the greatest affection, patting their cheeks and allowing them occasional puffs on their cigarettes.

The bus stopped with a jolt and the driver got out abruptly and walked away with the air of wishing to have nothing further to do with it.

'*Smitsek? Kuli?*' they would say to her, holding small bits of food in front of her face; the younger one tried to push dates between her teeth, but she laughed and shook her head, letting them fall on to the rug.

It is odd – and says something about the strength and the capaciousness of the novel – that there are all these things and others in it besides, and yet one's impression of it is of an unmarked – in the card-playing sense – and unliterary feature-lessness. The book seems to be as irreducible and as free from anything inessential as the little story Bowles remembers being told by Dali once:

Then he told a story about a small girl lost in a blizzard in the Alps. When she was more dead than alive, a fine St Bernard arrived with a keg of brandy around his neck. The dog then attacked and ate her.

Horrible, rational, queasily funny, a comedy of manners in that it too dramatizes a collision between two jurisdictions – isn't this like *The Sheltering Sky* in miniature?

The intensity of the book stems partly from, well, intensity, but also, perhaps even primarily, from how tightly drawn it is, from its rigorous exclusions. It has no future and no flashbacks, and only one single 'memory'. It has no other settings and no relationship to any other places, except the severed one to America. There is no social, financial or professional infor-mation about the characters, which are, in fact, impressively, well-functioning psychological organisms rather than charac-ters. The darkness that falls round the fringes of the story falls very abruptly; it is once mentioned that Port might be a writer of some sort – that's soon dropped; the *raison d'être* of the three of them (travellers, not tourists) in Oran – something to do with 'the mechanized age' – is so flimsy as to discourage further inquiry; the Arab words we hear – a minor, but again symptomatic point – are not translated for us. If our roads out

of the story, into other times and places, are all blocked off, nor
are we ever offered the comfort of familiarity or congruence.
The Sheltering Sky seems like a deliberately counter-mytho-
logical book: it seems impossible to match Port, Kit and Tunner
with any mythological trio: and, brilliantly, when Kit finds
herself in another trio, with Belqassim, nothing is made out of
that either! It seems to me that the book will countenance
nothing bigger than itself – not time, not character, not structure,
not technique, not philosophy, not meaning, not style – only
place. This gives it its intensity, and – paradoxically – its claus-
trophobic quality.

The Sheltering Sky is a book about people on the edge of an
alien space; somewhere, where curiously they are never alone;
somewhere full of noise and music and a sinister space-wind
that continually reminds them that they don't belong there. It
is not a confrontation between two civilizations or two ways of
being, it is too unequal and too sketchy for that. Besides, what
happens is not so much friction or collision as a reduced density,
incomprehension, the impossibility of communication. There are
the words: *talus, sebkha, bled, seguias, ereg, hammada, oued.*
Or there is the strange abstractness that is engendered in the
characters:

> The limpid, burning sky each morning when she looked out the
> window from where she lay, repeated identically day after day, was
> part of an apparatus functioning without any relationship to her, a
> power that had gone on, leaving her far behind.

Or there are the confusions that are somewhere in the middle:

> By the road sometimes were high clumps of dead thistle plants,
> coated with white dust, and from the plants the locusts called, a
> high, unceasing scream like the sound of heat itself.

It seems that, whatever their respective fates, Port, Kit and
Tunner are yielding to a vacuum with a soft, invisible edge like
terror or ozone. It's the story of an inverse conquest. Given a
whole world of sympathetic detail and heroic articulation, it
might have turned into an *Under the Volcano*; with an insistence
on spiritual value and sacrifice, it might have become a longer
version of 'The Woman Who Rode Away'. But Bowles doesn't

have the grandiose poetry of Malcolm Lowry or Lawrence's metaphysical errands and improvised emphatic clabber of style. *The Sheltering Sky* doesn't offer these consolations. It is Bowles's book. In its impersonal way, it is uncompromisingly personal, enjoined upon him from the moment when, as a very young man, he first caught sight of North Africa:

> Straightway I felt a great excitement; much excited; it was as if some interior mechanism had been set in motion by the sight of the approaching land. Always without formulating the concept, I had based my sense of being in the world partly on an unreasoned conviction that certain areas of the earth's surface contained more magic than others. [...] Like any Romantic. I had always been vaguely certain that sometime during my life I should come into a magic place which in disclosing its secrets would give me wisdom and ecstasy – perhaps even death. And now, as I stood in the wind looking at the mountains ahead, I felt the stirring of the engine within, and it was as if I were drawing close to the solution of an as-yet unposed problem. I was incredibly happy as I watched the wall of mountains slowly take on substance, but I let the happiness wash over me and asked no questions.

The Sheltering Sky is a most unlikely story for an American to tell ('the last frontier' and so forth), and much more unlikely now than it was even fifty years ago. Part of the interest of the book – and no doubt, part of the motivation for it – is Bowles's long-running argument with America. (He ran away from there after his first undergraduate year, swearing he would never go back, and though he did, it's many years now since his last visit.) There are a few digs at Americans here – 'There's something repulsive about an American without money in his pocket,' says the consular official sent to collect Kit – but two more important points too. Once, Port wonders whether 'any American can truthfully accept a definition of life which makes it synonymous with suffering', and later he asks: 'And whoever invented the concept of fairness, anyway?' (In *An Invisible Spectator* Bowles is quoted as saying 'Security is a false concept.') There is in the end only one thing we can be sure of. The same – evidently oracular – consular official remarks: 'It's funny. The desert's a big place, but nothing really ever gets lost there.'

CHRISTA WOLF

In the wall-month of November 1989 I translated two pieces from an anthology of East German writing for the magazine *Granta*, which in the end didn't use either of them. (These things happen.) One of them was by Christa Wolf, an extract, I think, from her book *Sommerstück*. It was just two pages long, nothing more than a preamble and image, but of a Shakespearean power and amplitude. A group of adults and children (Wolf's habitual, occasionally irritating, panti-social 'we'), driving in rural East Germany, stop by a beautiful old farmhouse that is in the process of being vandalized by the local youth: doors and windows, furnishings, the massive Dutch stoves in the corners, everything senselessly in ruins. As they leave, a little girl in the party sees a birdcage toppled over in a nettle-patch and walks over to have a look. Then she sees it: the furry remains (what remains) of a cat, locked inside the bird-cage and left to starve and rot.

I thought: could there be a better, more terrible image for what was happening, and what would happen to the East German state? Doesn't it fabulously contain everything: Honecker and his wife in Moscow, in the Chilean Embassy, stalked by reporters (that phrase, 'embassy compound'); the ransacking of the Stasi offices in the cities (the *runde Ecke* in Leipzig – they knew how to bend space); the Politburo huntsmen (hunting being the great GDR perk and hobby, equivalent to golf for the Japanese) now behind bars (the great GDR sanction and *raison d'être*: detention) – all in that one grisly cat? And then I thought: does she know? Could she see East Germany not just (rather obviously) as the abandoned and desecrated house, but as the defunct prison-state which the birds have flown and where the gaolers are now interned? Did she appreciate – or even share – 'the fury of disappearance', in a phrase of Enzensberger's? Was it her prophetic insight, or the construction put upon her words by the anthologist and reader? And could

Review of Christa Wolf, *What Remains and other stories*, trans. Heike Schwarzbauer and Rick Takvorian, and *The Writer's Dimension: Selected Essays*, ed. Alexander Stephan, trans. Jan van Heurk (London: Virago, 1993)

she see herself, even then, as the cat stuffed inside the empty
bird-cage of her oeuvre, maybe in Santa Monica now and a guest
of the Getty Foundation, but for all that still in the doghouse?

Reading the two books now published by Virago is a peculiar
activity and leaves a strange taste. They are neither of them new
– both cover the best part of thirty years – nor yet good. Christa
Wolf isn't a short story writer, or there would be more epiphanies
like the one about the cat: her best books are tissues she weaves
between people (*The Quest for Christa T.*), between themes
(*Accident: A Day's News*), between ages (*No Place on Earth*).
She proceeds by indirection – the short story gives her no space.
And then, you know more than you usually know as a reader,
and you are looking for still more, a tense and unhealthy
looking, a looking for tragedy: you read for dramatic irony, for
the Greek words, hubris, peripeteia, anagnorisis, catharsis; you
follow a person of stature, someone associated with an idea, the
representative of a society. Finally, you don't know quite where
you are – is it Act IV, or the second part of a trilogy, 'Christa
Wolf at Colonus'?

The discrediting of Christa Wolf is in large part a West
German achievement. With Unification, the West bought a cat
in a sack, is peeved about it, and complains. Everything from
the East has suffered revaluation, and East German literature –
which thought itself something special, was thought in the West
to be something special, even was something special – has been
degraded as well. Christa Wolf, as its *Aushängeschild*, its best-
selling literary export and the best-known spokesman – even
apologist – for the country, has copped her considerable share
of vilification.

The West has always had an ambivalent attitude to East
German writing: athletes, spies and writers were three things
the East seemed to be worryingly good at producing. East
German books were published in the West (some houses, like
Luchterhand, Wolf's publishers, specialized in them), and were
read in large numbers. My old copy of *Christa T.* is an 18th
printing, and that was 11 years ago. But East German literature
was always valued inasmuch as it offered criticism of the East
German state: reading it in the West was an exercise in ill-will.
On the one hand, there was the country, which you feared and

hated and claimed didn't exist (*die Zone*, 'the Eastern Zone');
on the other, there were its books (*Zonenliteratur*, disparagingly
– it sounds like science fiction), which you devoured. It is like
the principle of Mariolatry: 'There is no God, and Mary is his
mother.' Christa Wolf's work, implying criticism much of the
time, was highly prized, and partly it was her failure to 'deliver',
in West German terms, that provoked their anger. Having
wasted their time on a tool which didn't do what it was supposed
to do, and turned out not to be needed anyway, they threw it
away. The acknowledgment that had been extended to East
German literature (though never to the East German state) was
revoked in the *Frankfurter Allgemeine Zeitung* and elsewhere.
Christa Wolf surely knows what she is about, following Thomas
Mann to Pacific Palisades fifty years later.

Not that Wolf is completely without blame herself. It seems
to me that she did three things wrong: she retained her
allegiance to (an idea of) East Germany when it was too late
for that; she pulled out of her desk-drawer an old and lachry-
mose piece of writing, *Was bleibt (What Remains)*, written in
June-July 1979, revised in November 1989, published in 1990),
about how she was made to live for a time under the all too
visible eye of the security forces; and, in deadly contrast to that,
she herself – it emerged a little while ago – served the Stasi as
an informant between 1959 and 1962. The first of these is all
her: she was so constituted it would have been impossible for
her to do anything else. The third is all GDR and force of
circumstance – I can't see how anyone from the West, not having
had to suffer similar temptation and duress, can pass judgment
on her for that. Her only real 'error' – one she was free to
commit or not – was the publication of *What Remains*.

Within the GDR, Wolf's role was quite complicated. It seems
to me she was something like a tribune of the people, both
within the system and against it, establishment when seen from
outside East Germany, helpfully and tolerably anti from within.
Her essays refer many times to the letters she receives from
people all over the country; 'Reply to a Reader', for example,
is a letter to a West German medical student about peace and
the future of mankind; in that private-to-public, unknowns-to-
celebrity, MP's-postbag way, she was in touch with many

hundreds of people. *What Remains* has her being visited by a young woman writer, getting poems from a young man, discussing the future (What Remains) after a reading: unofficial channels – she was denied access (she says) to East German radio and television. She seems always to have been helpful to other writers; few can have had a bad word to say of her – she was like a slightly out-of-touch mother-figure to her younger East German colleagues. What she valued about East Germany was the feeling of being plugged into the life of the society. The readings in factories, which the Government probably grew progressively less keen on, may now sound chi-chi, but she was not 'alienated' and 'marginalized', as she felt Western writers were. Goethe's 'creativity without society' she glosses impulsively: 'what a horrible thought!' You could say that her need for the GDR to exist was greater than its own.

Reading through *The Writer's Dimension* (edited down from almost a thousand pages of speeches and addresses and essays in the original – what other writer speaks for a thousand pages!), one senses her attitude to her country cooling a little. It is worth checking the dates at the end of each piece. (The place is never cited, though many of these talks were given in the West or abroad. Wolf was a perfectly trustworthy recipient of the privilege of foreign travel, notably staunch at a colloquium in New York, say.) Still, such things as the terms in which she talks about 'science' – a key locution, which at times seems like a synonym or code-word for 'socialism' – change drastically in the course of the book: in 1968 she calls for a prose appropriate to 'the age of science'; by 1989 she is 'perfectly happy' to be 'highly critical' of it. When the crunch came in that year, she was in favour of continuity with spoonfuls of change: she had a hand in the appeal of writers and artists to which Egon Krenz and other Politburo members then stupidly and infamously added their names; she was booed for using the word 'socialism'; she asked the demonstrators 'to consider whom they would benefit'; and she called Reunification 'a dangerous nonsense'. At the same time, the bones she threw her listeners were laughably and amateurishly literary: she quotes a crowd's slogans back to them, calls for 'many samples of the popular literary creativity' to be 'collected and preserved', notes that 'incidentally, we writers can learn valuable lessons by associating with groups like these.' The note she sounds here is precisely that of the insincere and unteachable politician promising meaningless concessions. Her words as a writer are regularly vitiated by political clichés and considerations: 'grass-roots democracy in action'; 'Picture this: Socialism arrives and no one goes away!' (surely a crib from the sixties poster: 'What if they gave a war and no one came'); or the foul, licensing phrase 'subjective authenticity'.

There is a dichotomy in Christa Wolf's work between the politics of the day and the politics of the long view: in the latter she got nothing wrong – the role of women, freedom, peace, the planet – in the former nothing right. In the long run, it is senseless to be anything other than utopian; in the short term to be utopian is to be stupid. Christa Wolf ends her last piece, from February 1990, by lamenting that 'there is no motherland in sight, no more than before.' The nominal cabinet-representing, heavy-industry-dominated, goose-stepping and abortion-happy three-letter state (GDR) was never a candidate. It was carried by women, on the backs of women, but not for their benefit.

Christa Wolf's movements and thoughts in the last weeks of the GDR can be pieced together quite closely from her essays, and very revealing they are too: a radio interview with a Western journalist on 8 October; on 9 October to Moscow for a week (!) then a hard-hitting but uselessly late article on conformism and false education ('Perhaps now we will . . . admit that torch processions and mass gymnastic exercises are signs of an intellectual vacuum') for the East German *Wochenpost* on 21 October; on 30 October, a long and indulging and horribly ironic interview about a story of hers that had been adapted for Eastern television; a big speech in the Alexanderplatz on 4 November; and another on receiving an honorary doctorate at Hildesheim in the Federal Republic, where for the first time, and very oddly, we encounter the words 'opposition literature'. Imagine that in the original, after a thousand pages! – 'what we intended as our opposition literature'. And then: 'We seem to have been mistaken. Our uprising appears to have come years too late.'

In those months she must have got out her old manuscript,

Was bleibt, revised it and sent it off for publication. It was her decisive mistake: the one time she really tried to play to her audience, and played them false. The slim book appeared, blue sky through a net curtain on its jacket. It describes the course of a single day spent under police surveillance, 'the lowest level of surveillance, the warning kind, the instructions for those carrying out the task being: Conspicuous presence.' The men in the parked car in front of the window all day; the telephone; distrust of friends; an evening reading packed with the wrong people, with her real public locked out and provoked by the police. Its publication was a masterpiece of bad faith and bad timing, an arrant case of me-too-ism. At the very moment the West German press were asking 'Who's afraid of Christa Wolf?' she came forward with a tremulous, back-dated book about her own fears. Elsewhere, in the essays, she talked airily of 'the total commitment of one's personal moral existence', and of how 'strength of character and loyalty to convictions have the power to shape a person's writing style'. How could she begin a story with such a false crust of breathless excitement? The effect of the tenses is still more monstrous in German, with its stricter conjugations:

> Don't panic. One day I will even talk about it in that other language which, as of yet, is in my ear but not on my tongue. Today I knew would still be too soon. But would I know when the time was right? Would I ever find my language? One day I would be old. And how would I remember these days then? Something inside me, which expands in moments of happiness, contracts in fright. When was I last happy?

The enormous turning-circle apparent behind those questions made the politicians appear adroit. Did she actually have to live on Friedrichstrasse and wait for it to be dismantled to notice what had gone on there – entry-point for West Germans and exit for fortunate East Berliners, a less exalted Checkpoint Charlie? Then, later, it emerged that she had once allowed herself to be used as an informant in the way that she now, a kind of *demi-ingénue*, claimed to fear. The stone-throwing West Germans exercised their *Schadenfreude* to the full; they had always envied her success, but what they had found unendurable was the spectacle of her virtue, her decency, her incorruptibility. She had sought to bridge the historic German gulf between 'ideas' and 'the people': now it claimed another victim.

We won't judge Christa Wolf; we are too close, too remote. The subtle grey gradations of East Germany and its bizarre puncturing are lost, except to the imagination. Someone like Christa Wolf will come along one day – as she did for Günder-rode and Bettina von Arnim – and happen upon her case, the woman who was active in 'the most petrified decade' of the century (the 1830s, the 1970s). She will write uninvasively and enthrallingly – perhaps with some future style in her ear, the dream of scientific prose – of this bold woman living among 'an inwardly divided, politically immature people', where 'a well-organized government and security operation stifled every free impulse', and, impassioned by her heroine, she will say: 'We should change our lives. But we are not.'

GERT HOFMANN

After thirty years teaching German literature and writing radio plays, my father suddenly began to write fiction. *Our Conquest* was his fifth book in five years, and the second to be translated into English. (He has since published three others in Germany.) The sense of the possessive in the title is objective: it is we who have been conquered. The book plays for roughly the first 24 hours of peace in a small town in Germany, on a Wednesday in May 1945; and yet, as we shall see, and as the translation has it, a little fortuitously, because the word is *Ruhe* ('quiet'), 'there's never a moment's peace in our town.' There is a famous concrete poem/calendar which goes something like *Krieg/Krieg/Krieg/Krieg/Mai/Juni/Juli*, but to the world of my father's novel, things are rather less clear-cut and progressive. There, the fighting is over, but the war is still everywhere.

It appears that the small town of L. has been taken overnight. Or so it is said. In one of several weirdly sexual phrases, 'quite nonchalantly, the foreign soldiers are flowing in among us.' It is the same situation as in Kafka's short story, 'An Old Manuscript', where the imperial capital wakes up to find itself captured by foreign soldiers, 'nomads': only that, with my father, these soldiers are never actually seen at all. This is much to the regret of the book's central figures, or, better, of its voice or speaker, the 'we'-form that narrates. This plural voice, at once chorus and protagonist, is that of some boys of an unspecified age and indeterminate number. There seem to be enough of them, for instance, to take their friend Edgar in their midst or between them, but then again, they talk of 'our suit' and 'our cap' and even 'ourself'. They are the sons – or possibly just the son – of Frau Imbach, whose name, tacked onto that of the town of L., makes up my father's birthplace. My father does not set riddles, and I have little aptitude for such things: I offer the fact to the reader in all humility.

As well as this narratorial '*we*', which might go into the Greek dual, but, in German or English, continually discomfits the

Review of Gert Hofmann, *Our Conquest*, trans. Christopher Middleton
(Manchester: Carcanet, 1987)

reader, there is 'our friend' Edgar (although 'we' are not his
friends or friend: everywhere in the book is this failure of sym-
metry and equilibrium, of anything that might be thought
reliable or trustworthy). Edgar has been 'bombed out', and has
been sleeping in his friends' shed, or, just lately, with them and
their mother in the cellar. One would say he was older than
they are, and hungrier; at once more astute and purposeful and
less self-serving; that his social roots were at least one-and-a-
half classes below theirs; that he is a Huck to their Tom. On
both sides in different ways, their relationship depends on guilt,
weakness, secrecy and inequality. They seem at times to be little
more than his hostages; while he, with his family and home
destroyed, is an unfortunate and an inferior. For all his 'tall,
fair-haired, pristine skull', he suffers black-outs and headaches
and periods of dizziness; indeed, hunger and pallor and loss
seem to threaten him with becoming 'transparent'. I cannot
begin to say which predicament is closer to my father's, Edgar's
or 'ours' – or if they are both equally remote from it. I know
practically nothing about his story, his background, his war;
only that he was just into his teens when it ended. But a teenager
like Edgar, or like the wet Imbach boys? Or neither? In that
misalliance – somehow, however many they are, they aren't a
collectivity, aren't even the 'two or three gathered together in
my name' of Scripture – the only characters I can identify come
out of books: they are Huck Finn and Tom Sawyer, Hansel and
Gretel, the children of Hamelin, perhaps even Oliver Twist
and Fagin.

Anyway, what VE Day brings for these children is a chance
to get about in town, to indulge their long cooped-up curiosity,
morbidity, acquisitiveness and shame. There is a chance of spot-
ting a black soldier; of finding a nasty substance called
Butterschmalz at the slaughterhouse (I can't believe it's nothing
worse than my dictionary's 'run butter'); of wheedling her dead
husband's suit from a widow; of delivering a letter to an
associate of their missing father's, who owned and ran a whip
factory; of looking round the church and the theatre; of partici-
pating in a grisly atonement rite towards Edgar which involves
digging up his buried knife with the swastika in the handle,
heating it, and ritually wounding themselves (here, too, there is

the weird presence of an erotic element); of finding out who is alive and dead and missing and hurt; of experiencing for themselves the obscene geography of the town: Wundenplan (Wound Place), Siechentor (Sickness Gate), Kellerwiese (Cellar Meadow), though the very worst places have harmless names. Together, they walk through the town of L.

Our Conquest is an episodic book, opportunistic and casual, scenes following each other chronologically and geographically, as they do in my father's first translated novel, *The Spectacle at the Tower*, but with the incidents not subordinated to a single climactic incident (there, the spectacle itself), merely following each other in a series. The point is not character revealing itself in action, it is not even the eventual or abrupt revelation of one particular horror, it is the process – as elsewhere in my father's work – of the curious, obsessive, cruel and mechanical mind digging around in a soft and disordered world. Neither the world nor the consciousness can be said to have truly changed during the process of inquiry, or investigation. Both are much as they were before it began: there can be no question of 'loss of innocence' or anything like that, even the blurb's description of the book as 'a civilian war novel' strikes me as a little rosy. The Imbachs and Edgar resemble children as much or as little as the scarred children's choirs in some of my father's radio plays, or as the wizened little adults in some mournful genre painting. *Altklug* is the German word: literally 'old-clever', as wise as the old, an old head on young shoulders, precocious. Their dialogue moves as purposefully as a flow diagram. They ask questions like scrupulous logicians:

> For instance, which theatres have they played in, how long their longest applause lasted, what sort of people they've been while acting and helped by costumes, how they hit on the idea of theatre as a solution at all and then made it through to the theatre, and if they always know in advance what they exclaim or sing on the stage, suddenly everything at once, or if memorising it takes months and months. Or whereabouts in them or near them are the many persons they portray, when they themselves aren't on the stage – in the morning, for instance, or after a performance?

If the questions about applause and memorizing are innocent enough, the real thrust of the interrogation and that hard word

'solution' is absolutely without remorse: it is that of a prosecu-
ting counsel shredding a man's alibi – viz. that he is himself, an
actor, and not any or all of the questionable parts he would
have played under the Nazis. The actor turns out to be a ter-
rifying figure, with a dramatically unstable identity, an ability
to disappear and reappear at will, and a belief that the truth
can be left behind like a part once played. He is a typical figure
of my father's: at once powerful and ridiculous, with some
physical details but profoundly nebulous, and endowed with the
necessary metaphysics of his profession. Each of the ten or
twelve episodes in *Our Conquest* uncovers such types, each is
an investigation of part of the world; the result may be no more
than the sum of its parts – but nor is a ride on a ghost-train.

When I used the word 'opportunistic', I meant it to describe
the shadings of humour, of the fretful, the macabre and the
speculative, that darken each episode. One of my father's gifts
is to scatter among images or lines of thought that are mysterious
or wilful or decorative, some that are so challengingly straight
and direct that the reader has to treat them as allegorical. In the
slaughterhouse episode, there is a little excursus in which is
described, first how the music-school was relocated in the
slaughterhouse, and then how the butcher turns up, proclaims
his love of music, and wants to take the music-teacher out. Even
leaving history aside (say, the artistic preferences of Goebbels),
one reads this as the German body propositioning the German
soul, or, even worse, one part of that soul propositioning the
other. Or there is the feeling of the Imbach boys that 'a new
long suit, which we'd be able to pull right over [our wounds]
isn't something to be scorned': *Wirtschaftswunder* and sup-
pression of the past. Or, my own favourite, without
commentary: 'The church is just as it was before, including the
hole torn in the back of it that we always like to look at.'
Wherever the world is cut like this – incongruity, failure, poor
timing – it seems to bleed humour. On the very first page, one
blinks and mistrusts the translation, but yes, 'Perhaps, for all
the talk there'd been about it, our defence up on the Hoher
Hain had been *overlooked*' (my italics) is right: what a fantastic
and ignominious fate! Later on the same page, in the pirating and
parroting of their geography classes, the speakers say: 'we live

in an indeterminate, almost characterless upland region, imperceptibly polluted and sooted by a few not-so-distant industrial centres.' But here, what my father wrote is rather funnier, because the region is 'unobtrusively' or 'discreetly' polluted (*unauffällig*, not *unmerklich*). Imperceptible pollution isn't funny: it isn't 'the imperceptible charm of the bourgeoisie' either. All these grotesques and humoresques may seem rather sophisticated, but there are also some moments that are beyond explanation, being perfectly simple, as when, asked by the actor what part 'we' would like to play, 'we' reply 'the ocean'.

It is a peculiar moment, like a glimpse of blue sky from the ghost train or the darkened chamber of horrors, a tiny and unexpected escape from this rigged-up world, where there's a dead dog under the dead lilac, a buried knife in the Amselgrund, a dark liquid seeping out from under one of the doors of the slaughterhouse, and Herr Schellenbaum found in rigor mortis, and having to be buried in a sitting position. I talked about inquiring and excavating earlier, but really, there are numbered manhole covers over each of these exhibits. I used to think it might be the theatre behind it: a well-lit scene, the latest stage of the pilgrimage, a new interlocutor, a cardboard cut-out prop named for the convenience of the audience – Wundenplan, or Siechentor; or perhaps the radio dramas that my father has written for 35 years – a medium still more gruesome, still more mobile, *Kunstkopf* aping geography. But isn't it more the gaiety and violence and lust and unpredictability of the fairground, a garish non-nature, checkpoint for children and adults, animals and freaks, a thrilling and spilling, packed and faked and stuffed world that elicits *real* responses? In the scenes of Bosch and Brueghel the world of war and the fun of the fair are seen to be neighbours. The children in Beirut don't look especially downcast.

WOLFGANG KOEPPEN

It was the painter Kokoschka who said, 'If you last, you'll see
your reputation die three times, and even three cultures.' This
is just what has happened to Wolfgang Koeppen, whose career
has spanned six decades, from Weimar to post-Unification
Germany. Important critics have repeatedly hailed him as – with
Grass – 'the greatest living German writer', but in spite of that,
he has remained vastly less known and less read, a victim of
call it what you will: Kokoschka's 'Law of Longevity', the cen-
sorship of fashion, the tyranny of neglect, the neglect of fashion,
the fashion of neglect ... Articles on him have been published
with titles one might translate as 'Wolfgang Koeppen: the
Anatomy of a Failure'. However, the failure is not Koeppen's
but Germany's, and its circumstances are both specific and
illuminating.

Koeppen was born in 1906 in Greifswald on the Baltic coast.
He studied, in the German manner, various subjects at various
universities he doesn't seem to care to have publicized, and
probably never took his degree. From 1931 to 1934 he had
what he described as the only regular employment of his life,
when he worked as a journalist for the *Berliner Börsen-Courier*.
He published a novel, *Eine unglückliche Liebe (An Unhappy
Love Affair)*, left Germany for Holland in 1935, published
another, *Die Mauer schwankt (The Tottering Wall)*, but returned
to Germany before the war broke out. He then dropped out of
view until the 1950s, when, in the space of four years, he
published the three novels that (perhaps for the second time!)
made his reputation, all of them written very quickly, in no
more than three or four months apiece, he says. These books
are among the best things to have come out of post-war
Germany: *Tauben im Gras (Pigeons on the Grass*; there is an
English translation by David Ward, published by Holmes &
Meier in 1988), set in Munich in a single day, a modernist
jigsaw in 110 pieces and showing 30 figures; *Das Treibhaus
(The Hothouse)*, about the dilemma of a Socialist member of

Introduction to Wolfgang Koeppen, *Death in Rome*, trans. Michael Hofmann
(London: Hamish Hamilton, 1992)

the Bundestag during a rearmament debate, and something of a *succès de scandale*; and *Death in Rome*, the most accessible and I think the best of the three, about a German family reunion in Rome. The three books form a loose trilogy, an interrogation of the Federal Republic's phoenix act, the famous *Wirtschafts-wunder*. Since then, in almost forty years, Koeppen has published only one short work of semi-fiction, *Die Jugend (Youth)*, three travel books about Russia, America and France, and some essays and reviews. His silence – which is perceived as such – is one of the loudest things in German literature today.

So much for the fast-forward version. Taken a little more slowly, it shows the troubling shape of a career in twentieth-century German letters. Where Chancellor Kohl congratulated himself on being born late, Koeppen could lament being born early. He was formed by the 1920s, the great decade of mod-ernism, late expressionism and *Neue Sachlichkeit*. He read Proust, Kafka, Faulkner and Woolf as they appeared. *Ulysses* – the 1926 small-press edition of the first German translation – was the stuff his dreams were made of. By the 1930s his own career had begun. He went abroad. He wasn't a Nazi. He returned. He didn't have the reputation, the contacts, the command of foreign languages to enable him to make his way in exile. Nor did he lay claim to the condition of 'internal exile'. Along with the poet Gottfried Benn and a very few other significant writers he lived through the period in Germany.

This put him at a disadvantage later. One might have supposed that the *status quo ante* 1933 would be restored as a matter of urgency, but that isn't what happened. Instead, the story was one of discontinuity. It was as though the literature had been bombed as the cities had been. It took until the sixties and even the seventies for the classic books of the twenties and thirties – a Silver Age of German letters – to get back into print, for the still-living writers from that period to be 'discovered' and the dead ones to be exhumed. Precedence was given to the returning exiles – to Thomas Mann in the West, Brecht in the East – and to the work of new writers like the *Gruppe 47*. The preferred form for literature was a clean slate, with only the distinguished markings of a very few on it – the ones with cast-iron alibis. It was a very German solution – *Schwamm drüber!* – unjust and evasive and superficial, an extension of collective amnesia.

Koeppen's position was exacerbated by the nature of the books he wrote and published in the early fifties. Far from underwriting a fresh start, they connected stylistically with the twenties and politically with the thirties. They were works of memory and continuance and criticism – and they were savaged for it by the press. The response to them was characterized by 'hostility, even revulsion and repugnance' (*Neue Zürcher Zeitung*). Their detractors squealed at their ferocity and outspokenness, their self-conscious and difficult technique, their sexual content. 'Is this really what we need at such a time in our history?' (always an obnoxious argument in literary politics) was the gist, 'let's look on the bright side!' Even those praising Koeppen were embarrassed by the political content of his books, or sold their artistry short. And so the conservatism of the modish and dirigible German public won out. Koeppen's books never had anything like the currency and acclaim they deserved. Five years later, Grass's *Die Blechtrommel* appeared; another four, and Böll's *Ansichten eines Clowns*; and the internationally accredited commodity 'post-war German literature' had come into existence. The earliest and fullest and most drastic description of German post-war reality didn't figure in it. Anyway, whether for that reason or others, Koeppen gave up fiction. His travel books were respectfully reviewed – no one to tell him what he had and hadn't, could and couldn't see – but as a writer of fiction, in spite of the efforts of two determined publishers and a handful of *cognoscenti*, he has ceased to exist. It is a great scandal.

Death in Rome is the most devastating novel about the Germans that I have ever read, and one of the most arresting on any subject. It takes a German family – not a real German family, not even a caricature German family, but a prototypical German family that George Grosz would have had the bile but not the wit to invent, and Musil or Mann the wit but not the bile – and brings them to Rome, a city having an association with Germans that goes back hundreds of years, there to enact their conflicts.

It is a history book, a family book, a book about the battle over who gets to represent the authentic face of Germany.

Significantly, this German family is all male. (Of course there are women in it too, but they are minor, though also well done.) There is the older generation, consisting of Gottlieb Judejahn, the unreconstructed and unkillable old SS man, and his brother-in-law Friedrich Wilhelm Pfaffrath, who held office under the Nazis and is once more making his way up the greasy pole, this time as democratically elected burgomaster; and there are their respective rebel sons: Adolf Judejahn, who is on his way to becoming a Catholic priest, and his cousin, Siegfried Pfaffrath, a composer of serial music. (There is also Siegfried's conformist brother Dietrich, but let's forget about him for the moment.) These four represent the four principal areas of German achievement, or the four quarters of the riven German soul: murder, bureaucracy, theology and music. It is like having Frederick the Great, Bismarck, Luther and Beethoven in one family. Their movements, their meetings and remeetings in the alien city of Rome – which, interestingly, offers each of them what they want, so each of them sees it in a different version – are, as the novelist and critic Alfred Andersch pointed out, choreographed like a ballet: a macabre ballet of outrageous contrivance, viewed by the reader with growing horror, alarm and incredulity: how *dare* these people show their faces, how *can* they belong together . . .

This is part of Koeppen's point. Church and state. Music and the camps. You can't have one of them without the others. In the fifties when Germany wanted severance and disavowal of the past, Koeppen showed it bonds of steel and blood instead. He gave Germans a character at a time when they were supposed not to have one; he wrote the history of a period that strove for greyness, and – until invented by Fassbinder – had seemed invisible: whatever happened between 1945 and the World Cup in 1966?! There is something implacable, almost vindictive – like one of his Furies – about his pursuit of the Germans post-war, post-Holocaust, post-division, turning away from their crimes towards rehabilitation and the EC, once again exporting their goods and their culture and themselves. He shows them to us. All of them.

Death in Rome is a comprehensive and brilliant provocation of an entire nation (it's only a pity that the nation didn't respond a little better to it). It begins, like all the best German stories, with the words, '*Es war einmal . . .* ', 'Once upon a time', and it ends with a dirty, tawdry version of the last sentence of *Death in Venice* (the original of which is helpfully given as an epigraph). In between there are countless glancing references to German history, from Roman times to when the novel was written in 1954. There is a whole micro-plot about the German presence in Rome, from Alaric the Goth to the Holy Roman Emperor Charlemagne (who was also Emperor of Germany, is known as Karl der Grosse, and lies buried in Aachen), Henry IV's penitential visit to Pope Gregory VII at Canossa, the cultural trippers of the Grand Tour including Goethe, and finally Hitler himself on his fraternal visits to Mussolini. In their various ways – destroyer, ruler, penitent, tourist, warrior – these are all antecedents for the various Judejahns and Pfaffraths who have descended on the city now. As I said before, Koeppen is interested in establishing continuity and pattern.

Most of the German references concern the Nazi period – although the Nazis themselves, in their hunt for legitimacy and historical validation, had a deliberate policy of reinvesting old words, old places, old habits and old wars. For instance, they set up their élite 'Napola' schools in the old Teutonic fortresses in the East – which is why Adolf and Siegfried talk about their school as the Teutonic castle or academy; they revived concepts like the *Femegericht*, the 'Vehmic Court', first used in fourteenth-century Westphalia, then applied to political killings in the 1920s; they tried wherever possible to associate themselves with the military traditions of German history. And so the great majority of these terms and references are military or power-related, and are woven in around the figure of Judejahn, whose own immaculate National Socialist c.v. takes in everything that was anything in terms of right-wing murder and thuggery in the years after 1918: the Ruhr Uprising, the Freikorps, the Kapp Putsch, the Black Reichswehr. Of course, it's all too bad to be true – no single person can have participated in *all* of the above – but it tags, insists, calls to mind, reinforces the myth. Koeppen is calling the German language as evidence of the recurring violence and power-lust of German history.

I would like the English reader not to be too bothered by all this. If it's any comfort, I doubt whether most German readers would be able to explain half the references. It isn't necessary. You take in the principle of historical labelling and cross-referencing, feel the (foreign) texture of the word, take from the context whether it's a building or a political movement or a personality that's being referred to, and pass on. It can be read pedantically – by all means, consult an encyclopaedia – but it wasn't written in such a spirit, and the original didn't come with notes either. *Death in Rome* works as myth much better than as an agglomeration of allusions.

Koeppen seems to sit on the shoulders of his four main protagonists and parrot their thoughts and impressions: the brutal, rueful Judejahn (rueful for not having killed more); the discriminations – havering but also frank in their way – of Siegfried; pat Adolf and fearful Pfaffrath. In the modernist manner, they take up prismatically different attitudes to the same things: sex, dress, food, the gods and God, myth, Rome. Judejahn has his desert, and Siegfried the Africa for his black symphony. The spooky arms-dealer Austerlitz has his warmed milk, Siegfried and Adolf their ice-cream. Everywhere there is congruence and difference. The events and perspectives of the book are related in a wonderful, highly wrought and rhythmic prose – how many novels are there about which you can say they have rhythm? – short, spat-out sentences, and long, sweeping, comma'd-off periods, protocols of consciousness that are actually less difficult to follow than they seem. Koeppen's style commends itself both to the eye and the ear, as much as to the cells of memory and knowledge. It was the style – gorgeous, bristling, pugnacious – that got me sold on the book, and that from the very first sentence: 'Once upon a time, this city was a home to gods . . . ' If that worked, then everything else had to, too.

A note on the names. Both surnames are significant fabrications: 'Judejahn' from *Jude*, a Jew, and *jahn*, not a word but like a cross between *Wahn*, madness, and *jäten*, to weed out; and Pfaffrath, from *Pfaffe*, a disrespectful term for a priest, and *rath*, council or counsel. With the first names, there is an awful irony in the way the fathers have named the sons – and been named by their own fathers before them! – as they themselves should have been named. No one likes or fits his own name. There is a narcissistic syncopation in the way the Nazis have names from the pious empire, Friedrich Wilhelm and Gottlieb (love-god); and the rebels and expatriates are called Adolf and Siegfried. Siegfried's brother Dietrich is named by Koeppen after Diederich, the creepy and servile anti-hero of Heinrich Mann's novel *Der Untertan*; while the word 'Dietrich' means a picklock. Truly, he will inherit the earth.

BOHUMIL HRABAL

If totalitarian governments had been a little less assiduous, and Western publishers a little more so, we might have had a different literary history for the late twentieth century. In particular, the blend of allegory, surrealism, fantasy and exuberant narrative that we associate with Latin America, trace back to Faulkner, and call Magic Realism, might equally well be thought of as Central European, derived from Hasek and Kafka (both born in Prague in 1883), and called, I don't know, Celestial Provincialism or something. And then – 'this story of how the unbelievable came true' – the name of the Czech writer Bohumil Hrabal (1914–1997) would be as widely known as that of, say, Gabriel García Márquez.

Certainly, not since I read Márquez twenty years ago have I enjoyed an author so much as Hrabal. It was like revisiting the primal, irresponsible pleasure of reading in childhood. Whenever I wasn't reading, it wasn't the book I'd laid aside, but myself, it felt like. Hrabal's paragraphs had me sighing with contentment – I kept writing 'Ah' in the margins – I was too captivated even to look at the page numbers, and when I finished a book, I went straight on to the next one, or the last one, as I read and re-read back and forth among his seven books in English.

The spread of Hrabal's reputation has been hindered subtly and successfully in English; unsubtly and unsuccessfully in Czech, where he is – correctly – the most popular author of recent time, and has his writings collected – as they should be – in thirteen volumes. In English, the two things that spoke most loudly for Hrabal – the 1967 Academy Award given to Jiri Menzel's film of his novel *Closely Observed Trains*, and the advocacy of Milan Kundera – have been unluckily self-defeating. The film seemed, not least in recollection, such a completely satisfying thing in itself, that it didn't draw one to the book; typically, Hrabal himself remarked that he too preferred it!

Review of Bohumil Hrabal, *Dancing Lessons for the Advanced in Age*, trans. Michael Henry Heim (London: Harvill, 1997), and *Total Fears*, trans. James Naughton (Prague: Twisted Spoon Press, 1998)

While Kundera's praise, 'our very best writer today', coming from someone whom *we* in our unwisdom perhaps wanted to be that writer, probably met with a 'ho-hum' from us, when we should just have taken him at his word.

Such *malheurs* come to seem predictably trivial when set beside the chicanes that Hrabal and his books had to endure in his native land. Though he graduated from the Charles University with a doctorate of law, he worked, as the blurbs tell us, 'as a stagehand, postman, clerk, and baler of waste paper'. Parenthetically and acceptingly and with heroic absurdity, he relates in *Total Fears* how 'a crane fell on top of me in Kladno in fifty-two, after which my writing got better'. Even so, it wasn't until 1963, when he was almost fifty, that his first book was published. Thereafter, his books came out in unhelpful bursts – five in two years of the 'Prague Spring' – or not at all – he wasn't allowed to publish for some seven years, following 1968 – or they came out with long delays, or in censored versions – in his introduction to *The Little Town Where Time Stood Still*, Josef Skvorecky quotes a breathtaking example of that – or in samizdat editions, or from emigre presses: really, just about everything that could befall books under Communist regimes befell Hrabal's books. Even when reckoned together retrospectively it seems hair-raising; to live through and navigate it must have been impossible. The beautiful and informal late book, *Total Fears*, gives some sense of what it was like, especially in the title piece. Hrabal's method of dealing with the pressure he was put under from both sides – anti-method, really – was to give ground, to live in guilt and terror, and to drink. He describes himself as 'a man of no character', but his books have integrity. Except when he suffered them to be rewritten by the literary police he never wrote to please government or opposition. He functioned, in a chaotic, half-unintended way, as the lightning conductor for his books: 'and I couldn't drive the car, my wife had to drive, and I was shorter by ten centimetres, in a state of collapse . . . because I like to be afraid, it makes me write better, also writing is my only salvation from that gentle police terror.' It must have taken a terrible toll on him – not least on his sense of self-worth, having to endure pieces on himself like one by Ivan Klima called 'The Two Hrabals', whose

drift one can guess at all too easily – but it leaves his books
with their own gaiety and their own sadness, barely touched by
twentieth-century politics and ideologies. His refusal to play –
or, better, to do anything but play – must have been infuriating to
the authorities, and to the dissidents even a little disappointing.

In a subtle way, Hrabal's books are not escapist, as the
beautiful reflections of a kaleidoscope or a soap-bubble are
not escapist. He mockingly transcended the crude categories of
socialist realism. Such patent *Feindbilder* as Germans, Austrians,
Russians, gypsies, bourgeois are always treated kindly in his
books. Even in *Closely Observed Trains*, which doesn't quite
have the seamless freedoms of later novels, the first SS men are
'beautiful', while the soldier with whom the hero lies dying in
a ditch is pitiable, going '*Mutti, Mutti*' the whole time. Ditie,
the hero of *I Served the King of England*, is a waiter whose
favourite avocation is scattering flowers over naked women, and
whose ambition it is to become a millionaire and to open his
own hotel. If there is anything indoctrinating in this, it is hardly
the right sort of doctrine! When politics puts in a rare appear-
ance in a Hrabal book, there is something shrunken and almost
merry about it. In *Dancing Lessons for the Advanced in Age*,
the cobbler, brewer, soldier and ladies' man who speaks the
whole thing in one spellbinding sentence, describes himself as
'an engineer of human feet', deprecates most forms of progress,
and hankers after the days of the (Austrian) monarchy – into
which of course Hrabal himself was born, in 1914 – when 'there
were women who had to wear rucksacks filled with bricks to
keep from toppling over, they were really something those
bosoms, from morning till night the monarchy thought of
nothing but bosoms', and military uniforms were so exquisite
'the only possible competition would be nature wanting to show
what it could do and coming up with another kingfisher or
parrot'. This monster of gallantry – who also appears as Uncle
Pepin in 'The Death of Mr Baltisberger' and *The Little Town*,
and was apparently based on Hrabal's own Uncle Pepin – sits
there, addressing his 'beauties', with a book of dreams in one
hand and 'Mr Batista's book on sexual hygiene' in the other,
and makes 'strict reality' (Wallace Stevens's phrase) look pretty
sick: not, be it noted, because he is a creature of fantasy and

escape, but rather because he contains more reality in him than most writers and most regimes can manage.

Hrabal's great subject, it seems to me, is actually work. It is the dispatching of trains, with the traffic office 'always vibrating to the gentle humming and jingling and twittering of telegraphs and telephones, like the shop of some dealer in singing birds'. It is Pepin's description of brewing, Maryska's of sausage-making, Ditie's of waiting tables, Hant'a's of pulping books: 'For thirty-five years now I've been compacting old paper in my hydraulic press. I've got five years till retirement and my press is going with me, I won't abandon it, I'm saving up, I've got my own bankbook and the press and me, we'll retire together, because I'm going to buy it from the firm, I'm going to take it home and stash it somewhere among the trees in my uncle's garden.' It is stray descriptions throughout his work of barmen and lavatory cleaners, tram drivers, football players, readers, mechanics, motorcycle racers. It is a lovely description of Michael Jordan, whom he saw on American television, as related in *Total Fears*: 'Each time he magically caught the ball, which kind of hesitated in his pink palms for a bit, he went round his opponents with his bent smooth-shaven head, then suddenly he thrust up, with those hands and that leap of his – and the ball just swung into the net.' Whenever there is work, or someone working, Hrabal becomes sublimely attentive, gentle, sympathetic. It is a tragedy for the secret police who harried and wooed him – inasmuch as they did so with any discrimination – and for the so-called 'really existing socialism' of Czechoslovakia and elsewhere, that Hrabal could not be won for their persuasion: he was so gifted that he might have given socialist realism some aesthetic distinction. Or perhaps again, this too was something that he owed them, like the inspiring condition of terror in which he lived, for it was thanks to them, as he notes with cherubic irony, in his compact book about compacting books, *Too Loud a Solitude*, that 'the fourth estate was depopulated and the proletariat went from base to superstructure and . . . the university-trained élite now carries on its work'.

Over time and books, the point of focus or balance in Hrabal's novels moves back and back; it is the beginnings of his early books one remembers and returns to, and the endings of his later books. He loved jazz, and had the ability of jazz to bend and combine incompatible things till they go together. All his books, I think, begin and end in completely different places, moving from boisterous charm and levity to remarkable darkness. *The Little Town* seems little more than a series of gags – blood-gags, glue-gags, chimney-gags, wardrobe-gags, drowning-gags – but ends in a weirdly futuristic old people's home. *I Served the King of England* is, I think, the first book where the Hrabal ensemble really swings, from its witty and sexy *Krull*-like beginning, where the girl so wants our hero, she stands there pouring glass after glass of grenadine over herself, then all sorts of vicissitudes, to an ending of proper eremetic desolation. The movement in *Too Loud a Solitude* is from Hasek to Kafka, the voice of the indomitable Svejk-like subordinate shockingly cutting into the bleak ending of 'In the Penal Colony'. The constituents of the novel, mulched paper and beer, were the constituents of Hrabal's life. It is one of the great books of the century.

The conditions under which Hrabal created this *oeuvre*, their grievous, indestructible memory and final lifting with the collapse of Communism in 1989, are all recorded, along with visits to Britain and 'the Delighted States' in an extraordinary series of half-imaginary letters to 'Dubenka' – a visiting American student, who made a great impression on Hrabal – collected as *Total Fears*. Anyone interested in Hrabal or in Central European history in the period should read it. It is quick, rambling, spoken, but purposeful writing. The distant addressee makes it a little more accessible than a journal or memoir would have been. It reminds me of the Polish writer Tadeusz Konwicki's *Moonrise, Moonset* (published in translation in 1987); like Hrabal, Konwicki wanted freedom to record events, thoughts, responses, memories during a period of rapid and unpredictable change. Some people have called it Konwicki's best book, but I wouldn't go that far, nor with *Total Fears*, though both books are fully and fascinatingly circumstantial.

Between the years of '89 and his death in '97, Hrabal was blessed by the great efflorescence of his readership; but the Czechs were as blessed in having him. I envy them their Hrabal in thirteen volumes, and would like to think it will be possible to read more of his books in English. He has excellent and committed translators – Michael Heim in California, James Naughton at Oxford, Paul Wilson in Toronto – and I have bumped into many other titles that are, unfortunately, like *trompe l'oeil* doors, merely English titles for Czech works. Perhaps, with a little *glasnost* of our own, we can have them opened for us.

ADAM CZERNIAWSKI, JAKOV LIND, MANES SPERBER

These books are the autobiographies of three displaced persons. In terms of *anno domini*, they might make up a single, almost seamless life: childhood (Czerniawski), youth (Sperber) and manhood (Lind). But such a life would be a monster of contradiction. Two of the authors write in their acquired language, English, and one has been translated from German; two are individualists, one is a subscriber to causes, a disciple and a belonger; two are (rather dissimilar) Jews, one had a Catholic upbringing; two fetch up in England, one in France. I will be Anglocentric and begin with the English.

One of the points made in the coverage of Maastricht was that for the English, Europe is traditionally a place from which bad things have tended to come, invasions and rabies and so forth. Dover presents chalk cliffs rather than a Statue of Liberty. So protected, the English have remained relatively inviolate, the most settled and exclusive of peoples, enjoying the baffling and specialized condition known as Englishness, a thing at once glorious and unserious and – almost its first definition – eminently worth defending. It's a strange thing, then, in these days of the double opt-out and a Home Office policy so ferocious towards asylants that it has broken the law, to read the accounts of two men coming to England as a refuge and a new home, written in English by men born in Warsaw and Vienna. Czerniawski and Lind came here in the first post-war decade, and are – to me oddly and blithely – unconcerned about questions of entry, residence and nationality. (Lind marries an English girl who seems hotter than he is on the matter of aliens gaining work permits; Czerniawski drily describes the efforts of Ernest Bevin to get him and his family repatriated, 'now that Stalin has re-established independent Poland'.)

Perhaps, on balance, it really was a more decent age than the

Review of Adam Czerniawski, *Scenes from a Disturbed Childhood* (London: Serpent's Tail, 1991); Jakov Lind, *Crossing: The Discovery of Two Islands* (London: Methuen, 1991); and Manes Sperber, *The Unheeded Warning 1918–1933*, trans. Harry Zohn (London: Holmes and Meier, 1991)

present. I remember a Glasgow immigration official telling me, just turned 16 and half-way through the hermetic world of Winchester, 'to register wuth the pawlis', notwithstanding Common Market and all. I had to wonder what Cerberus at Dover would now swallow Lind's declaration of love for the English language, or Czerniawski, a Pole among Poles, to his consternation nicknamed 'the Englishman' in a camp in Gaza by a naive teacher. These books might almost suggest assimilation is possible, and Englishness an elective condition. You only have to want it badly enough. Perhaps the wicked Continent is actually full of Englishmen *in spe*?

Scenes from a Disturbed Childhood is the most modest of the books, and in some respects the most successful. Czerniawski has been prevailed upon, initially by a Radio Three producer, then by his publishers (it seems that writers, to their credit, usually need to be talked into writing their autobiographies), to tell the story of his childhood. In English terms, it is an extraordinary story; in Polish terms, it is one of a number of representative stories, and none the less interesting for that. Accordingly, and quite rightly, Czerniawski is writing it twice over: one version in English, perhaps from outside, deadpan, passive; and one in Polish, more intimate, more detailed and historical, I would hazard. Adam Czerniawski was born into a *grand bourgeois* family in Warsaw in 1934. When the war broke out, the family fled first East, where his father, by then mobilized, managed to get into Romania and join the Polish government-in-exile; then, unavailingly, West; and finally back to Warsaw. In 1941, just as Hitler turned on the USSR, permission came for the rest of the family, the author, his sister and his mother, to leave, which they did by way of Vienna and Budapest. They reached Sofia in Bulgaria only by the freakish chance that their urgent appeals to a Mr Zlotarev were misdirected to a man of the same name who happened to be Deputy Foreign Minister. The family was reunited in Istanbul, and spent the rest of the war in Turkey, Lebanon and the British Protectorate of Palestine.

This is where Czerniawski ended up spending five years – the remaining five years, one is tempted to say – of his boyhood. Names like Jerusalem, Ramallah, Tel Aviv and Beirut appear in the narrative, all touched with a strange innocence: the main action was still elsewhere. And yet, if anything, the region was even more riddled with ironies and tensions than it is now, because of the imposition of so many Europeans and *their* conflicts. At the same time, violence was not so readily available as a solution. A Polish Army was being set up in Palestine, and Jewish settlers from Poland found themselves living alongside emaciated hymn-singing Poles released from Stalin's camps. The young Czerniawski learned Hebrew and Arabic, and had to mind his p's and q's in both. Historical and racial strife were filtered down to the boy in striking linguistic and cultural brushes: 'I now have a long trek to the Polish school in Montefiore Street. Outside the gates at break time Arab ice-cream vendors bawl out Polish obscenities in the mistaken belief acquired from the schoolchildren that these words describe the colours and flavours of their wares. The school functions six days a week, and as I march there on a Sabbath with my prominent school satchel, I get stoned by Jewish children.' To a Polish reader, some of these complications must be familiar – from other reading, if nothing else. To the English they are an education in the ironies of history.

Czerniawski's progress through *Scenes from a Disturbed Childhood* is full of such little coloured sidelights. It is sensible, unquestioning and intrepid. There is no psycho- or emotional stuff, no playing to the reader – only some very English downplaying – no heightening or false embellishment. His use of the present tense throughout is astonishing and masterful. It acquires something provisional and modest – only the past tense claims to tell you everything. It is like a puppeteer's present, which makes safe, makes small and points up. I wonder if I have ever read an autobiography which makes so little *Tamtam* about the author; it is almost like an autobiography without the hero, enclitic, just Horatio or just Pylades. Events in Warsaw, for instance, he describes in a few pages of short quotations from a variety of sources – family members and politicians, soldiers, ambassadors. Some of the best lines are his sister's, an indication of some selflessness. One or two chapters have at the end of them small sections of 'random memories' of his own, a generous feature and more authentic than expanding them and incorporating them into his main text. And conversely, bits of that text leap out at you for their beauty, memorableness and suggestive power. Returning to bombed Warsaw in 1940: 'The cactuses on the balcony were covered in snow. Under the snow they were green but they collapsed like punctured balloons when the snow was removed.' That seems to me to be worth pages and pages of description and analysis. Similarly, a novel or play might be spun from this, about his father, a tobacco importer in peacetime, and now stuck in the Middle East and not allowed to fight: 'With time on his hands, he works on a tobacco blend agreeable to the palate of Polish troops and designs a board game based on the map of Europe, with Polish soldiers fighting their way to Warsaw on every front.'

So somehow, for circumstantial historical reasons, Czerniawski has wound up in England. The fact that he is a Polish poet, and translates Polish poetry into English might prompt one to situate him just offshore – where a ring of translators is working to defend England from foreign culture – but that would be unjust. In the English version of his memoir, at any rate, his Englishness is comically and consciously apparent. He describes his assimilation lectures of 1947: 'Now and then chaps from the British Council arrive to explain the British way of life to us.' Asked whether he feels homesick for Poland, he replies, having recently moved house in England, that what he really misses is Gloucestershire. In most cases of this kind, one's practical allegiances don't survive a period much longer than ten years.

Jakov Lind was 27 when he came to England, and having knocked around a bit, he was more purposeful about it (there are two previous volumes of his autobiography, called *Counting My Steps* and *Numbers*). What influenced him was the outcome and conduct of the war, which he, a Jew, had experienced at first hand, in Austria, Germany and Holland. As his friend Michael Hamburger wrote, 'no wonder Jakov Lind has become a specialist in the monstrous!' The Continent was insupportable, he couldn't live in Israel, indomitable Churchillian England was the place for him. And yet what brought him over was the most egregious misunderstanding of the nature of the English language which had beckoned to him as a child: 'Because of this discrepancy between spoken and written language, I had the impression that anyone could speak or write it; it was a free-for-all and not just made for Englishmen and Americans, Australians and Canadians. English seemed to know no rules and had a grammar one could apparently learn in four or five easy lessons.' I think English is exactly the opposite. Far from being without rules it is full of them, unwritten and unspoken for the most part, and the rules are full of exceptions. It is a language meant to discourage and to betray, full of class-traps, attitude-traps and provenance-traps. It is ruled by usage, the Queen and Pseuds' Corner, a language you use at your peril. Later on, Lind has many shrewd observations to make on England and the English: their sober mentality and love of ghosts, their pity for foreigners, their disapproval of anyone trying too hard, their utter incomprehension of Europe, the essentially negative qualities such as incuriosity and anonymity that make up for the want of such positives as, say, cafés. He has two lovely anatomies of individual Englishmen: the first, now deceased, the tobacconist who absolutely insists he is closed and refuses to serve his customer; the second, the odd, Coleridgean type who cadges a drink after hours and the next day denounces the publican to the police.

The burden of this volume of Lind's autobiography is the way he came to have a literary career, something he seems to have mixed feelings about, to say the least. To be someone in German post-war literature occasions him guilt and even repugnance. Twenty years after the original, sensational publication of *Seele aus Holz* (*Soul of Wood*), he refashioned himself as an English writer – since 1982, he has been writing in English. It is a long way to have to go, and even then, it isn't far enough. Lind seems uncommonly liable to wonder at the nullity of things – money, drugs, sex, success, America, the list of Martin Amis titles. They have come to him and he enjoys them, but at the same time, in some deep way, he wishes they hadn't. *Crossing* is the book of an unhappy Midas, a man unable to come to terms with this century and what he has done himself in order to adapt and survive in it. It is sloppily written – as though it might have been dictated – with little pride or joy. His books, typically, are barely mentioned, and the violent imagination that he displays in them – the golden touch – is absent here. The only rhythmically convincing passage is this:

> The publishers. The readers. The editors. They thought I could write. I thought I could write but now I see I can't write a line. I'm dumbfounded. I am silent. I'll never write another line. I'm finished. Fifteen thousand dollars have blocked my veins. I'm as good as dead. I'm burned out. I'm through. I'm busy, very busy, staring at the ceiling, praying for a global catastrophe that'll end it all.

Even if it was only said for effect, you know it's true anyway. Lind reminds me of another tall, handsome emigrant with a taste for the monstrous, cosmic disgust and *taedium vitae:* George Grosz. *Crossing* is an unintentionally shattering read.

George Grosz provides the cover for Manes Sperber's *The Unheeded Warning,* but the match is not one of temperament, merely of chronology. Sperber, born in 1905 and died in 1984, an Adlerian psychologist, engagé novelist and publisher, is the most formidably gifted of these three autobiographers, and the present volume, the second in a trilogy called *All Our Yesterdays,* is a rich piece of work reflecting the early years of an energetic and precocious young man. 'Even today I am able to re-experience the beginning of every friendship I have made since my youth.' His book is spontaneous, sincere and exhaustive. His method is self-analytical: he not only recreates the past, he interrogates his own role in it. It is demanding to read – and is written in a formal, three-piece style that is respected by the translator Harry Zohn.

Not the least part of what interests me in Sperber comes from the fact that he was born ten years after the novelist Joseph Roth, and that his life follows the same movements as Roth's: born in a village in Galicia, came to Vienna as a child, went to Berlin in the twenties, visited the Soviet Union, and went into exile in France. Almost inevitably, then, *The Unheeded Warning* describes many of the things familiar to me from Roth's books: the Europe of the time, cloven between Bolshevism and America; crowd scenes and demonstrations; the faddishness of Berlin, 'the most recognition-happy city in the world'; the spies and other sinister types that washed up there. Unlike Roth, though, Sperber was an ideologue and a believer, a 'Marxist Adlerian', he calls himself. From a very committed position, he catches all the dynamics of the myriad groupings of the time, the remote-controlled German Communist Party, referring to Moscow as 'home', just as much as the different Jewish and post-Freudian groups. The 'warning' of his title refers to the rise of Nazism, but also to Sperber's own feelings of culpability for his continued support of Stalin. He is brilliant on bigotry – *Kadavergehorsam* (literally, the obedience of the corpse), faith and loyalty carried to excess.

GEORGE KONRAD

After a lost war, Hofmannsthal said, one should write comedies, and in the twenties, within his limitations and against his genius, he did just that. I wonder what he would prescribe for the countries of Eastern Europe – many of them former Habsburg territories – after what is infinitely worse than a lost war: regional entropy; systemic collapse; an abrupt close brackets on an experiment that failed; a largely bloodless and painfully incomplete reversion to the *status quo ante* of forty, fifty, even ninety years ago; future generations exposed to the deleterious half-lives of political, industrial and human debris; the discrediting of one set of political ideas in favour of another, older, just as discredited and probably far more violent – the belief in race and nation. Riddle? Farce? Silence?

The regimes of Eastern Europe may have been oppressive and iniquitous, but the fiction and poetry written under them were for a time quite outstanding. This was partly because of the system, which was oddly literary in outlook and valued writers, though of course not as much as athletes; partly in spite of it – its preferences as regarded form and content needed to be surmounted if anything of value was to be produced; and partly nothing to do with it: the usual accident of who was born when and where. With the floating off of those countries into liberty and poverty and various degrees of crummy nationalism, that age is now over: perhaps it is the moment to apologize for having had a taste for its literary products. Publishers will go on pumping them out in translation for a few more years yet – perhaps even, briefly, at an increased rate – but I have no great expectation of them any more.

This is why: the New World Order finds the Eastern (or as he would prefer it, Central – it sounds more hopeful) European writer completely disorientated. He has lost the system in relation to which he defined himself, and that gave him censorship, sense of purpose and a measure of his effectiveness; official and underground publishers; paper-rationing and three-year waiting-times; a superhuman readership that bought up entire editions of his books before one copy could reach a bookshop

Review of George Konrad, *A Feast in the Garden*, trans. Imre Goldstein
(London: Faber and Faber, 1992)

and passed them round afterwards, that queued for shopping-baskets at bookshops and filled football stadia for poetry readings (this last is starting to sound apocryphal). Bizarre conditions in their mixture of favourable and unfavourable, but they provided the writer with readers and made him feel that what he was doing was important. This extended to 'abroad', and the foreign readership that gave his books a second life, if he was lucky; some wrote only for translation, acquired inaccessible hard-currency accounts and a disciplined and patient and somehow abstemious readership which probably understood just a fraction of what they read.

The landslip of 1989 transformed all this. Literature, having been promoted beyond its expectations, even beyond its capacity, has been abruptly relegated, almost wiped out, its domestic market wrecked by the withdrawal of subsidies, by competition from Western culture, by popular indifference and by uncertainty on the part of the writer himself, who for the first time finds himself in an artistic free-trade zone, a beggar-your-neighbour world, in competition not just with Moroccans and Ecuadorians and Italians and other exotics, but also directly with his fellow nationals. Previously, there seemed some point, both within, say, Poland, and outside, in reading seventeen Polish novelists: there was some cumulative effect, your money and attention were invested in something – not any more. By now the writer is like a ghost walking through walls. He doesn't know what is real, the past or the future, his own language or English, domesticity or national life. A kind of combi-book beckons, historical summary and Euro-fantasy, the triple-decker, poly-ideological, multi-generational national epic that reaches out to the rest of the continent, and preferably across the Atlantic: *Son of 'Zhivago'*. Inflation of length, mongrel form, the backward look to the Second World War – this time for scrapes and adventures, not anti-fascist credentials – the porno-historical schlockbuster that will sell in twenty countries, the definitive Ruritanian novel, now that all these countries have become Ruritanias, as indeed we are all Ruritanians now.

These fears weren't formulated in response to George Konrad's hefty new book, but they might have been. I don't know when I last felt so mutinous while reading a book. *A*

Feast in the Garden is an absolutely dire novel, misconceived, opportunistic, inflated, poorly written, cynical and floundering. Little G.K. in a prospect of history. Of course, there are occasional decent things in it – at almost four hundred pages, how could there not be – but even they are somehow routine, and what repeatedly struck me was the novel's stupidity, tactlessness and bad faith. Export-quality horseshit.

The rot wastes no time in setting in, a lingering and narcissistic introduction, the author for thirty pages reluctant to let his book go, even to hand it over to his fictional alter ego, David Kobra. He has a sub-Kunderesque divagation on his 'philosophy of ecstasy' before going on to the ownership of property – descriptions of remote and magnificent real estate are my hot tip for fiction-writers in this last decade of the millennium. Then, in case we don't know, he has the brass neck to tell us that his story is set 'in the heart of Central Europe'. It might be Hollywood speaking. All the time, he writes like an auction catalogue: 'A hundred years old, the house is made of quarry stone at the bottom, of bricks at the top. It has a wine cellar and an attic.' For sale separately, or as one lot. When talk turns to writing, self-love goes into overdrive. 'I keep my manuscripts in one closet, my clothes in another.' (Never trust anyone who talks to you about his manuscripts; still less anyone who wears them.) There is some terrible attitudinising:

> Writing, actually, is reading ... Writing turns observation into physical action ... I am writing my most hazardous book. I have been sentenced to examine myself. To dissect myself in the morgue of my own conscience.

And everywhere these little dickhead sentences: 'Before me, paper and pen, reckless calligraphy'; 'Death throes and bridal anticipation. I wait here, wait for inspiration'; or, haiku-style: 'On the spit: chicken legs, onions, and tomatoes.' It is poor style, but quite consistent with what Konrad says elsewhere about 'this book' being 'only the table of contents of another book'.

A Feast in the Garden, once Konrad lets go of it, is perfectly readable for quite long stretches, a ragbag of reminiscences of childhood in provincial Hungary, the war, the fate of relatives (the name Konrad is derived from Kohn), the boy's survival in a protected house in Budapest, his later relationship with his cousin, clever, Communist Zoltan, and much more. (The idea of the 'feast in the garden' is to assemble everyone, a kind of imaginary *This is Your Life*.) The later parts of the book are inevitably flat by contrast – everything that needs to be said is said in the one sentence, 'We all eat, drink and fomicate *à la hongroise*' – and are further spoilt by the recrudescence of Konrad's phenomenal vanity as well as the worst writing for a 'woman's voice' that I have ever read. The effect at first is shocking, almost exhilarating; later it is merely sad, like having to spend twenty years at Gatwick. Konrad's style, for ever tagging, jogging, praising, claiming – even if he only has someone saying: 'I am drinking a dry white wine' – is finally cringing, odious and unbelievable. 'My life, on the other hand, has been a series of border violations'; 'Women are drawn to his heat; dogs rub against his legs'; 'In her company, his manhood still soars, like Gothic art.' He has a chapter 'in which Melinda Kadron introduces herself', and another, 'in which Klara too gets to speak'. And what do they say, these women, what do they talk about? Why, their bodies, and then the men who are everything to them. It is gross, but also comically inept: 'I look in the mirror. Silvered black hair; gray lizardskin shoes' – it's a jigsaw of a Whistler speaking, not a person! Once he has put the pieces together, they proclaim:

I am, like my mother, a broad-shouldered, slim-waisted woman with strong thighs; neither small-breasted nor flat-bottomed. Dark brown eyes, deep voice, no moustache. I am five feet nine inches tall and weigh 132 pounds. My shoe size: eight and a half.

These women respond to chat-up lines like this, from a Swiss triceratops: 'By eight tonight I have to be back with my family. I have a beautiful wife and three children. My family happiness lacks only one thing. You.' And afterwards they say: 'He made every inch of my body sing.'

Konrad has written useful and acclaimed books in the past. *A Feast in the Garden* is a vivid hundred-page memoir of the war years, and after that is overwhelmed by stereotypes, folksiness and obsessive self-flattery. There is something deluded and

half-assed about it, like a running commentary on a game of
Subbuteo football; his dangerous seducer with his wheeled suit-
case; his pathetic nest-building sexpots of women; his terminally
self-admiring writers.

PÉTER NÁDAS

It's been some time since I felt much optimism about the prospects for foreign literature in English translation, but for the last three years or so, I've been in open despair. In the Eighties, there was still room for the kind of felicitous miscalculation that made the appearance of certain books in English possible – it seems to me these things were only ever done by mistake. The period we are now embarked on is quite possibly terminal. After it, we may expect a deluge – a deluge of nothing.

Houses with venerable names and cosmopolitan traditions seem quite unembarrassed about putting out catalogues that are wall-to-wall English-language originals. Chatto – home of Chekhov, Proust and Joseph Roth – recently went through three or four seasons without any translations at all. Obviously, publishing isn't what it was, the bottom line has risen inexorably, there were all the huge and much-bruited takeovers and mergers and acquisitions, but there are reasons more profound – even – than the state of publishing to explain why the number of foreign titles to appear in Britain is so low. The principal factor is the size and spread of the English language, which offers readers a delusive self-sufficiency. Why bother with anything else – apart from a handful of nineteenth-century French and Russian novelists, the only things that have ever really caught on – when there is so much to be read in English? Increasingly, it's only English that counts, not only in England and other English-speaking territories, but globally. Scores of English books get translated every year into every language under the sun – thereby wrecking the indigenous writers' domestic market – while pitifully few come the other way. English remains both the most highly sought reward and the basic measure of a foreign book, but, more and more, it denies access to itself.

Effectively, then, English is running a colossal and intolerable surplus with the rest of the world. (The abusive term 'dumping' comes to mind.) It isn't good for the rest of the world to be without its biggest potential readership and probably its only

Review of Péter Nádas, *A Book of Memories*, trans. Ivan Sanders with Imre Goldstein (London: Cape, 1997)

guarantee of posterity – but nor is it good for English. The loss
of the most distinguished, characteristic and classic books from
other languages will finally make itself felt, however richly
English is able to compensate itself from its multitudinous
sources. There is nothing like the strange bi-authorship of trans-
lation; the hapless, resourceful or wooden sense of words not
deployed by a single hand according to instructions from a
single mind; the demands on vocabulary, and, less predictably,
on syntax, that made the reading, for example, of Gregory
Rabassa's translation of *One Hundred Years of Solitude* such
an enlarging experience. Translation upsets expectation, it
extends the field of comparison, it forces even the sluggardly to
re-evaluate and to re-contextualize. A period of good writing
has to be a period of good and abundant translating also. The
fact that we're not presently living in the latter leads me to
qualify the large claims currently being made for British poetry
and fiction. It's written in a world language, but how much of
it is world literature? The low level of interest in translation
prompts the question.

For a long time, translated works were offered as part of a
bigger landscape: this is what Johnny Foreigner is doing, take
it or leave it. That's what shows in Frank O'Hara's great poem
of 1959, 'The Day Lady Died', when he buys himself a ham-
burger and a malted and 'an ugly NEW WORLD WRITING to
see what the poets/ in Ghana are doing these days'. Subsequently,
foreign titles had something of the status of evidence, or alibi:
an increasingly mendacious and half-hearted assertion that such
things were still part of the general scene, were still being culti-
vated. There was the token translation, like the token poetry
list, or the token volume of belles-lettres. You noted it and were
supposed to say: 'Look, it has come through.' It was a zoo (not,
alas, in the colloquial sense of the phrase), where you could see
the Márquez, the Grass, the Kundera, the Mulisch, the great
beasts, the kings of the jungle; again, as in a zoo, there was
something stale and old-fashioned about it, the animals were
getting on, they were grumpy and neglected, they kicked off and
weren't replaced, there was little sign of any fresh blood. And
now? The foreign novel is a novelty. It's a chimera or a yeti or
a unicorn. Over time, it has changed from being a cornerstone

to a decorative pillar to a perplexing functionless stump. It's produced and consumed in a bodiless way, as though it came out of some (English-language) test-tube: people don't read Hoeg out of an engagement with Denmark, or Gaarder to see what the writers in Norway are doing these days. There is something resolutely and manufacturedly singular about the books that are translated: one-offs like stumps and yetis and chemical clouds; pornographic or quasi-pornographic oddities. Foreign books are bought in as an occasional punt. The only publishers to continue to be committed to them being Carcanet and the inestimable Harvill Press. As easily expect discrimination and independent judgment from a row of skittles as from a cartel of international publishers. And so it is that there land in front of us – and less and less often, at that – such confections as *A Book of Memories*, wildly oversold ('claiming and extending the legacy of Proust and Mann', 'one of the great novels of modern times'), fantastically turgid, an all but unreadable version of the *versnobter* bonkbuster it so unmistakably remains.

Had I not been reviewing it, there is no stage at which I would not have stopped reading *A Book of Memories*. I ached not to read it. I would have stopped happily after one page, after five pages, after a hundred and five, after seven hundred and five. My marginalia grew more and more virulently obscene, before finally drying up altogether as I lapsed into apathy. For four weeks I put myself through it; I've never felt such a sense of waste when finishing a book. And then, for another four weeks, I was unable to contemplate the idea of writing about it.

It's hard to say what makes it so prodigiously unsatisfactory; length, long-windedness, evasiveness, over-structuring, mediocre expression, absence of humour, absence of voice, smugness and preachiness, the persistent withholding of such ordinary amenities as names and ages and settings and incidents, a dully and vauntingly cerebral book about bodies (how disgusted D. H. Lawrence would have been with it!), racking up more and more about less and less, semi-colons adrift in bloated and fussy prose. It is a book about sexual disloyalty or sexual distraction, written without heart and, barring two short scenes that are like a dentist's dream of pornography ('can swab and scrub the tight

yet slippery cave of the vagina'), without sex, as portentousness
and delay and sheer dropsy get in ahead of lubriciousness. And
yet the book turns on sex, and is about sex: the narrator's
homosexual relationship with an East German poet, Melchior,
against the background of female interest in them from the
actress Thea; flashbacks to his adolescence in Hungary, on
the periphery of a group of girls and a group of boys, and a
mother and father both interested in other partners; the corrupt
fin-de-siècle narrative he is writing, about a similarly placed
bisexual hero Thoenissen; the hackneyed device of a framing
epilogue by Krisztián, one of the Hungarian boys, since grown
up to be another (completely indistinguishable) self-regarding
sex maniac; the scriptural epigraph about 'the temple of the
body'. *A Book of Memories* would like nothing better than to
be shockingly truthful, gaily polymorphous-perverse, but it's
tedious and repressed. The Priest of Love would have loathed
it for its timid omni-sexuality, its do-nothing mind-fuckery: 'The
reason for this, he went on, may have to do with the fact that
the first thing every living thing takes into its mouth, is its
mother's milk-filled breast; and that's why we want our father's
red-veined cock in our mouth, too.'

Nádas's calamitous formal innovation is the first-person
omniscient narrator who is also largely his own subject. It is
impossible to convey just how deadly this speaker and vantage-
point are, how his orotundity anaesthetizes the reader and
annihilates and makes incredible whatever it touches on. His
particular foible is to begin relating something, switch to some-
thing else, go back to the first thing, then the second again, and
in such a mechanical and impersonal way that the reader, feeling
the contempt with which Nádas treats both subjects, his strategy,
himself and his audience, is reduced to helpless fury in short
order: Stalin's death and a landscape; adultery and a scene from
childhood; and most contemptuously, the 1953 riots in Berlin
and the 1956 uprising in Budapest. For hundreds of pages
nothing very much happens, then there is a sudden flash of
action, scandal or *guignol*: 'especially since I who, let's not mince
words, was the son of a murderer, a common ravisher' or 'When
years later I came across the little teddy bear, I looked at it; it
hurt too much; I threw it away.' This works to the mutual

disadvantage of both sorts of writing: the quick, lurid inserts are incredible, and the surrounding descriptions inflict unnecessary suffering on the reader. The book is a bastard of romantic schlock and watered-down Modernism. To describe this as 'claiming and extending the legacy of Proust and Mann' is quite breathtaking. Yes, Nádas's sentences are long and relatively abstract, but they have none of Proust's open-ended inquisitiveness or the purpose and design of Mann. They are without risk, without discovery, without grandeur. Far from resembling or – ha! – outdoing Proust and Mann, this is utterly epigonal writing, a third-generation *Zweitaufguss* for middlebrows.

A Book of Memories must have been grindingly unpleasant to translate – I couldn't face getting hold of the German version at least to compare translations – but Sanders and Goldstein haven't done badly, though they haven't been above such things as 'back on track' or 'total eating pleasure' or the description of a flaccid penis 'lying on my thigh with infantine disinterest'. The impression they give – faithfully, I assume – is of a book that is nowhere as good as it believes itself to be, with its moronic pseudo-epigrams ('the most elemental need in a crowd is to close ranks') and bungled crescendos: 'I believed my life was so miserably hopeless, so over, so terminated and therefore certainly terminable.'

A feature of the writing throughout is a certain flagellated quality: 'We talked, as I say, though it would be more correct to say that we told each other stories, and even that would not be an accurate description of the feverish urging to relate and the eager curiosity to listen to each other's words.' It is an automatic upping, a tyranny of enhancement. Things that might be perfectly commonplace are garnished with meaningless mark-ups for a kind of *faux* intensity: 'an unusual and for me perfectly typical relationship'; 'studied coyness, no doubt, but not the usual kind'; 'lighting up, for us, was not simply the act of common puffing on a common cigarette but the very essence of smoking pleasure'; 'she had one of those female voices that have a very strong effect on me.' The poverty and inadequacy of this writing are self-evident: it's an overblown bubble, vibrato on an air-violin, going 700 pages with an auctioneer. Nádas has a gift for making nothing matter. He gives us the long-winded *épateur*, the over-psychologized psychological moment, the phantom sexual voracity, the political and mythological tie-ins, the closet worldliness, the logomachic belly-flop, but there is nothing there between his mirrors. In Sylvia Plath's phrase from 'Death & Co.' he is 'masturbating a glitter'.

None of this would matter much if it were against a background of engagement with other languages and literatures, of a cornucopia of translation, of a continuing search for interesting and worthwhile books. It's the fact that there is no such background, and that this book isn't merely bad but rotten while being called not merely good but great, that makes it worth writing about. It deforms a void.

TADEUSZ KONWICKI

For a year or more, I was haunted by the outline of a story: someone is told to immolate himself as a political protest. All day he runs around whatever city it is, as it were Leopold Bloom with a can of petrol, wondering whether to go through with it, waiting for the appointed time, saying his goodbyes. I didn't know where this idea had come to me from; no one I asked knew anything about any book along these lines, and I was just beginning to think that I must have dreamed it and (God forbid!) that I should write it myself, when I came upon a copy in a second-hand shop: the book is laughingly entitled *A Minor Apocalypse*, the city is Warsaw, the liquid is not petrol but, unpleasantly, 'thinner', and the author of this terrific and almost unknown masterpiece is Tadeusz Konwicki.

In all, six books by Konwicki (born in Wilno in 1926) have appeared in English. I propose to leave the first two out of discussion: *The Anthropos-Spectre-Beast*, 'a fantasy for young readers' that is as hard-edged and adult as everything else of Konwicki's; and *A Dreambook of Our Time*, once chosen by Philip Roth for his Penguin series 'The Other Europe', but long unobtainable. (My own copy of it has gone missing, but I remember it as a slightly flowery rooming-house novel about zero-hour Poland.) It seems barbaric to ignore any books by a foreign author, like re-burying archaeological material: when not everything of his has been preserved for us by translation; when translation affects what has; when a writer has had such a chequered career as Konwicki, who was a Party member in the fifties, the author of approved socialist realist books, as well as of eerie and untidy films (he directed some of his own, as well as writing scripts for Wajda). But perhaps it is too much to hope – to reconstruct the career of a foreign author under circumstances so unfathomably alien to our own. Like rebuilding Knossos or Troy. This brooch, that awl, these shards? God knows. The point is the particular historical moment of the last ten years, and that, out of whatever moral and ideo-

Review of Tadeusz Konwicki, *Bohin Manor*, trans. Richard Lourie
(London: Faber and Faber, 1992)

logical and stylistic background, Konwicki found himself able
and equipped to take it on. The test of writing from another
country is the degree of reality and interest it gives to that
country. The four last books of Konwicki give a fascinating
picture of Poland – no, they *are* Poland, as Juan Rulfo is Mexico,
or Patrick White Australia. Further, they contain some of the
funniest, most outrageous, acid and lugubrious writing I have
ever read. I don't think I have ever been spoken to by an author
the way I have by Konwicki.

The first of these four books is *The Polish Complex* (1977 –
the translation by Richard Lourie in 1982), the first of Kon-
wicki's books to be banned by the authorities in Poland; later
on, he graduated to being banned by the Underground. Its basic
situation is less extreme than that of *A Minor Apocalypse*, but
just as dramatic and suspenseful: practically the whole book is
set in a queue. It begins: 'I was standing in line in front of a
state-owned jewellery store. I was twenty-third in line.' What
Konwicki and his fellow Poles are queuing for is gold wedding
rings, a consignment of which is rumoured to be on its way
from the Soviet Union. There is no particular occasion for them
to be wanting these rings: the queue isn't about to get itself
hitched, individually or collectively. They are there because the
goods are (or, strictly speaking, aren't), because a queue is an
opportunity, because anything is better than the money freezing
a hole in their pockets: Konwicki is always prodigal with money
in his novels. It is hard not to think that these gold wedding
rings from Russia have a symbolic aspect as well: something
like the legitimisation of the Russian-Polish relationship, Russia
doing the decent thing after years of crass occupation. In general,
Konwicki is not a hermetic or even an indirect type of writer:
but a symbolic reading does suggest itself. Anyway, the rings
never come. There are electric samovars instead.

The ironic thing about the queue is that it becomes a great
way for the people in it – the Poles – to get to know one another.
Divisions break down, and the queue talks – how preferable,
from the Soviet point of view, the conspicuous or furtive con-
sumption of goods would have been. Konwicki has given us a
magnificently warped sample of his countrymen. There is
Kojran, a rather well-informed and grumpy reader of Konwicki's

work (and Konwicki himself is preparing to defend himself in a lawsuit brought by another reader who feels his own character has been maligned in the books); there is a one-time security man, Duszek, once instructed to eliminate Konwicki in the early days after the war, but now thoroughly mellowed out, and given to uttering gnomic pieces of folk wisdom about the Poles, little gems like 'Drink makes a Pole merry,' 'When a Pole complains, he feels better right away,' 'When a Pole sees a balcony, he wants to jump.' These have a moronic profundity about them. There is also a serving security man, a 'stoolie', Grzesio the provocateur, who doesn't fool anyone for a second with his 'Do you people know the joke about the Party Secretary?' and whom Duszek has well in hand. Then there are lesser characters: a peasant woman of astounding wealth, elegance and sexual appetency; a student with a French anarchist in tow, someone for the Western reader to identify with:

'He says,' said the student, still interpreting for the anarchist, 'that there's something in Poland. Some sort of spirit. Some force of eternal unrest. He's seen Polish films, he knows about the Polish school.'
   'Many unprejudiced people become quite taken by our country,' said the woman in the pelisse.

All of life is in the queue, in its rapid and brilliant cross-talk, and shifting relationships and alliances. People eat, drink and sleep in the queue, they make love – a typically Konwickian coupling, sexy, improbable and half-consummated, with the shop assistant – and they suffer heart attacks that take them to death's door. Intercut with this life, this wonderful heightened repartee, the sumptuous deciphering of detail are passages of reflection and prophecy in a rhetorical and splenetic rush, and a couple of fictionalized scenes from the rebellious and betrayed history of nineteenth-century Poland (the 1863 Polish Revolt against Russia). The effect is at once seditious and pessimistic, a combination that underwrites Konwicki's absolute and uncompromising independence. His pessimism is actually his worst sin, because it antagonized government and opposition in equal measure: sedition 'only' upset the regime. 'Don't make us any sadder, godamnit, write something to give us strength,' his faithful reader Kojran beseeches him, but after his work in the fifties – of which only one suggestive title, *Authority*, is known to me – Konwicki is through with giving strength. He might give it to the wrong people.

A Minor Apocalypse is one of the great works of fiction to have come out of the late, half-lamented eastern half of Europe. Its daunting, unforgettable and joyful first sentence, 'Here comes the end of the world,' has its truth confirmed throughout the rest of the book – confirmed personally, medically, alcoholically, politically, architecturally, folklorically, nationally, sexually and cosmically. Many of the themes and tropes of *The Polish Complex* recur in it, in heightened and perfected form: the relationship of Russia and Poland, a man's life and death, the presentation of the author in conversation, daily life in Warsaw, political debate, the state of the universe 'where rusted Sputniks and astronaut excrement, frozen bone hard, go gliding past'. Compared to its predecessor, *A Minor Apocalypse* has been given one more twist of desperation. Once again, the action is all in the waiting – but waiting for the end. And it has been elevated. From being a cross-section of anybodies, a queue of men in the street, everybody here is 'somebody'. In Poland the book was read as a *roman à clef*, and even to us, without inside information, it is peopled with high-ups in the regime and opposition, the arts and censorship, philosophy and the film industry.

On the day the author is approached by Hubert and Rysio, two old lags from the Underground, the self-styled 'keepers of a dying flame', themselves ironically three-quarters dead, with their outrageous and bland request that he sacrifice himself for their cause – he is after all, expendable – on that day, Poland is receiving a state visit from its eastern neighbour. It would be; it often did; and this is also what gives the protest its occasion. Konwicki experiences in his own person all the encroachment and duress inflicted on – and transmitted by – Poland. He is leaned on by the Underground, picked up by the Police, the water and gas are disconnected in his flat, he meets censors, Politburo members, big-cheese film directors – it seems that everyone in the book except himself is some kind of authority figure, has some kind of crummy power vested in him, forms part of an infernal and cannibalistic machine. At the same time,

he witnesses Poland's national humiliation: the placards WE
HAVE BUILT SOCIALISM! amidst the rubble of Warsaw, the over-
rehearsed crowds, the quasi-homoerotic antics of the two heads
of state on the numerous television sets all with the sound turned
off.

One of Konwicki's great themes is the way his country has
been fucked by Russia: 'I came out onto Nowy Swiat, which
was overgrown with a shrubbery of flags, red flags and red-and-
white flags. But in those red-and-white flags of ours the red has
slowly increased over the years, while the white has diminished.
And now our flags are red, too, with just a little white band at
the top.' Hence his interest in outer space, which might be
'twinned with Poland', for all the Soviet detritus swimming
around in it. The occasional Polish flag peeps out 'shyly' from
between its red neighbours. The Polish leader has the demeanour
of a concierge or a catamite. The crowds in the street chant
'Poland!' in Russian and Polish. People break into Russian at
moments of stress, speak Polish with Russian accents, even when
performing in folkloric representations of Polish culture: 'The
leader of the dance was tapping his foot and singing in a low
voice with a Russian accent: I'm from Krakow, yes, I am!' The
Russian is marked out everywhere in the book, and identified
with power and scale. There is (the unnamed) Brezhnev with
his 'Kalmuck face', 'the tsar of tsars, master of half the world';
the wife of a Politburo member is chatted up by a reference
to her 'Soviet tits'; the official banquet features 'an enormous
sturgeon, a tsar of a sturgeon': 'The sturgeon was covered by a
shimmering pale-green aspic, which reminded me of the depths
of Lake Baikal.' Even when consorting with the Underground
Konwicki meets the beautiful Russian Nadezhda (or Hope),
framed by pictures of 'the stern and bearded faces of the Russian
dissidents'. The unwearying identification of things Russian is
comic in itself, and further comedy comes from the way they
have been shamelessly substituted for Polish things, their grisly
virtue, their scale, their austerity. None of it is authentic, and
none of it is even plausible:

A bunch of guys, not young but dressed as newspaper boys, were
fast approaching us from Aleje Jerozolimskie. It was a group of some

sort of activists, probably from a youth organisation. They were
scattering a special edition of *Trybuna Ludu* and calling out shame-
facedly:

'Poland awarded honorary title of First Candidate for membership
in the Union of Soviet Socialist Republics!'

'Extra! Poland a candidate for membership in Soviet Union!'

Konwicki careers through his day, stumbling from drink to
drink, from one encounter to the next, like an all-comprehending
pinball. He has nothing, he represents nothing, he is alone, he
believes in nothing he sees, he is a transcendental or romantic
nihilist. To those who nominated him, the Konwicki character
seems like the perfect victim – written-out, hungover, on the
skids – but he plays the victim's last best trick of accepting his
fate and devaluing it at the same time. His obedience, both to
the authorities and the opposition, comes over as a sublime
insult. His refusal to be surprised or deceived or enraged is
absolutely maddening to both sides. Somehow, a combination
of passivity, shrewdness and vast indifference have made him
free, and as a free man he is invulnerable. When the police haul
him in and stick a needle in his arm, he is grateful that they use
a clean one:

> He injected the entire large dose. I didn't feel anything. It wasn't out
> of the question that the ampoule was a dummy. They used injections
> like that which contained no drugs, only a salt solution. Our domestic
> pharmaceutical industry had also been on the skids for some time.

How do you duff up a man so unimpressed and so analytical
that the subject of his unselfish musings is 'our domestic pharma-
ceutical industry'?

I am conscious of having made *A Minor Apocalypse* sound
rather like a monodrama: in fact, it is a Babel. Just as in *The
Polish Complex*, everyone gets to talk, though this time not in
short, joky lines but more often in long, dazzling and ironic
speeches. There is cutting and parrying and thrusting, like some
intellectual Punch and Judy show; the best action of the book
is in the talking. Everywhere there is amazing articulacy and
sophistication from the most unexpected sources. The torturer
perorates like this: 'You represent noble passivity while I am
trivial action.' The censor invites Konwicki to work for the

Censorship: 'They'd appreciate you. You had a flair for allusions.' The opposition is attacked as 'apparatchiks', 'dissidents with lifetime appointments. The regime has grown accustomed to them and they've grown accustomed to the regime.'

A Minor Apocalypse is both generously polyphonic and a curmudgeonly aria. Konwicki appears as the antagonist of a whole country, and the supreme expression of its cussed spirit. When I finally read the book for the first time, I was amazed that Konwicki was still living in Poland, not because I thought he hated it and wanted to leave, but because I couldn't think of any organization or power or sectional interest that would put up with him any longer. I could think of no one from the town planners of Warsaw to the priests 'of the new dispensation' to the Polish-Arab Friendship Society whom he hadn't offended. Like the speaker in Joseph Brodsky's poem 'Plato Elaborated', here was someone to throw the book at:

> And when they would finally arrest me for espionage,
> for subversive activity, vagrancy, for *ménage*
> *à trois* . . .

It was Brodsky again who archly pointed out that 'a translation, by definition, lags behind the original work.' In Konwicki's case, the lag has been five years for each book. Five years is an eternity, given the recent rapid transformations in Poland and the rest of the Soviet imperium, and it may be that Western readers may question the relevance to them of books so outdistanced by political developments. (In 1989 I was aware of an ugly and sub-intellectual wash of resentment against Brecht: 'with Communism on the way out, why do we still have to put up with him,' people seemed to be saying. Of course, they were the people who could never be bothered with Brecht in the first place, knavishly using politics as an excuse.) The argument for Konwicki – and the same goes for Brecht – is the artistic one. His books are more than reportage, and survive the conditions from which they sprang. If Gierek had never lived, and Poland never existed, Konwicki would be worth reading. *A Minor Apocalypse* has, in Edmund Wilson's phrase, 'its place among the books that set a standard'. My own belated 'discovery' of it seems a case in point: but even if I'd read it punctually, it would still not have been 'topical'.

This is highly ironic, given that some of Konwicki's bitterest criticism is reserved for himself and his own writing. In all his books, he presents himself as a soon-to-be-ex writer in one way or another: beset by disappointed readers; selected for an *auto da fé*. *Moonrise, Moonset* begins with a constatation of his failure:

> I am being rejected. I am being rejected from literature. With the force of a jet engine I am being ejected from fiction. To maintain your prestige you must produce a novel every so often. It's high time I stammered out another work of prose. But I can't. But I can't.

This diary-book, itself an imitation, according to Konwicki, of a similar and far more successful earlier book called *The Calendar and the Hourglass* (never translated – if it even exists), is the work of a disgruntled journalist manqué, 'a columnist forced by an unfortunate set of circumstances into becoming a novelist'. Without the stomach for the struggle with form, he lets himself go, produces a hodge-podge of actuality, reminiscence and malice, improvises a 'Slavic pizza'. And yet even his earlier work is unreadable, he declares; he himself has never managed to read a word of it: 'I am spur-of-the-moment, short-run, temporary. In life and in my misshapen writing. My books start to die as soon as the ink dries on the page.'

Konwicki makes, as one would expect, a devastating case against himself, but one should hold out against it. I would put *Moonrise, Moonset* in a slightly different class from the two previous books, which were, after all, achieved novels – although, to make the opposite case, it only continues their *démontage* of the form, and should perhaps be more highly prized for refusing all compromise. The *New York Times* did say 'it has to be considered Konwicki's best book.' The Western reader could use a little help with some of the names and references, although Konwicki's entanglements with Brzezinski ('the Great Zbig', who is unable to find time to meet him, thereby causing Jimmy Carter to lose the election, according to Konwicki) and the Laureate Milosz ('It looks as if I'll be making a film of Milosz's *The Issa Valley* – a jolly leap into a simpatico abyss') need less explanation than most. Still, for all one's ignorance of many of the cast, *Moonrise, Moonset* is a gripping read: for the utter clarity and extreme wilfulness of Konwicki's positions; for the headlong and perfervid rush of his prose; for the tonic bleakness of his observations; and for the material of Martial Law Poland and World War Two Wilno (Konwicki fought in the Home Army), and brilliant episodes like his visit to the Soviet Union in the fifties. Konwicki's translator in all four of these books, the American Slavist Richard Lourie, is once again quite superb: translations can be an alibi or an experience, and Lourie provides an experience, no question, with his wonderful colloquialisms ('Get up, you provincial dink') and his matching of Konwicki's foul, matey and rhetorical style. If an author tells you, 'The sex will come later, my little blindworms' (a hint of Edna Everage?), you know there's really no lag or loss in the translation, and that such stuff just doesn't die or dry on the page. Konwicki writes about coming round to the style of the actor Zbigniew Cybulski, star of *Ashes and Diamonds*, after first finding him too American, with too much of James Dean and Montgomery Clift, but his own writing matches Cybulski's performance in Lourie's hip and confessional American English.

Konwicki's latest book, *Bohin Manor*, really may be his last. The author has been crying 'Wolf' and 'Uncle' for a long time now, but in a way that becomes more credible for each repetition. Others of his prophecies – the rise of nationalism in a period of global trends, the collapse of the Soviet Union brought about by 'the collective self-immolation' of the Poles, and glimmerings of a more hopeful future for Poland – have all come to pass. Now, in his 'last voyage in literature', Konwicki has returned to the past and to Wilno and told the story of his grandmother, Helena Konwicka.

It is a tale of decayed gentlefolk, with a will-she, won't-she marriage plot that might be out of Wodehouse, but acquires a strongly allegorical bent in Konwicki's hands; Richard Lourie observes that it is his most deeply Polish work. The young woman lives with her father on the small estate of Bohin, having been displaced there (like Poland, shunted this way and that) from their original home of Milowidy. Her mother has died, and her father, a patriotic Pole, has taken a vow of silence following the quelling of the last uprising. In an atmosphere at once paradisal, repressed and mysterious, she finds herself variously courted: by a rich, unenthusiastic neighbour; by the Russian Korsakov, drunkenly guilty about occupying Milowidy; and by a young flame-haired Jew Elias, a rebel and émigré returned from Paris and Australia (suggestions of the Polish patriot leader, Kosciuszko).

Konwicki picks out her story in fragrant, rather old-fashioned prose, now and then putting in an appearance himself in his lassitude and uncertainty. It is all oddly hesitant and tremulous, like the work of a beginner, a worshipper of the nineteenth century, a believer in romance, tradition and Poland. Konwicki's other books are ragged, triumphant shows of the pointlessness, tedium and extinction of pedantic conventional narrative: now he has written one himself! It is a strange and in a way triumphant ending – if it is to be an ending – to a brilliant and tempestuous late career. Having previously described (and welcomed) his ejection and rejection from literature and seen no future for himself but 'And me? I'll go looking for a country with censorship, where I can write modern allusive prose for the rest of my days' – to have gone on to accomplish a sweet, Chekhovian romance that ends happily and with, of all things, himself. 'Still, it all ended well, because, despite everything, I do exist and am among the living.' And then, noting the improbability: 'But how can *I* be the upbeat ending to any story?'

ROBERT MUSIL

Of all the great European novelists of the first third of the century – Proust, Joyce, Kafka, Mann, Woolf – Musil is far and away the least read, and yet he's as shapely as Gibbon, as mordant as Voltaire, as witty as Oscar Wilde, and as indecent as Schnitzler. *The Man Without Qualities* (a title almost as off-putting as Italo Svevo's *Senilità*) is an extraordinary amalgam of the formidable, the delicious and the unfinished, and no doubt each of these attributes is in some measure dissuasive, especially to admirers of one of the others. Now, it is to be hoped that this magnificent new edition, expertly and devotedly translated by Sophie Wilkins and Burton Pike, shrewdly packaged in two volumes, and valuably containing some six hundred pages of drafts and fragments that have never previously appeared in English, will find him something like the readership he deserves.

If we take it that the characteristics of twentieth-century life are fatuity, doubt and confusion, the 'barbaric fragmentation' of the self, where 'impersonal matters [. . .] go into the making of personal happenings in a way that for the present eludes description', a crisis of individual identity and collective purpose, then it is Musil's astonishing achievement to take all this and, yes, to make a comedy of it. This book that begins with a baroque meteorological description; whose first action is a car accident; whose hero is first seen looking out of the window, stopwatch in hand conducting a statistical survey of the passing traffic – can there be any doubt that it is a prophetic book about us and our world? Musil is us. The world of 'global Austria' and the Parallel Action – the plan, in the novel, to claim 1918 for the celebration of the Emperor's 70th jubilee before the Germans get it for Kaiser Wilhelm's 30th, made a nonsense of, of course, by the supervention of World War One – is our own world of the International Decade for Natural Disaster Reduction (with a quarter of a million Dutch evacuated from their homes, at the time of writing) and an international conference scheduled for March 29 to pay tribute to the achievements

Review of Robert Musil, *The Man without Qualities*, trans. Sophie Wilkins and Burton Pike (New York: Knopf, 1995)

of Douglas Hurd and, as it were, 'global Britain'. While Musil's contemporaries, Proust and Joyce, chose interiority and the private world of memory, Musil is uncannily prescient about modern life, where sportsmen and criminals are indifferently idolized, where quantity sits in judgment on quality (so that an author 'must have an awful lot of like-minded readers before he can pass for an impressive thinker'), where we sit and stew among 'bobsled championships, tennis cups and luxury hotels along great highways, with golf course scenery and music on tap in every room'.

So far, I have stressed the satirical side of *The Man Without Qualities*; as one of the characters says, 'the man of genius is duty bound to attack.' However, it is not harsh satire, still less sour. Rather, there is something loving about it, it is sweetly satirical, like paisley. Musil's tone is unlike anyone else's. Partly it is the Austrian melancholy that underlies the book – the melancholy of a defunct state, the melancholy of a closed conditional. What if, instead of expressing itself in the carnage of the First World War, human folly had chosen this other form, the novel implies. Partly it is the equable irony that plays over every single character and institution and group in the book that makes reading Musil such an exquisitely flattering experience. At last someone who understands me, you think, even as you read something amiably puncturing like 'A young man needs to shine, far more than he needs to see something in the light' or again 'She was one of those charmingly purposeful young women of our time who would instantly become bus drivers if some higher purpose called for it'. There is nothing sneering about these characterizations and generalizations; it is mockery, but more akin to the self-mockery these characters might produce, if they – or we – could only briefly stand outside themselves. The fact that *The Man Without Qualities* was never finished, could never be finished, is germane here too: nowhere do we have to endure the spectacle of Musil the master-baker clapping the sugar of superiority off his hands.

In the book, there isn't a character who is presented without mockery – not least for taking themselves so seriously. Who is Ulrich, for instance, the eponymous 'man without qualities' and central figure of the novel that, at 32, in superb physical condition and dauntingly intelligent, he is already a veteran of three careers, in the army, engineering and mathematics, and asks for a time-out to think about life – only to find himself relentlessly courted by the world! Or Bonadea the bluestocking society hostess, likened by one of the other characters to 'a gigantic power station in whose mysterious function of spreading light one did not meddle'? Or her long-suffering husband Hans – never Giovanni! – Tuzzi, with his dry smell and Foreign Office conceit? Or Arnheim, the Prussian industrialist and *penseur*, whose name is alarmingly liable to crop up on practically any page of a newspaper? All of these are skewed and partial, but none are caricatures (perhaps the book's almost complete lack of physical description plays a part here – and yet in spite of it, you feel you could pick them in an identity parade, Clarisse, Walter, Rachel). They are Musil's puppets, but each of them – even stupid Bonadea, Ulrich's one-time mistress – embodies a certain part of Musil's intelligence. All of them have dignity, consistency and a partial grasp of the truth, that truth which, incidentally, 'is not a crystal that can be slipped into one's pocket, but an endless current into which one falls headlong', just as one falls into this book. Musil makes other writers look either very black and white, or just quite grey. Still in his twenties, *à propos*, he invented a chromatometer.

The Man Without Qualities took up the last two decades of Musil's life. He died in exile in Switzerland in 1942, at the age of 61. Two volumes of it were published, to acclaim but few sales, in 1930 and 1932; a third reached the proof stage in 1938 when he withdrew it. He was working on it when he died. It was not that he lost faith in it, it was more the circumstances in Europe and the difficulties of his own situation. It was from its beginnings an unmanageably open and metamorphic project – this is part of its greatness and its charm. It proliferated continually – once it was to be called 'Die Zwillingsschwester', 'The Twin Sister', but in the end the appearance of Ulrich's sister Agathe is delayed for over seven hundred pages! – and the longer he lived with it, the more it changed. The book is like a carbon chain, major new characters – Lindner the Christian schoolmaster, Schmeisser the Socialist – continue to appear, and all the time with the book's external dramatic clock running down towards August 1914. Alternative versions are written: Ulrich and Agathe, Ulrich and Diotima, Ulrich's attempt to free the murderer Moosbrugger, Ulrich and Clarisse. It is strangely enriching to read on as the book frays into alternatives – after all, isn't Ulrich's philosophy that of 'possibilism', not what is but what might be! – and to read Musil's exhortations to himself, 'Dramatize! Make all this present!' or 'And no way at all of framing this in cycles!' This is a quite overwhelming book, commensurately translated and published, that ideally everyone would read.

JOSEPH ROTH

With the appearance of *Rebellion*, we now have all of Joseph Roth's completed novels, fifteen of them, in English translation, sixty years after his death. It has taken a dozen translators and a score of publishing houses, in Britain and America, but the intermittent, idealistic, and determined enterprise is complete, and a classic accolade has been assembled for a classic writer. One might think of a relay race – one in which the baton is neglected for the best part of forty years, between the thirties and the seventies – or the efforts of a willing, if amateurish, team of skittles players. Briefly atop this heap of literary coral, I feel a modicum of triumph, a degree of shame, and a strong sense of being at a loss. '*Und dann? Und dann?*' as my father would sometimes say, 'What next? What next?'

Rebellion was Joseph Roth's third novel. The first was *The Spider's Web*, published in serial form in the Viennese *Arbeiter-Zeitung (Workers' Newspaper)* in 1923, but never as a book, and later repudiated by Roth. The second was *Hotel Savoy*, serialized in the *Frankfurter Zeitung* – for which Roth began to write in 1923, and which was to be his principal employer for most of his life – and published in 1924 by Die Schmiede (the Smithy), a renowned, if short-lived house in Berlin, that also brought out Kafka and Proust in the same series. *Rebellion (Die Rebellion)* was serialized in the German Socialist newspaper *Vorwärts (Forward)*, and published by Die Schmiede in the same year, 1924. These three books make up Roth's early period.

Over the next two or three years, his life and opinions changed profoundly. He wrote more and more for the 'bourgeois' *Frankfurter*, and less and less for the left-wing papers to which he had first gravitated as a very young man after the war. He quickly became one of the star journalists of the period, making the *Frankfurter*'s name almost as much as it made his. In 1925, he was given the heady job of Paris correspondent (it was soon taken away again, but it didn't matter, as Roth stayed on in

Introduction to Joseph Roth, *Rebellion*, trans. Michael Hofmann (London: Granta, 1999)

France, and was only an occasional visitor to Germany from that time). In 1926, like many Western writers, he went to the Soviet Union, where he spent a disillusioning few months. Walter Benjamin, who also wrote for the *Frankfurter*, and was a little in awe of Roth, as well as a little disapproving, secured an audience with him in Moscow. It took place late one night in Roth's hotel room, full of unobtainables to eat and drink, and Benjamin came away with the impression – overstated, but perhaps only a little – that Roth had gone to the Soviet Union a convinced Communist and was leaving it a Royalist!

Certainly, the little spate of *Neue Sachlichkeit* (New Objectivity) novels that Roth published next – *Flight Without End, Zipper and his Father, Right and Left* – are already recognizably different books, moving away from politics and political action where the early books were going toward it, and resigned where the early books were up in arms. Thereafter, Roth forsook his documentary manner and his interest in contemporary themes, and discovered the past, his own and that of Austria, in what are often advertised as his 'great' books, *Job* (1930) and *The Radetzky March* (1932), and in the string of exquisite and sad novels that he wrote in his brief but astonishingly fertile period in exile. He died in Paris on May 27, 1939.

Early Roth is an unexpectedly opposite commodity. The way we think of him – largely conditioned by what he became later – is already sufficiently paradoxical and crowded (the self-styled 'Frenchman from the East', the Jewish Catholic, the onetime pacifist with a cavalry officer's bearing, the newspaperman and novelist for posterity, the hardworking drinker, etc., etc.) without the addition of yet another facet: Roth the 'bleeding heart Socialist,' red Roth, '*der rote Roth*', his sometime early nom de plume. It is, admittedly, a bigger factor in his journalism and his other writing than it is in his novels, but one still can't read the early books without being aware that their author was a man of certain preoccupations, beliefs, and – to put it no higher – hopes.

The Spider's Web is set among the bigots, spies, and terrorist militias of Weimar. The hotel in *Hotel Savoy* has a strangely dual function as a representation of capitalism and a wonderfully atmospheric internment camp for soldiers returning from the war. And *Rebellion*, in its classical, Brechtian way, charts one man's fall and another's rise in the yeasty, nervy post-war atmosphere.

While none of the three novels could be described as agitprop, all of them portray the disillusionment of their heroes with a society for which they had risked their lives and shed their blood. 'For this is war,' Roth wrote, 'we know it is, we, the sworn experts in battlefields straightaway sensed that we have come home from a small battlefield to a great one.' Over time and many books, Roth's preoccupation shifted or clarified from social justice to fate. In *Rebellion*, a squared circle, both are present, the one still, the other already. In a fine, no doubt sneering phrase of Walter Benjamin's (applied not to Roth, but to Erich Kästner), the book is informed with a 'melancholy of the Left', '*linke Melancholie*': a condition as fanciful and illogical as the unicorn, but then, what could be more like Roth?

Where *Rebellion* scores over its two predecessors is in its ferocious concentration on a single destiny. The earlier books are marked by a charming inattentiveness that was to beset Roth in many of his novels: a major new character is belatedly introduced, and practically steals the book from under the hero's nose; such crucial things as lottery tickets, American billionaires, and dancers by the name of Stasia are all simply left dangling while the author sets off in pursuit of new prey. Early Roth – or that side of Roth – is like a manic juggler, picking up characters, incidents, objects, keeping them in the air with speed and dexterity, then distractedly letting them go as he stoops to collect different ones. This doesn't happen in *Rebellion*. There is a brusque and initially disorientating switch at the beginning of chapter 7 – you think a piece of a different book has got into the one you're reading! – but that turns out to be merely the lead into what Roth's biographer, David Bronsen, considers one of the best crux/catastrophes in the whole of the oeuvre. No, throughout *Rebellion*, Roth is intent on the downward path of Andreas Pum, the encounter with Herr Arnold, the equivalent rise of Andreas's friend Willi, and his belated coming-to-consciousness as a 'rebel'. But even here, in this diagrammatically simple story, Roth displays his ability to stretch the boundaries of his novel; in a couple of places, when Andreas becomes habituated to the darkness of his cell, and when he replays the images of his distant childhood and his work as a night watchman, it's as though Roth makes the book go to sleep for a while, dream vividly, and wake up refreshed! The sudden breaks in tempo and level seem to give it a depth of reality that at other moments it would appear to scorn. They lend credibility, too, to the otherwise inexplicable ageing of Andreas in the course of a six-week gaol sentence.

This is typical of the way *Rebellion* manages to keep a slight edge over the typical products of the period, while seeming to resemble them entirely. One expects, maybe, from the German twenties, Roth's Grosz-like caricatures of the lady on the tram, or the police officer at his desk; the wide array of style and diction; the switches of tense, the '*O Mensch*' addresses to the character, and the first-person plural meditations. 'From their midst, as by a miracle, they suddenly produced a policeman' is like a moment out of a Chaplin film, while the idea of a character's descent to the level of toilet attendant actually *is* the story of Fritz Murnau's film *The Last Man*, which came out in the same year as *Rebellion* and starred one of the silent cinema's great masters of pathos, Emil Jannings. But what is unexpected and distinctive and 'Rothian' in *Rebellion* is the lyrical cynicism with which Herr Arnold is described in chapter 7; the way that, purely through suffering, the character of Andreas Pum deepens into a third dimension; and the shocks of irony and poetry that accompany the story, in the breathtaking savagery, say, of the sentence, 'It may be said that that evening she was completely happy,' or the pathetic resonance of the image: 'On Andreas's little dish, everything was all mixed up, and a large bone stuck out of the mess like a broken rooftree from the ruins of a house.'

Ingeborg Sültemeyer, the critic who has done the most to – quite literally – discover and habilitate early Roth, makes the clever point that to Andreas in *Rebellion*, God and State occupy reversed positions: there is something like a business contract with God, while the State is the object of faith and worship – hence Andreas's unexpected word, 'heathens' for those veterans who, unlike himself, are dissatisfied and rebellious. The relationship with this 'deity' and the great, Job-like final scene seem to be freighted with more than the misprision of a purely secular authority.

While there is no suggestion that Andreas is *actually* a Jew – and indeed, the casually anti-Semitic aspersion of the old man on the tram would seem to rule it out – critics have pointed out that his intimate and vexed and accusing relationship with his 'God' is the same as, and is perhaps modelled on, that of Eastern Jews with theirs. It is this unexpected congruency that lends support to James Wood's interesting contention that 'all of [Roth's] self-defeating heroes, even if gentile, are ultimately Jewish'.

Here, anyway, in its dealing with the extremity of a man's life and his dealings with the Almighty, however constituted, *Rebellion* seems to look forward to *The Legend of the Holy Drinker*, the charmed tale that Roth completed in the weeks before his own death in 1939. It is uncanny what the two books have in common: a hero named Andreas, an unexpected reflection in a mirror, a barbershop, parrots, suits, money (coins in *Rebellion*, paper in the *Holy Drinker*), God, an individual's destiny in a group of people similarly placed, church, a woman, prison, friendship, policemen, documents, wallets, a little girl (here Anni, there Therese), a dying confusion. It's as though the same ingredients have been recombined to create two completely different dishes. If I may leave the reader of *Rebellion* with a suggestion, it is that he or she might care to go on and read *The Legend of the Holy Drinker* and catch a prismatically different writer to try and reconcile with '*der rote Roth*', and briefly recapitulate a remarkable oeuvre. Alternatively, of course, he or she might read the whole of that oeuvre, now that it is possible to do so.

RYSZARD KAPUŚCIŃSKI

In Warsaw a year ago, I happened upon the P.A.P. building, and stopped for a moment in a show of respect for the unhappily initialled Polish Press Agency, whose one foreign correspondent had presumably sent off his stoical wires and dispatches to just this address.

That said, Ryszard Kapuściński's new book, *The Soccer War*, was a disappointment. His customary energy and his drive to understand were stretched over two decades and two continents. I lost my belief in his ability to respond afresh to new countries and new situations. Against its own principles, his writing seemed to fall into a pattern of repetition. The continual brushes with death were actually tedious to read.

It sent me back to his Angola book, *Another Day of Life*, with its amazing description of a city awaiting attack – Luanda – being picked clean and abandoned by its inhabitants. It is – *mutatis mutandis* – the subject of Cavafy's poem 'Waiting for the Barbarians' and Kafka's tiny story 'ein altes Blatt'. In length, proportion, sobriety, handling of himself, observation, it is flawless. Kapuściński catches human beings behaving in a way one might have expected of insects. Reading him, one becomes aware of the triangle formed by terror, due process and absurdity. Those thirty pages stood out for me in a year in which a great deal happened, and I read the newspapers and not much else.